We Shall Overcome

HERB BOYD

NARRATED BY
OSSIE DAVIS & RUBY DEE

sourcebooks
mediaFusion

An Imprint of Sourcebooks, Inc.®
Naperville, Illinois

Published by Sourcebooks, Inc.
P.O. Box 4410, Naperville, Illinois 60567-4410
(630) 961-3900
FAX: (630) 961-2168
www.sourcebooks.com

Library of Congress Cataloging-in-Publication Data

Boyd, Herb.
 We shall overcome / by Herb Boyd.
    p. cm.
 Includes bibliographical references.
 ISBN 1-4022-0213-X (alk. paper)
 1. African Americans—Civil rights—History—20th century. 2. African Americans—Civil rights—History—20th century—Sources. 3. Civil rights movements—United States—History—20th century. 4. Civil rights movements—United States—History—20th century—Sources I. Title.
 E185.61.B774 2004
 323.1196'073'009046—dc22
                                    2004012509

BOYD

Printed and bound in the United States of America
VHG 10 9 8 7 6 5 4 3 2 1

This book is dedicated to those who dreamed—and dream—of a better America.

Contents

On the CDs

DISC 1

TRACK

1   **Introduction**
Narrators Ossie Davis and Ruby Dee.

2   **Slave Narratives and Freedom Songs**
Hear the voices of former slaves and
their songs.

3   **A. Philip Randolph and the Roots of
the Movement**
Hear A. Philip Randolph, soldier Hosea
Williams, President Harry S. Truman,
and a news report on voting.

4   **Brown v. Board of Education**
Hear Thurgood Marshall, President
Dwight D. Eisenhower, and a news
report on the decision.

5   **The Little Rock Nine**
Hear a news report on the students,
President Dwight D. Eisenhower, and a
panel discussion of black and white students from Central High.

6   **Martin Luther King Jr.**
Hear Dr. King speak during the Montgomery bus boycott.

7   **Sit-ins**
Hear Greensboro sit-in participants Ezell
Blair Jr. and Franklin McCain, protestor
Jesse Jackson seek admittance to a
restaurant, a news report on sit-ins, and
James Farmer on the effect of boycotts.

8   **Freedom Riders**
Hear Freedom Rider Chuck Person and
Reverend Fred Shuttlesworth.

9   **The Albany Movement**
Hear a sheriff's arrest in Albany, an
Albany official on "outsiders," Dr.
William Anderson, and the voices of
the Ku Klux Klan.

10 **James Meredith in Mississippi**
Hear President John F. Kennedy and
Mississippi Governor Ross Barnett's
negotiations and speeches by Barnett
and Kennedy.

11 **Birmingham**
Hear "Bull" Connor, Reverend Fred
Shuttlesworth, and Martin Luther
King Jr.

12 **George Wallace and John F. Kennedy**
Hear George Wallace, Wallace and
Deputy Attorney General Nicholas
Katzenbach at the University of
Alabama entrance, and President John
F. Kennedy.

13 **Medgar Evers**
Hear Medgar Evers, Myrlie Evers-
Williams, and Bob Dylan's "Only a
Pawn in Their Game."

DISC 2

TRACK

1 **The March on Washington**
Hear President John F. Kennedy and remarks by Bayard Rustin, A. Philip Randolph, John Lewis, and Martin Luther King Jr.

2 **Four Little Girls**
Hear Martin Luther King Jr. speak about the tragedy.

3 **Mississippi and Freedom Summer**
Hear President Lyndon Baines Johnson, FBI Director J. Edgar Hoover, Senator James Eastland, and Mississippi Governor Paul Johnson.

4 **Fannie Lou Hamer**
Hear the firsthand experiences of Fannie Lou Hamer.

5 **Mississippi Freedom Democratic Party**
Hear the MFDP's demands, Fannie Lou Hamer, Senator James Eastland, and Fannie Lou Hamer's "Walk With Me, Lord."

6 **Selma, Alabama**
Hear Martin Luther King Jr., a Selma police order to disperse, and Selma mass meeting participants sing "We Shall Overcome."

7 **The Civil Rights Bill**
Hear President Lyndon Baines Johnson.

8 **Black Power**
Hear chants of "black power" and Stokely Carmichael.

9 **Watts Riots**
Hear Los Angeles police tapes and a news report on the riots.

10 **The Black Panther Party**
Hear Huey Newton and Eldridge Cleaver.

11 **The Assassination of Martin Luther King Jr.**
Hear President Lyndon Baines Johnson, Robert F. Kennedy the night of the assassination, and Martin Luther King Jr.'s last sermon.

12 **Epilogue**
Author Herb Boyd and narrators Ossie Davis and Ruby Dee.

Author
to Readers

Long before the civil rights movement officially emerged in the United States in the 1950s and 1960s, African Americans struggled to be free, to achieve equality, and for their rights. There is no way to say for sure when the first cry was raised, particularly if by civil rights we also mean human rights. To this extent, the Africans who were snatched from their homelands during the Atlantic slave trade and found themselves captives in the Americas certainly had their human rights brutally violated. The countless rebellions and acts of resistance stand as a testament to the African captives' determination to be free. **CD**

The demand by African Americans for justice and equality can be traced to the Reconstruction era, and most directly to the passage of three amendments: the Thirteenth Amendment abolished slavery in 1865; the Fourteenth Amendment, adopted in 1868, affirmed black citizenship under the Constitution; and in 1870, the Fifteenth Amendment guaranteed blacks the right to vote. These three amendments provided the U.S. Congress with the power and authority to enact civil rights legislation. On paper it seemed African Americans had gained full citizenship, and the subsequent election to Congress of such notable black politicians as Mississippi senators Hiram R. Revels (1870–71), who replaced Jefferson Davis, and Blanche K. Bruce (1875–81); South Carolina Congressmen Joseph Rainey (1870–79) and Robert Brown Elliott (1871–74); and Governor P. B. S. Pinchback (1872–73) of Louisiana lent credence to the notion of black progress, though he served only about a month.

However, the presence of a handful of elected black politicians—a mere twenty-two served in Congress from 1868 to 1901—was enough to strike fear in the hearts of many white southerners,

Thirteenth Amendment to the U.S. Constitution: Abolition of Slavery (1865). "Neither slavery nor involuntary servitude...shall exist within the United States, or any place subject to their jurisdiction"

who viewed this political change as "nigger domination." Even when blacks constituted a majority of the population, as they did in South Carolina, they never controlled any of the states' political machinery. Moreover, these black elected officials had very brief tenures in office, and the two senators from Mississippi did not serve at the same time in Congress. Wrote historian William Z. Foster, "Actually, the Negroes got only a small percentage of the local, state, and federal posts—and those of less importance—than their numbers entitled them to."

The myth of "Negro domination" is further refuted in each southern state's judiciary, which ostensibly remained in the hands of whites. Though the white southern aristocracy had been toppled by Union forces, they retained control of the political apparatus, the economic means, and the cultural life. The esteemed historian John Hope Franklin wrote,

"In failing to provide adequate economic security for the freedmen, Reconstruction left them no alternative but to submit to their old masters, a submission that made easier the efforts of Southern whites to overthrow Reconstruction and restore a system based on white supremacy."

When these misconceptions fomented by white historians or "apologists" were embellished in such fiction as *The Clansman* by Thomas Dixon, the source of D.W. Griffith's *Birth of a Nation*, the lies and distortions reached an even larger audience. Telling examples of the failure of Reconstruction were apparent everywhere. Radical Republicans such as Thaddeus Stevens and Charles Sumner had introduced legislation to guarantee the recently emancipated slaves forty acres and a mule. That bill never made it to committee. When it was tabled millions of blacks were mired in peonage, relegated to sharecropping which kept them in perpetual debt.

Vagrancy laws were enforced in many of the major cities in the South. Freedmen or women without visible means of support and a place to live were arrested. To escape this injustice, many former slaves returned to their previous owners; others left the South, hoping for better opportunities in the North or the West. Although thousands of them were skilled mechanics, barbers, barrel makers, wagon masters, masons, and carpenters, these jobs were now only available to white men. Before the Civil War, these same white men gained their livelihood and often their wealth from slavery. With the system for the most part abolished, they had to fend for themselves, taking the jobs that were once performed by those in bondage.

Even more perilous, the ex-slaves were vulnerable to racial violence from the Ku Klux Klan and other night riders seeking revenge against unarmed blacks. One of the most terrifying acts of the Klan was to surround a black home at night and throw a lit torch through the window, setting the house on fire. There are hundreds of reported instances in which mobs of whites would forcibly take a black man or woman from their homes or off the streets, accuse them of some crime, and lynch them from the nearest tree. At this time, it was not possible to count the number of blacks who were lynched by mobs or the Klan. Author Ralph Ginzburg in his book *100 Years of Lynching*, published in 1962, offers a partial listing of approximately five thousand blacks lynched in the United States since 1859.

When the former slaves were not at the mercy of a lynch mob, they were being fleeced by unscrupulous bankers, even by the Freedman's Bank, which was founded to safeguard their savings. At first the bank thrived, sustained by deposits from black farmers, servants, mechanics, and washer women. But gradually, as branches grew and the supervision became more lax, the bank began to unravel.

Unscrupulous managers and bank presidents approved loans that were never repaid, unwise investments were made, and soon the savings of black workers and merchants were stolen or shrewdly siphoned from the bankers by speculators. "Money was loaned recklessly to the speculators in the District of Columbia," wrote W. E. B. Du Bois in *Black*

Entered according to act of Congress in the year 1872 by Currier & Ives, in the Office of the Librarian of Congress at Washington.
ROBERT C. DE LARGE, M.C. of S. Carolina.   JEFFERSON H. LONG, M.C. of Georgia.

U.S. Senator H.R. REVELS, of Mississippi   BENJ. S. TURNER, M.C. of Alabama.   JOSIAH T. WALLS, M.C. of Florida.   JOSEPH H. RAINY, M.C. of S. Carolina.   R. BROWN ELLIOT, M.C. of S. Carolina.

THE FIRST COLORED SENATOR AND REPRESENTATIVES,
In the 41st and 42nd Congress of the United States.

An 1872 Currier and Ives lithograph showing African American politicians

A 1939 Ku Klux Klan rally

Reconstruction. "Jay Cooke and Company, the great bankers, borrowed half a million dollars, and this company and the First National Bank of Washington controlled Freedman's Bank between 1870 and 1873. Runs were started on the bank and then an effort was made to unload the whole thing on Frederick Douglass as a representative Negro. This was useless and the bank finally closed in June, 1874."

Depositors were able to recoup only 30 percent of their savings, which was better than the dividends Douglass got from his attempt to save the doomed bank. As president of the bank, Douglass tried to stop black depositors from withdrawing their savings, even depositing $5,000 of his own money. It was too little and too late. He was widely admired and many had faith in his judgment, but Douglass could not save Freedman's Bank. Its collapse was symptomatic of the Reconstruction period and its failure to provide for the millions of ex-slaves. "Despite my effort to uphold the Freedman's Savings and Trust Company it has fallen," Douglass recounted in a letter to Gerrit Smith, a prominent white abolitionist, "it has been the black man's cow, but the white man's milk. Bad loans and bad management have been the death of it. I was ignorant of its real condition till elected its president."

Losing their life savings when Freedman's Bank closed proved disheartening, and thousands of blacks never recovered from the setback. Many were left homeless, without any means of subsistence, and thus vulnerable to the vagrancy laws that would be but one of several statutes imposed as part of the bulwark of Jim Crowism and segregation.

Black rights further unraveled with the Compromise of 1877. In the presidential election of 1876, Democrat Samuel J. Tilden of New York led Republican Rutherford B. Hayes in popular votes, and 184 to 165 in electoral college votes. However, because of fraud and violence in South Carolina, Louisiana, and Florida, as well as questions about the eligibility of electors in Oregon, twenty electoral votes were in doubt. When a special commission was created to sort out the dispute, Hayes was given all twenty votes. This prompted a filibuster from the Democrats. To settle the impasse, representatives on both sides convened a meeting at Wormley House, a black-owned establishment in Washington, D.C., to concoct a deal.

Eric Foner and John Garraty, editors of *The Reader's Companion to American History*, summarized the outcome: "The South would accept Hayes's election, back Republican James A. Garfield for House Speaker, and protect black rights; Republicans would provide federal aid for internal improvements, patronage, especially, home rule. But Garfield was defeated for Speaker, the government failed to subsidize improvements, and Hayes dispensed patronage and followed existing policy by removing federal troops from the South. The final southern Republican governments, all in the disputed states, collapsed, leading to the Democratic Solid South and violence and discrimination toward blacks."

For black Americans, as Professor Rayford Logan concluded, it was the beginning of the "nadir."

Despite the efforts of the National Association for the Advancement of Colored People to challenge in court the inequities of voting procedures, restrictive covenants, separate public education, and segregated interstate and local transportation, very little change occurred until just before World War II. In the interim, blacks experienced such widely publicized incidents as the Tulsa Riot in 1921, in which there were many black fatalities, and black businesses and homeowners suffered great losses; the attack on Dr. Ossian Sweet and his family after they moved into an all-white neighborhood in Detroit in 1925; and the

Freedman's Bank Passbook, 1873

No. 1614th

Ledger W

Ann Blue

BANK BOOK

OF THE

Freedman's Savings

AND

TRUST COMPANY,

Chartered by Act of Congress, approved March 3d, 1865.

ISSUED BY THE AGENCY AT

Lexington, Ky.

Keep this Book in good order; do not fold or roll it; give notice at once, if lost.

Wm. MANN, STEAM-POWER PRINTER PHILADA.

conviction of the "Scottsboro Boys," who were falsely accused of raping two white women in Alabama in 1931. All were dramatic examples of how vulnerable black life had become in America. Black Americans could not rely on law enforcement agencies or the courts to protect them from those intent on abrogating their civil rights.

With no support from the authorities, black Americans began finding new ways of getting their message heard. By the mid-thirties, Reverend Adam Clayton Powell Jr. led a brigade of protesters in Harlem against white store owners who refused to employ blacks. "Don't Buy Where You Can't Work!" was a slogan they popularized that sparked similar demonstrations in other cities.

Black Americans discovered how to place pressure on the federal government when the great labor activist A. Philip Randolph assembled his legions and threatened President Franklin Delano Roosevelt with a march on Washington in 1941 unless he put an end to discrimination in the defense industry. Roosevelt capitulated to Randolph's demand and signed Executive Order 8802 prohibiting discrimination in the defense industry.

While Roosevelt's New Deal relieved millions of white Americans from the menace of the Great Depression, for black Americans it was the same old "raw deal." Placing a few blacks in his administration, including the redoubtable Mary McLeod Bethune, a prominent educator and founder of Bethune-Cookman

THE ANTI-LYNCHING CAMPAIGN OF IDA B. WELLS

1935 Lynching

In March 1892, nearly thirty years after the Civil War, three close friends of Ida B. Wells—Thomas Moss, Calvin McDowell, and Henry Stewart—opened the People's Grocery Company in Memphis, Tennessee. Their store competed with a white-owned grocery located directly across the street from them. Angered over the loss of business, a white mob gathered to run the black grocers out of town. But the blacks were warned of the raid and armed themselves. During the ensuing shootout, at least one white man was wounded. The black store owners were arrested.

An already aroused white community was further incensed when the local papers sensationalized the incident. Once more a white mob assembled, stormed the jail, and snatched the three black men from their cells. They were lynched. Wells, who had earned a reputation for her uncompromising editorials in the *Free Speech and Headlight*, a paper she partly owned, responded to this atrocious act of violence by writing an editorial urging blacks to leave Memphis. This was the beginning of her anti-lynching crusade that brought her international acclaim.

College in Daytona Beach, Florida, was widely appreciated, but it wasn't enough to lift the majority of black Americans from the pit of poverty.

President Harry Truman would sign a similar executive order ending discrimination in the armed services. Later, shortly after the end of World War II, and in response to the NAACP and other civil rights organizations, he formed a committee of notable Americans to secure the rights of black citizens. Chief among the concerns was the continuing pattern of discrimination in housing and education. Black Americans were jubilant on May 3, 1948, when the Supreme Court sounded the death knell of restrictive covenants in its *Shelley v. Kramer* decision, forbidding state and federal courts from enforcing such agreements. The NAACP was largely responsible for this success through the *Shelley v. Kramer*, *Hurd v. Hodge*, and *McGhee v. Sipes* cases.

Two years later, in 1950, the Supreme Court ruled that the University of Texas could not bar Herman Marion Sweatt from its law school because of race. Moreover, it ruled that the separate law school that the state had established to accommodate Sweatt was not and could not be equal to that of the University of Texas. Another significant step toward overturning the "separate but equal" doctrine mandated by the Supreme Court's 1896 *Plessy v. Ferguson* decision occurred when the high court ruled that the University of Oklahoma could not segregate G. W. McLaurin within its graduate school once he had been admitted.

The favorable decisions for blacks at higher educational institutions spurred the NAACP to action against the widespread segregation in the nation's elementary schools. By 1952, with the resourceful Thurgood Marshall at the helm, the NAACP argued five cases from different school districts before the Supreme Court. The cases involved Clarendon County, South Carolina; Prince Edward County, Virginia; Wilmington, Delaware; Washington, D.C.; and Topeka, Kansas, whose name would be attached

Mary McLeod Bethune

to the landmark *Brown v. Board of Education* decision two years later on May 17, 1954.

Though the highest court in the land ruled to eliminate segregated schools, the law would meet with stubborn and sometime violent resistance, particularly in the South. Each progressive move by the federal government was countered by segregationists demanding state's rights. In the middle of this impasse, and those who figured so prominently in this battle, was the emerging civil rights movement. More than a year after *Brown v. Board of Education* became the law of the land, the segregated transportation system of Montgomery was challenged. Rosa Parks took a stand by remaining seated.

Many believe this event triggered the rapid rise of the civil rights movement. Others contend that it was only the second phase of a reaction following the murder of Emmett Till in Mississippi, three months before Rosa Parks refused to move to the back of the bus. We begin our excursion into the history of the civil rights movement with this incident that links the North and South through the innocence of a black youth who unwittingly stepped over the long-standing, lethal boundaries separating blacks and whites in Mississippi.

THE SCOTTSBORO BOYS

The Scottsboro Boys

Prospects of employment have always been difficult for African Americans, and job opportunities were even fewer during the Great Depression. The search for work is what prompted several of nine black youths to hop a train in Chattanooga, Tennessee, bound for Memphis in 1931. When they encountered a band of white men on the train, insults were exchanged and then a melee erupted. The white men were incensed when the blacks got the better of them and reported their plight to railroad officials. A conductor at the depot phoned ahead to Paint Rock, Alabama, where the boys were taken from the train and charged with assault.

But when the boys were later jailed in the nearby town of Scottsboro, they faced new charges. Traveling on the train with them were two white prostitutes—Victoria Price and Ruby Bates—both dressed in men's overalls. They claimed they had been assaulted. The nine youths were charged with rape.

Despite the lack of incriminating evidence, the accused, now called "The Scottsboro Boys," were convicted by an all-white jury and sentenced to death (though one received a mistrial). Within weeks, the boys were a *cause célèbre*, particularly among leftist organizations and the Communist Party. The rallies, marches, and fundraisers on behalf of the boys intensified after the Alabama Supreme Court upheld the convictions.

A number of retrials ended without any justice for the boys. Even after Ruby Bates recanted and testified for the defense, and two reversals by the Supreme Court, the convictions stood. In 1935, after the second Supreme Court ruled that black residents had been systematically excluded from the jury pool, the NAACP, along with the boys' legal team from the International Labor Defense, stepped up its campaign to free them. Two years later, the rape charges were dropped against five of the defendants. The rest received life sentences. In 1976, Alabama Governor George Wallace finally pardoned all the Scottsboro Boys—only one of whom was still alive.

1

The Murder of Emmett Till

t was near the end of August, 1955, about four months after the Supreme Court had ruled on the second version of *Brown v. Board of Education*, or *Brown II*, in which segregation would be ended with "all deliberate speed." Fourteen-year-old Emmett Till arrived in Money, Mississippi, from his home town of Chicago. He had come to Money, a small town in the Delta where tiny shacks stood amid miles of cotton fields, to spend two weeks of his summer vacation with an aunt, uncle, and cousins. One day Till, his cousins, and some friends ventured down to the Bryant Grocery Store.

Simeon Wright, one of the cousins with Till that day, recounted what happened. "Lots of books have the facts all wrong about what Emmett did and said," Wright said during an interview. "He did whistle at Mrs. Bryant, but it had nothing to do with us daring him to do it. To this day, I'm not sure why Emmett did that." Mamie Till Mobley, Emmett's mother, offers an alternate version, explaining, "Emmett had a speech impediment, and I told him that when this occurred for him to whistle." Apparently Till was asking Mrs. Bryant for some bubble gum and stammered on the "b-sound" and whistled in order to continue his purchase.

"That's not true," Wright continued. "Emmett wasn't stuttering. He whistled at her, but it had nothing to do with his stuttering."

Days later, according to Till's great uncle, Moses Wright, Simeon's father, two white men—Roy Bryant, Carolyn's husband, and J. W. Milam, his half-brother—abducted Till from Wright's home early Sunday morning, August 28. By some reports, with Till still not home hours later, Wright called Sheriff George Smith of Greenwood and reported him missing. On Monday, less than forty-eight hours after the abduction, Sheriff Smith arrested Milam and Bryant on kidnapping charges. Bryant confessed that he had taken Till from the Wright's house, but later contended he had released him when he found out that he wasn't the boy who had "insulted" his wife.

Till was missing for four days before his body was found by Robert Hodges while fishing in the Tallahatchie River. Hodges was twelve miles north of Money. Till's body was weighted down by a seventy-five-pound cotton gin fan that was looped around his neck with barbed wire. Till had apparently been brutally beaten before he was shot through the head. Mose Wright identified his nephew's body. Bryant and Milam were held in jail pending a grand jury session on possible murder charges.

Till's mother was informed of her son's tragic death, but rather than traveling to Mississippi decided to wait in Chicago for his body to be delivered. She didn't want to see her son's body in Mississippi. When it arrived in Chicago, the body was taken to A. A. Rayner and Sons Funeral Home. She said she could smell his remains before she got there. "It was the most terrible odor," she recalled in her autobiography. "We began to smell it about two blocks from the funeral home. At first, I thought about the stockyards, where they slaughtered hogs and cattle….This was much worse. This was overpowering…it was the smell of death and it was everywhere."

"They had him in a box, larger than any one I've ever seen," Mrs. Mobley said. "I asked them to open it and I discovered that it was covered with lime (to make it deteriorate faster). I told them to remove

Above: Mamie Bradley at arrival of body

Left: Emmett Till

OBERTS TEMPLE

THE INTERNATIONAL BOARD of FOREIGN BISHOPS OVERSEERS
OF THE CHURCHES OF GOD IN CHRIST
1st ANNNUAL CONVENTION HERE
SEPT.14 THRU THE 19 1955
DAILY SESSIONS 11:30 A.M.
EVENING SESSIONS 8 P.M.

GOD IN CHRIST †

Mourners enter Till's funeral

the lime so I could see his face." What she saw was what the world saw in *Jet* magazine in 1955. Till's face was battered beyond recognition. Till's mother recalled: "His left eye was hanging down on his cheek, his nose was bashed in and it was if someone had taken an axe and chopped his face away from the rest of his head."

Bryant, age twenty-four, and Milam, age thirty-five, pleaded not guilty when arraigned. They were indicted for kidnapping, with a ten-year maximum sentence, and murder, with a possible life sentence. The outrage from the crime rocked the nation, particularly in northern cities. Wrote Marty Richardson in the Cleveland Call and Post, "Much of the outrage expressed in Chicago, and in thousands of letters, wires, and telephone messages to President Eisenhower, Attorney General Herbert Brownell and congressmen from all states, came over the fact that the murder of the boy was the third one since Mississippi first began showing a savage resentment over the

Supreme Court ruling on segregated schools and Negroes began a stepped-up voting program."

Roy Wilkins, executive secretary of the NAACP, termed the murder a "lynching" and he was further infuriated when a local sheriff charged that the NAACP was using the incident to "embarrass" the state of Mississippi.

Mrs. Mobley insisted on having an open-casket funeral for her son. For three days, tens of thousands of people, blacks and whites, lined up outside Roberts Temple Church of God in Christ on South State Street in Chicago to view his bloated and battered corpse. While her son lay in his coffin, Mrs. Mobley, sobbing inconsolably, told the press, "I'm not bitter against all white people. Many good white people will help me, I know, but I do want these lynchers of my boy punished. And it's the federal government's job to punish Mississippi for its refusal to protect colored people. I want to go to the Mississippi trial; I want other people to go with me to see this thing

Roy Bryant, right, and J. W. Milam, second from right, exit the courthouse in Greenwood, Mississippi

through. I'm willing to go anywhere, to speak anywhere, to get justice." And she did.

The trial of Roy Bryant and J. W. Milam lasted five days, from September 19 to September 23, 1955. The defendants were represented by five white attorneys. More than seventy reporters and thirty photographers, from all over the world, crowded in and around the courthouse in Sumner. Historian David Halberstam, then a young reporter, wrote that the trial "became the first great media event of the civil rights movement."

As the trial opened, the defendants swaggered into the courtroom, confident that they would be acquitted. They were just as jovial as the 250 friends and relatives packed into the courtroom.

All the black reporters, including Jimmy Hicks, later to be an editor of the *Amsterdam News*, sat in segregated chairs behind a railing, apart from the white reporters, trial principals, and other spectators. Along with Hicks, there was room for only three other black reporters. Sheriff H. C. Strider, a huge man of nearly three hundred pounds, and his deputies, made sure everyone was thoroughly searched. There had been a series of death threats against the blacks who were scheduled to testify and they didn't want to take any chances. There were about fifty black spectators at the trial, all of them seated to the rear of the two-story courthouse, some standing in the second floor hallway outside.

After two days, the jury of all white men was finally selected. Most of the delay was due to excusing potential jurors who either knew the defendants and had donated money to their defense or who clearly showed definite opinions about the case. Judge Curtis Swango then requested a recess because the state had learned of the existence of other possible witnesses to the kidnapping and the murder. The final pretrial disruption occurred when Till's mother arrived in court accompanied by Congressman Charles C. Diggs of Michigan. One press account described her as "a demure woman whose attractiveness was set off by a small black hat with a veil folded back, a black dress with a white collar. In the more than ninety-nine-degree heat of the courtroom, she fanned herself with a black silk fan with a red design."

On the third day of the trial, the prosecution called its first witness—Moses Wright, Till's great uncle. Murray Kempton wrote in the *New York Post*, "Moses Wright, making a formation no white man in this county really believed he would dare to make, stood on his tiptoes to the full limit of his sixty-four years and his 5 feet 3 inches yesterday, pointed his black, work-worn finger straight at the huge and stormy head of J. W. Milam and swore that this was the man who dragged fourteen-year-old Emmett Louis Till out of his cotton field cabin the night the boy was murdered. 'There he is,' said Moses Wright. He was a black pigmy standing up to a white ox. J. W. Milam leaned forward, crooking a cigarette in a hand that seemed as large as Moses Wright's whole chest, and his eyes were coals of hatred. Moses Wright took all their blast straight in his face, and then, for good measure, turned and pointed that still unshaking finger at Roy Bryant, the man he says joined Milam on the night ride to seize young Till…'and there's Mr. Bryant,' said Moses Wright and sat down hard against the chair-back with a lurch which told better than anything else the cost in strength to him of the thing he had done. He was a field Negro who had dared try to send two white men to the gas chamber for murdering a Negro."

"Some accounts of my father saying 'Thar he is' and speaking in broken English are exaggerated to make him sound like a country hick," Simeon Wright said. "But my father was a minister who preached in

The all-white jury

around the county, and he was very articulate. However, they are right about his courage."

Such an accusation—a black man charging a white man with a crime—was unheard in the South at that time. "He was a brave man and unafraid," said his son.

Till's mother also took the stand, recalling when she first saw her son's body and how she was able to identify him by the ring his father had given him. The prosecution's surprise witness was a black man, Willie Reed, an eighteen-year-old farm hand, who testified that he saw J. W. Milam enter a barn in Sunflower County on August 28 and seconds later heard screams coming from the barn. His grandfather, Ed Reed, corroborated Reed's testimony.

After the prosecution rested its case, the defense wasted no time in putting Mrs. Carolyn Bryant on the stand, but without the jury being present. Writing for the *Washington Afro-American*, Jimmy Hicks captured her testimony. "A slight brunette, she charged that young Till used obscene remarks when addressing her but refused to quote the exact words. She left the impression that to use such words would defile her. Mrs. Bryant said that on August 24, a colored man entered her store in Money. She said she

asked him what he wanted and she got it for him. She never testified, however, just what purchase the colored man wanted." She said that when she put her hand out for the money for the purchase, Till grabbed her arm and said, "How about a date, Baby?"

Hicks continued, "The woman testified that she struggled loose and turned from the colored man but he chased her around the counter and caught her at the cash register. She said he placed his arms around her hips and then quoted the man as asking: 'What's the matter, baby? Can't you take it?'

"It was at this time Mrs. Bryant was asked to repeat some of the exact language used by the boy but she declined. She even refused to repeat one obscene word used. 'You needn't be afraid of me,' Mrs. Bryant quoted the colored man as saying later. She said that he then told her: 'I've been with white women before.' It was then, according to Mrs. Bryant, that another colored fellow entered the store and caught the alleged attacker by the arm and led him out." Mrs. Bryant said that Till, in the company of several other black men, made another obscene remark outside the store, thus prompting her to go to her car to get her pistol.

Moses Wright identifies Bryant and Milam as Till's kidnappers

On the fifth day of the trial, the jury heard closing arguments from the defense and the prosecution. In a loud, booming voice that carried out to the streets where many of the black townspeople listened, District Attorney Gerald Chatham said he was not "concerned with the pressure and agitation which the trial has produced, either within or outside the state of Mississippi." But he said he was concerned "with what is morally and legally wrong." Referring to Till's mother sitting at the card table with the black reporters, his final words to the jury were: "The next time it may be you who will be sitting there crying."

Throughout the trial, the defense had contended that Till was still missing and that the corpse in question belonged to someone else. John Whitten, one of the defendants' lawyers, framed his argument around this contention, saying, "There are people in the United States who want to destroy the way of life of southern people. There are people...who will go as far as necessary to commit any crime known to man to widen the gap between the white and colored people in the United States. They would not be above putting a rotting, stinking body in the river in the hope it would be identified as Emmett Till."

Either before, anticipating the defense's argument, or after—the reports are not clear about the order of the closing statements—prosecutor Gerald Chatham hammered: "If there was one ear left, one hairline, one part of his nose, any part of Emmett Till's body, then I say to you that Mamie Bradley [Mamie Till Mobley had remarried] was God's given witness to identify him."

After a little over an hour of deliberations, the jury came back with its verdict. They were all standing when the foreman spoke: "We the jurors find the defendants not guilty." A buzz of voices rippled across the humid courtroom, but it ceased as if heeding Judge Swango's stern expression. Acquitted of murder, the defendants were turned over to LeFlore County officials to face possible federal kidnapping charges. Friends and relatives crowded around the defendants, embracing them, shedding tears of joy.

MYRLIE EVERS-WILLIAMS ON THE TILL MURDER

"I never completely understood what it was that made the murder of Emmett Till so different from the ones that had preceded it," wrote Myrlie Evers-Williams, widow of assassinated NAACP Mississippi state field secretary Medgar Evers, in her memoir *For Us, The Living*. "In part, I suppose it was his youth. Medgar was convinced that the existence of our office in Jackson and the enormous efforts of the NAACP to get out the news made a tremendous difference. Whatever the answer, it was the murder of this fourteen-year-old out-of-town-visitor that touched off the worldwide clamor and cast the glare of a world spotlight on Mississippi's racism. Ironically, the deaths of George Lee and Lamar Smith, both directly connected with the struggle for civil rights and killed while registering voters in Mississippi, had caused nothing like the public attention attracted by the Till case."

None of the reports recorded the reaction of Till's mother, who wept during the closing arguments.

After the verdict, former First Lady Eleanor Roosevelt wrote in the *Memphis Press-Scimitar*, "I think the jury that allowed itself to be persuaded that no one had really found and identified the body—though it was granted that a boy had disappeared but the body found might not be his—and therefore, the accused men could not be convicted or punished in any way, will find their consciences troubled. It is true that there can still be a trial for kidnapping, and I hope there will be. I hope the effort will be made to get at the truth. I hope we are beginning to discard the old habit, as practiced in a part of our country, of making it very difficult to convict a white man of a crime against a colored man or woman."

Within several weeks of their acquittal, Milam and Bryant avoided a second trial after a grand jury refused to bring indictments against them for kidnapping. Despite their prior confessions to the charge, no indictments were issued, nor did the grand jury offer any explanation why the case was not sent to trial. Even more disturbing, the two men would later confess to the crime in a widely reprinted story written by William Bradford Huie for *Look* magazine. They would die without ever being convicted of the crime.

Following his testimony, Moses Wright was spirited out of town, his relatives fearing retribution. As for Till's mother, she waged a relentless campaign, not only to vindicate her son's name but to protect the human and civil rights of other black children. "My son was a sacrificial lamb," she often told reporters, "he was sent to play a special role and I don't think he died in vain."

Before the year of 1955 was out, Till's tragedy would be supplanted in the press by an incident involving Rosa Parks in Montgomery, Alabama. Several years later, as the civil rights movement continued to gain momentum, the incident would be memorialized by folk singer Bob Dylan in his song, "The Death of Emmett Till."

It was not until new evidence uncovered by documentaries of two filmmakers, Keith Beauchamp and Stanley Nelson, that the Till case was reopened by the Justice Department in 2004.

If Till's murder wasn't the spark, it was the flint against which the emerging civil rights movement would find its source to ignite. It must also be seen in the context of a century of black men who had been lynched after being accused of raping a white woman. Moreover, the murder of Emmett Till cannot be separated from *Brown v. Board of Education* that had roiled segregationists all over the South. Till's presence and his comportment may have been too bold for his abductors and murderers, reminding them of black people's demands for respect and equality that was so much a part of the first March on Washington in 1941.

"THE DEATH OF EMMETT TILL," BY BOB DYLAN

'Twas down in Mississippi not so long ago,
When a young boy from Chicago town stepped through a Southern door.
This boy's dreadful tragedy I can still remember well,
The color of his skin was black and his name was Emmett Till.

Some men they dragged him to a barn and there they beat him up.
They said they had a reason, but I can't remember what.
They tortured him and did some evil things too evil to repeat.
There was screaming sounds inside the barn, there was laughing sounds out on the street.

Then they rolled his body down a gulf amidst a bloody red rain
And they threw him in the waters wide to cease his screaming pain.
The reason that they killed him there, and I'm sure it ain't no lie,
Was just for the fun of killin' him and to watch him slowly die.
And then to stop the United States of yelling for a trial,
Two brothers they confessed that they had killed poor Emmett Till.
But on the jury there were men who helped the brothers commit this awful crime,
And so this trial was a mockery, but nobody seemed to mind. I saw the morning papers but I could not bear to see
The smiling brothers walkin' down the courthouse stairs.
For the jury found them innocent and the brothers they went free,
While Emmett's body floats the foam of a Jim Crow southern sea.

If you can't speak out against this kind of thing, a crime that's so unjust,
Your eyes are filled with dead men's dirt, your mind is filled with dust.
Your arms and legs they must be in shackles and chains, and your blood it must refuse to flow,
For you let this human race fall down so God-awful low!

This song is just a reminder to remind your fellow man
That this kind of thing still lives today in that ghost-robed Ku Klux Klan.
But if all of us folks that thinks alike, if we gave all we could give,
We could make this great land of ours a greater place to live.

2

The First March on Washington

I t is not possible to find the first moment of African resistance to captivity during the more than three hundreds years of the Atlantic slave trade. Nor can we document the first revolt on a slave ship, or the first rebellion on a plantation. African captives found a number of ways to show they would not passively abide oppression. Long before Malcolm X proclaimed his dictum, "By any means necessary," black Americans employed a variety of tactics and strategies to secure their freedom.

In the early years of our nation's history, marches against racism, discrimination, and segregation were among the most visible and easily organized forms of resistance. From the handful of blacks who assembled at Boston Commons in the 1770s to voice their protest against British tyranny to the aroused thousands in the 1920s and 1930s demanding the nation honor its promise of liberty and equality, African Americans have been on the march. Their determination to achieve justice reached massive proportions in the 1940s when Asa Philip Randolph began to galvanize his forces for a March on Washington.

A native of Florida, Randolph arrived in New York City in 1911 and attended City College, where he came into contact with a number of progressive political activists. A few years later he co-founded the *Messenger*, a weekly newspaper with a socialist outlook. In 1918, he was jailed for expressing anti-war sentiments. Three years later he unsuccessfully ran for the secretary of state of New York. Randolph's early claim to fame occurred in 1925, when as a union organizer, he helped launch the Brotherhood of Sleeping Car Porters, some 10,000 black workers. It took the black porters ten years to win a contract with the Pullman Palace Car Company. Through his work with the union, and with World War II looming even larger, he began to think of ways to further empower black workers, particularly in the defense industry where they had been systematically excluded. To remedy the situation, he thought public pressure on the White House might be effective, though there were detractors who felt such a tactic might not be appropriate during wartime. CD

DISC 1
TRACK 3

Randolph's anger and resentment grew during a decade of blatant hostility against black Americans, beginning with the Scottsboro Boys incident in 1931. Nine black youths were accused of raping two white women on a train in Alabama. Despite strong evidence of their innocence, eight of them were convicted. Subsequent trials before the Supreme Court gave the case national exposure and aroused a protest movement to free them. After many years of trials, the men were gradually released from prison.

Randolph must have been further infuriated to hear reports of hundreds of black men being lynched throughout the South while segregation and discrimination made blacks second class citizens. "Where there was once tolerance and acceptance of a position believed to be gradually changing for the better, now the Negro is showing a 'democratic upsurge in rebellion,' bordering on open hostility," the *Amsterdam-Star News* reported in 1941. The racial climate in America was seething.

DISC 1
TRACK 3

Nowhere was this racial explosion more ominous than in the military, where black soldiers had for generations complained about unfair treatment, the lack of promotions, and the disproportionate number of African Americans put in the stockades or dishonorably discharged. These were the racist conditions that greeted activist and author Nelson Peery when he entered the service in 1940. "The military never dreamed of using black soldiers as anything but hewers of wood and drawers of water," Peery recounted in his autobiography. "They sent them into the Quartermaster, Port, Water Supply, Graves Registration, Laundry, and Engineer Battalions. These combat sup-

A. Philip Randolph addresses the sleeping car porters

port groups freed up white men to fight white man's war in defense of a white man's country." CD

Later, when unrest was reported at several Army training camps, Peery knew the source of it firsthand at Fort Huachuca in the high desert of Arizona. "They say a healthy army gripes," Peery related. "We griped about the chow, the heat, the dust, the water, and the things that made the army the army. Most of all, we griped about the white supremacist attitude of most of the white officers.

"The War Department, dominated by the Southern elite and Northern reactionaries, followed the old discredited line that the segregated Negro outfits functioned best if staffed by Southern officers because 'they understood the Negro,'" Peery continued.

"Most of these officers were reservists. Many were Klansmen. Some of them tried to treat the regiment as if it were their antebellum plantation. They expressed their belief in white supremacy with body language and tone of voice. The worst expression was their slave term 'boy.' Sometimes, the officer would catch himself and change the 'boy' to 'soldier.' Most of the time when the braver of soldiers would carefully say, 'Sir, my name is Private Johnson,' the officer would glare at the insolence, realize he was wrong, turn on his heel, and walk away."

The mounting tension in the armed services sent waves of resentment among blacks throughout the nation. The exclusion of black workers from the defense industries caused considerable concern to civil rights organizations and militant community activists. The National Association for the Advancement of Colored People sent a statement to President Franklin D. Roosevelt charging that "equitable employment of minority racial groups in defense industries was more than an issue of racial policy." This was a radical departure from the organization's previous policy, which was still holding to the time-worn position of separate-but-equal disengagement. But a committee formed by the Pittsburgh Courier, in an alliance with black college fraternities and sororities, and led by Dr. Rayford Logan, fell in step with African American public opinion. This prestigious committee, combined with a newly enlightened labor movement, swayed the NAACP to challenge racist policies.

The Congress of Industrial Organizations (CIO) was the pivotal force in this more militant view. Union leaders were gradually learning they needed black workers if they were going to be successful in

The all-black 99th U.S. Fighter Squadron, 1944

organizing mass production industries. This lesson became vividly clear during the union's attempt to organize the Ford plant at River Rouge outside Detroit. When the UAW–CIO struck in 1940 at the huge Rouge industrial complex, black workers, having been denied opportunities in the past, crossed hostile picket lines seeking employment.

As the turmoil threatened to boil over into a full-fledged melee, the union called on the youth wing of the city's NAACP, which was more sympathetic to the union, to stem the mounting dissension. Ultimately, Walter White, the organization's national secretary, arrived in River Rouge and convinced the black workers to walk out of the plant. White's efforts were significant, but so was the role played by a cadre of black union organizers who were on the ramparts years before the civil rights workers took notice. The appearance of actor, singer, scholar, and political activist Paul Robeson in the days preceding the strike was always a source of inspiration.

The climate was set for the entry of A. Philip Randolph. Randolph's prominence as a national leader had already been established by the founding of the Brotherhood of Sleeping Car Porters union. In January 1941, he issued a call for a massive demonstration on the nation's capital to end discrimination in employment in the defense industry. The march was set for July 1. Randolph's call came in the wake

DISCRIMINATION BEYOND THE MILITARY

Outside the military, the situation of black Americans was no better. Even in the nation's capital, racism and discrimination were rampant. "At that time racism bulged in Washington, D.C.," filmmaker/photographer Gordon Parks recalled. It didn't take Parks long to discover that even a talented, easy-going black man was unwelcome in the city's municipalities and upper echelons of society. "In a very short time Washington was showing me its real character," he said. "It was a hate-drenched city, honoring my ignorance and smugly creating bad memories for me. During the afternoon my entire childhood rushed back to greet me, to remind me that the racism it poured on me had not called it quits." Like, Peery, Parks had spent a portion of his youth coming of age in Minneapolis, where the black presence was small compared to the major cities where they would later reside.

If circumstances were deplorable for gifted young black men, for black women (with or without the best education) times were terrible, particularly opportunities for employment. In 1939, Dorothy Height moved from New York City to Washington, D.C., to take a position as executive secretary of the YWCA Phillis Wheatley Home. Concurrently, she became a member of the Delta Sigma Theta, an all-black sorority founded on the campus of Howard University in 1913.

During a sorority committee meeting in the summer of 1940, Height proposed that the sorority analyze the reasons why black women were excluded from so many of the jobs available to women. The project was considered important because at that time many black women over the age of fourteen were working, and most married black women held employment outside of their homes.

of the NAACP's sputtering attempts to launch its own campaign. Soon, the NAACP, the National Urban League, and black leaders of the YMCA endorsed the movement.

"We call upon you to fight for jobs in National Defense," the call began. "We call upon you to struggle for the integration of Negroes in the armed forces, such as the Air Corps, Navy, Army, and Marine Corps of the nation." Randolph was a fiery orator and he took the hustings. With a deep, resonant baritone voice, perfect enunciation, and great passion, the impeccably dressed Randolph could move a crowd with his conviction.

"Now, let us be unafraid," he said at a rally in Detroit. "We are fighting for big stakes. Our stakes are liberty, justice, and democracy. Every Negro should hang his head in shame who fails to do his part now for freedom. This is the hour of the Negro. It is the hour of the common man. May we rise to the challenge to struggle for our rights. Come what will or may, let us never falter."

When Randolph insisted that the march be all-black, the demand slowed its momentum. Randolph's decision had come in part because of his virulent anti-Communism. Perhaps still gnawing at him was the penetration of the Communists, especially "black reds" in the National Negro Congress, and their subsequent domination of the organization, that prompted Randolph to take such a firm position on the race issue. While he was mindful that such an exclusionary policy could prove a detriment and unwittingly exclude influential white liberals, he was guarding against the possible heavy influx of white Communists "who would use the March for ulterior purposes."

Though Randolph was an imaginative and indefatigable leader, he wasn't solely responsible for the orchestration of the march and its objectives. He had a number of resourceful aides, but none more reliable than Bayard Rustin. It was within weeks of Randolph's denunciation of the white Communists

Bayard Rustin

that twenty-nine-year-old Rustin quit the Young Communist League and returned to the ranks of the March on Washington, renewing his acquaintance with Randolph. Things had been cordial, but lukewarm in their first encounter a few months before as they disagreed about the role of Communists in the movement for social and political change. Now Rustin was back seeking to join his considerable organizing skills with his mentor's. Having put aside his former political ideology because of the sudden shift in Soviet policy after Hitler invaded Russia, Rustin was ready to admit his mistake and assume whatever task Randolph assigned. Immediately, he was placed in the youth arm of the movement.

Rustin threw himself passionately into the March's plans, even though much had been done and decided by the time he arrived. President Roosevelt had been warned by Randolph that the only way he would cancel the march was the issuance of an executive order ending all racial discrimination in the nation's munitions factories. A few weeks after Rustin returned to the ranks, Roosevelt capitulated, mainly because his wife, Eleanor, had alerted him to the extent to which he would injure himself politically at home and abroad. It was Eleanor who had also arranged a meeting on June 18, 1941, that brought the president, Randolph, New York City Mayor Fiorello La Guardia, and Walter White together to discuss the ramifications of the march.

"Mr. President, time is running on," Randolph told Roosevelt as they sat in the Oval Office of the White House, June 18, 1941. "You are quite busy, I know. But what we want to talk with you about is the problem of jobs for Negroes in defense industries. Our people are being turned away at factory gates because they are colored. They can't live with this thing. Now, what are you going to do about it?"

After Randolph made clear to Roosevelt that he wanted nothing short of an executive order making it mandatory that blacks be permitted to work in the plants, and that he fully intended to march one hundred thousand people on Washington, the men set about finding a remedy.

On June 25, a week after this meeting and three days after Hitler invaded the Soviet Union, the president announced that he was issuing Executive Order

MARIAN ANDERSON AND THE DAUGHTERS OF THE AMERICAN REVOLUTION

Marian Anderson performs at the Lincoln Memorial

In the 1930s, Marian Anderson was a contralto who had performed on all the great stages of the world. But such renown was not enough for the Daughters of the American Revolution (DAR), or at least not enough to supersede the "white artists only" clause in the contract of one of their performance halls. In 1939, they denied Anderson from appearing at Constitution Hall in Washington, D.C., which the DAR owned. Eleanor Roosevelt, the president's wife, was so incensed that she resigned from the patriotic group. She then helped arrange an Easter Sunday appearance for the singer at Lincoln Memorial. More than 70,000 people attended the event. "There seemed to be people as far as the eye could see," Anderson recalled in her autobiography. "I had a feeling that a great wave of good will poured out from these people." In time, Constitution Hall would change its policy, and Anderson performed there on several occasions. Years later, though, it was disclosed that the DAR did not discriminate against Anderson because of her race—it was a scheduling conflict.

8802, declaring that "there shall be no discrimination in the employment of workers in defense industries or government because of race, creed, color, or national origin." The president also appointed a Committee on Fair Employment Practices to administer the order, although White was denied a seat and a white Mississippian chaired the committee.

Even so, Randolph called off the March.

"The deceit in this maneuver was that the march had been organized as unconditional," observed Conrad Lynn, a highly regarded political activist and lawyer, who handled as many controversial cases as Clarence Darrow. "Many of us backed the preparations because we felt it would provide the opportunity for a revolutionary confrontation with the government. This, of course, was the last thing the Socialists had in mind." Three months later, Lynn and several other activists walked from New York City to Washington, D.C. It took them fifteen days to walk 250 miles. Their feet aching and bloody, theirs was a protest of what they believed was a unilateral decision.

Millions of black Americans were bewildered by the sudden turn of events. "Plans had been completed for a march of some one hundred thousand Negroes from all sections of the country," an editorial in the *Amsterdam-Star News* lamented. "[This paper] having initiated the demand for an executive order from the President to check discrimination in National Defense, has also supported the 'March on Washington' since its inception." Several of Randolph's top lieutenants were baffled by the decision and voiced their concern. They believed that nothing tangible had been gained and insisted that the movement continue. Rustin, in particular, was disappointed. Like the other members of the organization's youth brigade, he felt the immediate desegregation of the armed forces should have been among the demands. But their attempts to keep the march alive failed, and Randolph began purging them from his movement. The great leader chastised them, calling

them "dilettantes" and "dupes of the Communists." These remarks were enough to incense Rustin and he stomped back into the arms of the pacifists.

Once more Rustin and Randolph had come to loggerheads, but they would eventually join forces and play vital roles in an actual March on Washington in 1963, when Dr. Martin Luther King Jr. would rise to immortality. Randolph attempted to revive his larger goals by calling for a series of forums and mass meetings around the nation, and while it effectively

Executive Order 8802: Prohibition of Discrimination in the Defense Industry (1941): "I do hereby declare that it is the duty of employers and of labor organizations...to provide for the full and equitable participation of all workers in defense industries, without discrimination because of race, creed, color, or national origin."

applied pressure on certain issues in various parts of the nation, the momentum of the threatened march had long been squandered. Still, neither Randolph nor Rustin at that time realized that the aborted march would come to symbolize the inauguration of the modern civil rights movement.

For countless workers there were some immediate results of the movement and the president's edict. Within weeks, the Fair Employment Practices Committee was besieged with complaints. They averaged more than five thousand annually during the committee's five-year existence. The NAACP was the chief beneficiary of these civil actions. However, an enactment of the FEPC didn't mean anything to segregationists in the South. The ink was barely dry on Roosevelt's Executive Order when the offices of the NAACP were alerted that a soldier had been found hanging in a tree in a wooded area at Fort Benning, Georgia. More incidents followed, as black soldiers were stoned, shot at, insulted, and threatened, despite protests from the NAACP. Clearly, much more enforcement was needed from the legislative, judicial, and executive branches of the government if blacks were going to receive fair and equitable treatment.

But on December 7, 1941, the Japanese bombed Pearl Harbor, and the nation was soon deeply involved in World War II. Important domestic issues

NAACP FIGHTS FROM 1941–45

A fight during the 1943 Detroit race riots

- It took pressure from the NAACP to get the Secretary of the Navy to commend the bravery of black mess attendant Dorie Miller. Miller, who was aboard the USS Arizona when it was attacked by the Japanese at Pearl Harbor, shot down enemy planes with a machine gun after having moved his captain from the line of fire. Admiral Chester W. Nimitz presented Miller with the Navy Cross.
- When race riots erupted in Detroit and Harlem in the summer of 1943, the NAACP rushed to quell the violence. Walter White and Thurgood Marshall arrived in Detroit in order to protect the civil rights of black residents. In Harlem, Roy Wilkins worked closely with Mayor La Guardia to stifle any further disturbance, which was mild compared to what happened in Detroit. In thirty-six hours of rioting in Detroit, thirty-four people were killed, most of them African Americans.
- After helping to quiet the situation in Detroit, White left on a three-month tour of Europe and the Mediterranean to investigate the status of black troops in the theaters of war. Upon his return, he submitted a fourteen-point memorandum, recommending improvement of opportunities for black soldiers.
- In the first months of 1945, the NAACP continued its attack on racial discrimination against black soldiers, demanding that the Veterans Administration end hospital segregation and other forms of racial bias. It fought to free fifty black seamen who had been convicted of mutiny at Port Chicago, California, and to reverse the convictions of fifty-two soldiers who had also been convicted of mutiny in Hawaii, where they were stationed.

that were not war-related were pushed aside. Still, the unresolved racial problems would continue to crop up in the military and throughout the war the NAACP would have a full agenda investigating case after case of racial discrimination at home and overseas. **CD**

But the NAACP, which was also involved in a flurry of cases against segregated schools, came to a halt—as did the rest of world—when it was announced on April 12, 1945, that President Roosevelt had died in Warm Springs, Georgia. It was not until the summer of 1947 that President Harry Truman renewed some of the civil rights issues Roosevelt left undone. In fact, there was a pronounced shift in policy on race matters from the White House and the federal government with Truman in office, though he had to be prodded by leaders of civil rights organizations. "We can no longer afford the luxury of a leisurely attack upon prejudice and discrimination," the president said during his June 1947 address to the NAACP's 38th Annual Conference in Washington, D.C. "There is much that state and local government can do in providing positive safeguards for civil rights. But we cannot, any longer, await the growth of a will to action in the slowest state or the most backward community. Our national government must show the way."

President Truman speaks at the NAACP conference

DISC 1
TRACK 3

3

To Secure These Rights!

Despite small gains from a threatened march on Washington, led by the indomitable A. Philip Randolph, which forced President Roosevelt to end discrimination in the war plant hiring process, black Americans were still a long way from full equality. Randolph's action had emboldened many civil rights factions, particularly the NAACP and religious groups. At the close of World War II and with a new administration in the White House, it was time to apply pressure to gain further concessions. To some extent the Truman administration anticipated the nation's heightened mood for social change and quickly appointed a committee to assess and possibly improve the civil rights situation.

Two nationally publicized atrocities involving black soldiers and white racists may have prompted Truman to such action. The first occurred on a warm July evening in 1946 in Monroe, Georgia, just as the sun was setting. Along a dirt road on the outskirts of town, a mob of white men yanked two black men and two black women from an automobile, took them down by the river, lined them up, and riddled their bodies with shotgun pellets. One of the men was a recently discharged Army veteran. U.S. Attorney General Tom Clark ordered a full investigation, which reportedly resulted in a couple U.S. attorneys poking around briefly and concluding that the case was not covered under federal civil rights laws.

Another black veteran, Isaac Woodard, had only been discharged from the Army for a few hours on February 12, 1946, before he was taken from a bus near Aiken, South Carolina, when the driver complained he was making too much noise. Woodard was among several soldiers from Camp Gordon, black and white, who were celebrating their new status as civilians. When the driver

The funeral for lynching victims George Dorsey and Dorothy Dorsey Malcolm

asked one of the white soldiers to come to the front of the bus—in keeping with the state's segregation laws—the soldier refused. Later, Woodard requested the driver make a rest stop so he could relieve himself. The driver refused and cursed Woodard, who in turn cursed him back and demanded he be treated like a man.

At the next town, the driver called the sheriff and reported the exchange he had with Woodard. The sheriff forcibly removed Woodard from the bus. According to the sheriff's testimony, Woodard resisted arrest and tried to take his blackjack, which the sheriff then used to subdue him. Woodard offered the all-white jury a different account in this, the first civil rights case ever heard in South Carolina. The jury believed the sheriff, not the blinded Woodard, who had been beaten and then had his eyes gouged out by the sheriff's billy club.

Woodard's case aroused the black community and it also enraged many white Americans. Many wrote

letters to President Truman demanding that he intercede and mete out justice.

One such letter was written a week after the incident by Major R. R. Wright Sr., president of the citizens Committee, Citizens and Southern Bank and Trust Company, a bankers' association located in Philadelphia. In the letter, Major Wright wrote, "I understand that this matter has been reported to the Secretary of War and it is alleged that he has said there is no jurisdiction, because of the fact that the veteran had been discharged only a few days before the dastardly act was committed by the police officers. Hence, it seems to me that we are compelled to call upon the Chief Executive to instruct or request the Attorney General to look into this case so that justice may be meted to those unfaithful officers whose duty it was to keep the peace and protect the citizens of our country. Mr. President, I am not able to put this matter before you, even as I feel it. To 'gouge out the eyesight' of a man who had used his eyes to safeguard the freedom of his country is surely a disgrace unheard of in any other country of the world."

In response, David K. Niles, Administrative Assistant to the President, wrote that the matter would be thoroughly investigated. "The War Department made an investigation when the episode was first reported," Niles replied. "The investigation disclosed, as you say in your letter, that Mr. Woodard had been discharged at the time of the incident, so that the War Department is without jurisdiction." He went on to say that "the Civil Rights section of the Department of Justice has taken charge of the matter and is conducting an investigation to determine whether the entire civil rights statute has been violated."

By September, President Truman wrote a personal letter to his Attorney General: "I had a caller yesterday [from] some members of the National Association for the Advancement of Colored People and they told me about an incident which happened in South Carolina where a Negro sergeant who had been discharged from the army just three hours was taken off a bus and not only seriously beaten, but his eyes deliberately put out, and that the mayor of this town had bragged about committing this outrage.

"I have been very much alarmed at the increased racial feeling all over the country," the president continued, "and I am wondering if it wouldn't be well to appoint a commission to analyze the situation and have a remedy to present to Congress—something similar to the Wickersham Commission on Prohibition [established to evaluate the possibility of repealing the Eighteenth Amendment which prohibited the sale of liquor].

"I know you have been looking into the Tennessee and Georgia lynching, and have also been investigating the one in Louisiana, but I think it is going to take something more than handling each individual case after it happens—it is going to require the inauguration of some sort of policy to prevent such happenings. I'll appreciate it very much having your views on the subject."

Truman's urgency was fed by an increasing number of rallies and demonstrations, occurring mainly in northern cities, demanding an end to the unchecked violence sweeping the land, particularly in the South. Out of these protestations a National Emergency Committee Against Violence was formed that included a coalition of some forty religious, professional, labor, veterans, and civil rights organizations. Truman met with their representatives in September and thoughtfully considered their pleas for federal action.

Rather than await the outcome of the various investigations being conducted by unions, on December 5, 1946, Truman issued a statement on the Freedom From Fear and the subsequent Executive Order 9808.

Many questioned Truman's motivations. Was he merely being politically expedient, anticipating the presidential run two years down the road or was he genuinely sympathetic to the plight of black veterans because he was once in uniform? In any case, he wanted something done immediately. "I want the bill of rights implemented in fact," he declared. Earlier, in 1945, when the Fair Employment Practices Committee (FEPC) was threatened, Truman had taken a firm position to keep it intact.

To carry out this task, Truman appointed a blue ribbon committee, which included black members Dr. Channing Tobias, a prominent leader in the YMCA movement and later director of the Phelps-Stokes Fund, and Dr. Sadie Alexander, who had been the secretary of the National Bar Association, among her many firsts as a black woman.

In keeping with the charges set forth in the executive order, the Committee held public and private meetings, thoroughly examining many pressing civil rights issues. In October 1947 the committee submitted its one hundred and seventy-eight page report

EXECUTIVE ORDER 9808

1. Freedom From Fear is more realized in our country than in any other country on the face of the earth. Yet all parts of our population are not equally free from fear. And from time to time, and in some places, the freedom has been gravely threatened. It was so after the last war when organized groups fanned hatred and intolerance, until, at times, mob action struck fear into the hearts of men and women because of their racial origin or religious belief.

2. Today, Freedom From Fear, and the democratic institutions which sustain it, are under attack. In some places, from time to time the local enforcement of law and order has broken down, and individuals, sometimes ex-servicemen and even women have been killed, maimed, and intimidated.

3. The preservation of civil liberties is a duty of every government—state, Federal and local. Where law enforcement measures and the authority of Federal, state and local governments are inadequate to discharge this primary function of government, these measures and this authority should be strengthened and improved.

4. The Constitutional guarantees of individual liberties and of equal protection under the laws clearly place on the Federal government the duty to act when state or local authorities abridge or fail to protect these Constitutional rights.

5. Yet, in its discharge of the obligations placed on it by the Constitution, the Federal government is hampered by Civil Rights statutes. The protection of our democratic institutions, and the enjoyment by the people of their rights under the Constitution require that these weak and inadequate statutes should be expanded and improved.

6. I have, therefore, issued today an Executive Order creating the President's Committee on Civil Rights and I am asking this committee to prepare for me a written report. The substance of this report will be recommendations with respect to adoption or establishment of legislation or otherwise of more adequate and effective means and procedures for the protection of the civil rights of the people of the United States.

entitled "To Secure These Rights" that stressed a ban on lynching and the poll tax, the establishment of a permanent FEPC, the formation of a civil rights division in the Department of Justice, the desegregation of the military, and several other matters of national and international importance. 🄲🄳

Much of the onus for applying the safeguards of civil rights was placed on the federal government. But this "does not mean exclusive action by that government," the report noted. "There is much that the states and local communities can do in this field, and much that they alone can do. The Committee believes that Justice Holmes' view of the states as 48 laboratories for social and economic experimentation is still valid. The very complexity of the civil rights problem calls for much experimental, remedial action which may be better undertaken by the states than by the national government. Parallel state and local action supporting the national program is highly desirable. It is obvious that even though the federal government should take steps to stamp out the crime of lynching, the states cannot escape the responsibility to employ all of the powers and resources available to them for the same end. Or again, the enactment of a federal fair employment practice act will not render similar state legislation unnecessary."

President Truman enthusiastically welcomed the broad recommendations, deeming the report "an American charter of human freedom." In effect, these recommendations were great in theory and on paper, but there remained the practical application and the required compliance to make them effective. The real challenge would be forging a federal anti-lynching law and putting an end to state-mandated segregation.

The most immediate result of the Committee's report was the formation of more committees. Truman created another interracial committee to tackle the glaring inequalities in higher education, and then, with far more tangible results he appointed yet another committee in 1948 to study the possibility of integrating the armed services, one of the recommendations proposed by Tobias, Alexander and others. Truman, with one eye on the looming elections and the armed services moving at a snail's pace to end segregation, sought to speed up the process with the appointment of Lester Granger, then head of the National Urban League, and John H. Sengstacke, publisher of the *Chicago Defender*.

On January 12, 1949, the committee to desegregate the armed forces held its first meeting. It was widely believed that Truman's victory over Thomas Dewey was a vote of confidence on several civil rights initiatives previously announced by the re-elected president. With Major League Baseball's racial barriers having finally toppled less than two years before with the Brooklyn Dodgers' signing of Jackie Robinson, one could excuse black Americans for feeling a little more optimistic about the future. By the spring there was another hopeful sign when the Air Force announced a new policy of equal treatment for all its personnel. But it would be a tug of war between the committee and the Navy and the Army, both of which were resistant to making even minor concessions, suspending racial quotas, and beginning the process of integrating its various units. Some meager advances were made, but it would take the Korean conflict to bring about substantial change in the number of black soldiers and the gradual erosion of the age-old policy of racial separation.

On June 25, 1950, the North Korean People's Army swarmed across the 38th Parallel into South Korea. One of the first units into the fray was the still-intact all-black 24th Infantry Regiment. After the unit had been engaged in several major battles, there were reports that the black soldiers were less than valiant; that many of them had abandoned their weapons and fled from the enemy. These accounts, however, were contradicted by the heroism of Private William Thompson, the first American soldier to earn the Medal of Honor in Korea. When a company

DISC 1
TRACK 3

of rifle men panicked before the advancing North Koreans, Thompson set up his machine gun and kept firing until he was killed.

If the American commanders were disturbed by the allegedly poor combat performance of the 24th, the NAACP was troubled by the frequency of court martials involving members of the unit as well as the severity of punishment they received. As a result, Thurgood Marshall, an attorney with the NAACP, was appointed to conduct an investigation of military justice. He received cooperation from General Douglas MacArthur, the commander in chief of the Army's far eastern theater. Marshall was appointed in response to the request of thirty-nine soldiers of the 24th Infantry who had been convicted of serious breaches of discipline, including running away from the enemy. Tireless and diligent, Marshall was able to reverse or reduce the sentences for most of the accused.

With the Korean War underway, the Army soon determined that segregated regiments were not the answer to a successful military campaign. That was the upside. On the downside, the process of integration could not be quickly put into effect, given the complexity of reorganizing units and the further training needed for soldiers who had been denied promotions on the grounds of their race. In far too many instances, integrating the forces was left to the discretion of company commanders who often put off such measures as long as possible, fearing a loss of morale among troops. Completing the process of integration took almost to the end of the war.

But compared to the European theater, integration in Korea was on a fast track. In Europe it was not until 1953 that the changes would affect a sizable influx of African American soldiers. Eventually, the exigencies of the war made it impractical to abide to a strict code of segregation. Black enlisted men and

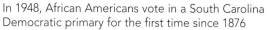

In 1948, African Americans vote in a South Carolina Democratic primary for the first time since 1876

Above: An April 14, 1947, memorandum from the President's Committee on Civil Rights, concerning the civil rights of Army personnel and requesting information on "the possible and probable effect of the unification of the armed forces" and "the role of the Army in controlling civil disturbances growing out of race riots"

some women—even a few officers—were being deployed in fairly equal percentages throughout the armed services. That is, overseas. Back home the military outfits were often islands of integration located in virulent racist communities.

"Racial integration in the armed services came to embrace even the schools operated on military or naval bases for dependent children," military historian Bernard Nalty concluded. "During the final years of the Truman presidency, Hubert Humphrey, now a senator from Minnesota, had urged the armed forces to do away with racially segregated schools on federal property, but nothing happened until a new chief executive, Dwight D. Eisenhower, decided to look into the matter. Shortly after taking office early in 1953, President Eisenhower declared that 'all must share, regardless of such inconsequential factors as race and religion,' in any federal assistance to education."

President Eisenhower had touched a nerve of contention that would soon be a vital element in the civil rights movement: education.

To a large degree the education battleground had already been broached by nonviolent activists affiliated with the Congress of Racial Equality (CORE), one of the first civil rights organizations, founded in 1942. Son of a Methodist minister from Texas, co-founder James Farmer received his political indoctrination from his participation in the Fellowship of Reconciliation (FOR), a group formed after World War I to promote pacifism and international understanding. Farmer joined the group in 1941 and was appointed race relations secretary. At the same time, Bayard Rustin was made secretary of student and general affairs. It was in this environment that Farmer and Rustin honed their organizational skills that would be so indispensable in the emerging fight for social reform.

In fact, Rustin, a versatile organizer who had been active in the pacifist movement headed by A. J. Muste, conducted a one-man crusade for civil rights as he traveled across the country on behalf of FOR, which, essentially, was more concerned with anti-war measures than with the plight of African Americans. When Randolph, finally prepared to release his restless followers, announced a massive civil disobedience campaign as a continuation of the first March on Washington Movement, Rustin was jubilant. FOR willingly endorsed and supported Randolph's civil disobedience campaign, even when some prominent mainstream black leaders and publishers denounced the idea. Randolph's major conference in Chicago ended on July 4, 1941, and the hundreds of delegates pledged to campaign nonviolently against all forms of racial discrimination in public accommodations. Rustin and Farmer, the latter with some envious reluctance, addressed the delegates and lectured them on the finer points of Gandhian mass resistance. This propitious beginning was stillborn, and the plans evaporated in the race riots that ripped through Harlem and Detroit in 1943. Several years later, Randolph's movement would fade from the scene, and Farmer's CORE and subsequently Dr. King's nonviolent protests would fill the void he left behind.

But with the intrepid Rustin forever in motion and agitating, the Fellowship of Reconciliation con-

ON THE FRONT LINES

Curtis Morrow, in his autobiography *What's a Commie Ever Done to Black People?* captures a moment in Korea when black soldiers are ensconced in their barracks talking about racial conditions in and out of the Army:

"'Well, if I get out of this shit alive, this is going to be one Negro that's going to send some of them whites to hell ahead of him.' It was Sergeant Bedgood, our platoon sergeant, joining the conversation. 'Meanwhile, we're in Korea, supposedly fighting the evil forces of communism and defending the cause of freedom, justice, and all that shit—for others.'

"There was a moment of silence, as we digested the sergeant's words and waited for him to continue.

"'You hear those sounds?' asked the sergeant, looking at the two replacements. He was referring to the distant sounds of exploding artillery and bombs, sounds always heard up front.

"'Yes sir, Sergeant,' both newcomers answered in unison.

"'Well, you'll be hearing it as long as you are here, although you won't hear the one that gets you. Or the bullet that kills you. That's about the only thing you can be sure of here. And the only chance we all have of surviving this motherfuckin' war is sticking together. And that means joint fire power. In a fight, the more there is, the better our chances of living to see daylight....That talk about fighting for liberty, justice, and all that bullshit is another fight, one we'll have to fight when and if we survive this one...."

tinued its relentless fight against racism, waiting for an opportunity to take on the formidable forces of Jim Crow. That moment arrived in 1944 when Irene Morgan, a black woman recently released from the hospital after surgery, boarded a bus in Gloucester, Virginia, bound for Baltimore, Maryland. She took a seat within the black section of the bus, but in her weakened condition, she refused to give it up for a white couple when ordered to do so. The driver had her arrested in the next town. At her trial, she was convicted of resisting arrest and violating the state's law against integrated seating. She gladly paid a fine of ten dollars on the first count of resisting arrest, but, with the counsel of the NAACP, she appealed the second one of violating the state's law against integrated seating. After the Virginia Supreme Court upheld the conviction, the NAACP, with Thurgood Marshall as the lead attorney, took the case to the U.S. Supreme Court, arguing not that the Fourteenth Amendment offered equal protection, but that the segregation impeded interstate commerce. The court ruled in Marshall's favor. But it was a pyrrhic victory since the bus companies ignored the decision and blacks had little wherewithal to challenge the existing state laws.

In *Morgan v. Virginia*, Rustin and FOR found the issue to mount its "Journey of Reconciliation," a series of bus rides through the South. It was hoped that this form of nonviolent direct action would make an opening in the Cotton Curtain and provide a wedge into the backwaters of racial hatred and bigotry. FOR and its organizers realized this endeavor could not be done without the legal assistance of the NAACP, then under the leadership of Walter White, who had reservations about direct action. Marshall voiced his objection to the tactic, insisting it was foolhardy and that no good would be achieved.

"Unjust social laws and patterns do not change because supreme courts deliver just decisions," Rustin wrote in response to Marshall's critique. "One needs merely to observe the continued practice of Jim Crow in interstate travel, six months after the Supreme Court's decision, to see the necessity of resistance. Social progress comes from struggle, all freedom demands a price."

Despite Marshall's recalcitrance, FOR went ahead with its plans to make a two-week pilgrimage through Virginia, North Carolina, Tennessee, and Kentucky, beginning April 9, 1947, Paul Robeson's 49th birthday. The team assembled was composed of eight blacks and eight whites—all men. Among the blacks joining the tour's coordinators Rustin and George Houser were journalist William Worthy, who had been a stalwart with Randolph's March on Washington Movement; Rev. Nathan Wright, a religious social worker; attorney Conrad Lynn; and Homer Jack, a Unitarian minister and a charter member of CORE from Chicago. Rustin and Houser, who was white, laid out the guidelines and procedures during their two-day orientation session. "If you are a Negro, sit in the front seat. If you are white, sit in a rear seat. If the driver asks you to move, tell him calmly and courteously: As an interstate passenger I have a right to sit anywhere in this bus. This is the law as laid down by the United States Supreme Court."

The other instructions included how to respond when accosted by the police. The protesters were to willingly cooperate with the police, and upon reaching the station call the headquarters of the NAACP or one of their lawyers. Part of the orientation was often done in song with Rustin's mellifluous voice and strummed guitar leading the singers.

As expected, the arrests began within two days of the start of the journey when Lynn was taken into custody in Petersburg, Virginia and Jim Peck, Andrew Johnson, and Rustin were arrested in Durham, North Carolina. The first instance of violence occurred in Chapel Hill. After Rustin and several others were dragged from the bus, Peck eluded attention and later went to the jail to post bail for the others. When he arrived to pay the bail he was surrounded by the bus drivers. "'Coming down here to stir up the nigger,' snarled a big one with steel-cold grey eyes," Peck recalled. "With that, he slugged me on the side of the head. I stepped back, looked at him, and asked, 'What's the matter?'...My failure to retaliate with violence had taken him by surprise."

Rustin exercised a similar tactic when he was convicted of violating the segregation laws and given a thirty-day sentence on a chain gang in Roxboro, North Carolina. Since his case, after he surrendered to authorities, was well-publicized in local newspapers, the superintendent of the work camp expected Rustin to be haughty and difficult, but the activist had something else in mind. "My aims were really far different," Rustin recalled in *Down the Line*, his collected writings. "I wanted to work hard so I would not be a burden to other chain-gangers. I wanted to accept the imprisonment in a quiet, unobtrusive manner. Only in this way, I believed, could the officials and guards be led to consider sympa-

thetically the principle on which I was convicted. I did not expect them to agree with me, but I did want them to believe I cared enough about the ideals I was supposed to stand for so I could accept my punishment with a sense of humor, fairness, and constructive good will."

Except for Peck's beating, Rustin's time on the chain gang, a few fines, brief arrests, and trials, the Journey of Reconciliation was judged a success by the participants and some of their detractors. "The Journey of Reconciliation achieved no dramatic breakthroughs," author Jervis Anderson concluded. "Blacks did not suddenly begin flocking to the front seats of interstate conveyances, and it would be some time before the bus companies began enforcing the Supreme Court decision in *Morgan v. Virginia*. The Journey's achievement was mostly psychological or symbolic, signifying the possibility of future nonviolent mass action in the South."

4

Brown v. Board of Education

The Rev. Oliver Brown was nervous after being sworn in to testify in a case that would become a catalyst for profound changes in the education of black and white children in the United States. It was a very warm morning in June 1951, and as he struggled to get comfortable on the witness stand, tiny beads of perspiration formed on his forehead. The heat in the courtroom was almost as unbearable as the heat in the Santa Fe railway shops where he worked as a welder. With attorney Charles Bledsoe as his guide, he slowly told the court why he had chosen to remove his daughter, Linda, from all-black Monroe Elementary School, located more than a mile from his home, and enroll her at all-white Sumner Elementary School, which was only a few blocks from where they lived in Topeka, Kansas.

In his landmark study of *Brown v. Board of Education*, Richard Kluger recounted Oliver Brown's testimony: "Linda had to leave home at 7:40 am to get to school by nine. She had to go through the dangerous Rock Island switching yards to get to the bus pickup point by eight o'clock, but often the bus was late and 'many times she had to wait through the cold, the rain, and the snow until the bus got there.' It was a thirty-minute ride to school, and so if the bus was on time, Linda got to wait—sometimes as long as an half hour—in front of the school until it opened at nine."

Bledsoe, who was assisted in his direct examination by attorneys Robert Carter and Jack Greenberg, the point men on the case, asked Brown whether his daughter would confront any such hazardous conditions if she attended the nearby Sumner School. "Not hardly as I know of," said Oliver Brown. "And how far away was the Sumner School? Seven blocks."

After a few more minutes of testimony, there was a heated cross-examination from the city's attorney, and that morning, just before noon, Brown stepped down from the witness stand into the pages of history.

The class action suit was filed in U.S. District Court in February 1951. Brown's name led the list of plaintiffs thereby earning his family everlasting fame. It should be noted that this case was by no means the first legal action to desegregate the nation's schools. Cases had been argued and re-argued in South Carolina, Virginia, and Delaware without any redress. Within six months, the Brown case would face a similar fate when the District Court ruled against them, deciding that the schools in Topeka, whether for black or white children, were equal.

Undaunted, the NAACP appealed the decision, regrouped, and took their complaint to the highest court in the land. The difference now, however, was the suit included all the other suits that had been filed, thus making the issue much larger and representing the interests of hundreds of deprived children. In addition, the suit was now under the legal guidance of Thurgood Marshall, who had been so successful defending Irene Morgan in her case involving interstate travel and the black troops overseas charged with cowardice. By this time, Marshall—aided by such outstanding lawyers as Robert Carter and Constance Baker Motley—had acquired considerable experience arguing before the Supreme Court, which gave him an advantage few advocates possessed. Overall, he would present thirty-two cases before the high court, winning twenty-nine of them.

"I am as certain as I'm sitting here," Marshall said of the opposing forces, "that governmentally enforced segregation…governmentally imposed discrimination because of race, creed, or color, so far as

Above: Supreme Court Implementation Decree: "Take such orders…as are necessary and proper to admit to public schools on a racially nondiscriminatory basis with all deliberate speed the parties to this case. Per Mr. Chief Justice Warren, May 31, 1955"

Left: Linda Brown

enforcement by government is concerned will be off the books within the foreseeable future....Once the whole problem is laid bare and clear then democracy will take over." 🄲🄳

At issue was the question of whether segregated schools resulted in an inferior education for black children. To prove their case, noted psychologists Kenneth and Mamie Clark were summoned to testify for the plaintiffs. As early as the mid-1940s, the Clarks had begun testing the racial self-awareness of black children with their "doll experiments." In one significant study of black children, the Clarks tested 134 from segregated public schools in Arkansas and 119 from racially mixed public schools in Springfield, Massachusetts. "The children were given one of four dolls, each identical except for gender and skin color," Ben Keppel explained in *The Work of Democracy*. The children were asked questions in the following order:

1. Give me the doll that you like to play with.
2. Give me the doll that is the nice doll.
3. Give me the doll that looks bad.
4. Give me the doll that has a nice color.
5. Give me the doll that looks like a white child.
6. Give me the doll that looks like a colored child.
7. Give me the doll that looks like a Negro child.
8. Give me the doll that looks like you.

George E.C. Hayes, left, Thurgood Marshall, center, and James N. Nabrit, the lawyers representing the school integration cause

What the test showed was that the African American children in both northern and southern samples expressed a preference for the white doll over the brown doll. While under oath, Clark offered this conclusion about students he had interviewed as part of the *Briggs v. Elliott* case, one of five cases that made up *Brown v. Board of Education*: "The conclusion which I was forced to reach was that these children in Clarendon County [a rural section of South Carolina] like other human beings who are subjected to an obviously inferior status in the society in which they live, have been definitely harmed in the develop-

ment of their personalities; that the signs of instability in their personalities are clear, and I think that every psychologist would accept and interpret these signs as such."

When this evidence was presented to the justices of the Supreme Court it was persuasive enough to show how segregation and negative images had damaged the self-esteem and personality of the children. The Clarks' research and findings had been submitted to the Court as an appendix to the NAACP's brief, over the objections of some of the lawyers on the team. "Some of the lawyers felt the case should

DISC 1
TRACK 4

The *Topeka State Journal*, May 17, 1954

not be 'contaminated' by psychological evidence," Clark said in an interview years later. "Other lawyers, particularly Robert Carter, argued that you couldn't overthrow (*Plessy v. Ferguson*) by just sticking to the law. To show damage and a violation of equal protection under the Fourteenth Amendment, you had to show that being segregated actually damaged children. Carter felt that the test results were evidence of the damaging effect of segregation on children."

Marshall agreed with Carter, and leaned on the evidence as a key part of his deliberations before the Court.

On May 17, 1954, Chief Justice Earl Warren, only recently appointed to the position by President Eisenhower, read to a tense courtroom the historic eleven-page decision declaring that segregation was unlawful under the provisions of the Fourteenth Amendment. Warren was determined to get a unanimous opinion, perhaps hoping the example of a uni-

fied court would influence southern opponents to act accordingly. But such a goal was not an easy one. The court was badly split. To begin with, wrote constitutional law expert Jack Balkin, "five justices—Hugo Black (a southerner and former Ku Klux Klan member from Alabama), William O. Douglas, Harold Burton, Felix Frankfurter, and Sherman Minton—wanted to overturn Plessy. They believed that segregation was unconstitutional per se, and not only if facilities for blacks and whites were unequal."

On the other hand, Justice Stanley Reed, a Kentuckian, did not think that segregation was unconstitutional, a position Justice Tom Clark of Texas supported, but not as passionately. Many had anticipated that Robert Jackson, a former attorney general and prosecutor during the Nuremberg trials, would join the liberals on the court. But he was a moderate, and was conflicted by race. Warren's monumental task was to find the middle ground and write an opinion that would appeal to both sides. Declaring that separate but equal facilities were inherently unequal satisfied Black, Frankfurter, Douglas, Burton, and Minton. Warren's decision to move slowly on a remedy appealed to Clark. Only Jackson and Reed were left to win over.

At one point Jackson strongly considered writing a concurring opinion, which would have presented the disunity that worried Warren. When Jackson had a heart attack in March 1954, Warren visited him in the hospital, bringing him a copy of his opinion. Jackson thought it was a masterful work of brevity and simplicity. With a few minor changes, he accepted the draft. (Jackson suffered a fatal heart attack in October and was replaced by John Marshall Harlan, whose grandfather was a dissenter on *Plessy*.)

Reed was of the opinion that segregation would disappear on its own. He remained firm in this view despite repeated prodding by Warren. But when the chief justice convinced him that segregation would be dismantled gradually, Reed joined the rest. Warren had the court speaking in one voice.

This victory was the culmination of a long fight that had been waged by individuals and organizations since colonial times. In effect, the decision, which eradicated the operation of segregated schools in the states and the District of Columbia, also reversed the longstanding *Plessy v. Ferguson* decision of 1896, the so-called "separate but equal" law that had kept black Americans mired in second class citizenship. "In the field of public education," said Chief Justice Earl Warren, speaking for the court in its unanimous decision, "the doctrine of separate but equal has no place. Separate educational facilities are inherently unequal. Therefore we hold that the plaintiffs and others similarly situated are, by reason of the segregation

Above: Birmingham billboard calling for Warren's impeachment

Left: Justice Earl Warren

complained of, deprived of the equal protection of the laws guaranteed by the Fourteenth Amendment."

In October 1954, President Dwight D. Eisenhower, after soundly defending his selection of Warren to the Supreme Court, conveyed his sentiments about the decision. In a letter to childhood friend E. E. "Swede" Hazlett, he wrote, "The segregation issue will, I think, become acute or tend to die out according to the character of the procedure orders the court will probably issue this winter. My own guess is that they will be very moderate and accord a maximum of initiative to local courts." **CD**

DISC 1
TRACK 4

To some degree Eisenhower's statement proved prophetic. While the decision in *Brown I* was widely praised, it had to await *Brown II* to weigh the aspects of implementation and to avoid the ruling's potential chaos in the southern school system. The first round of *Brown v. the Board of Education* had said that segregation was unlawful, but did not suggest how or how quickly the old segregated system might be rebuilt into something fair and workable.

At the core of the Court's 1955 compromise in *Brown II* was Justice Felix Frankfurter's line stating that schools should be desegregated with "all deliberate speed." With this condition, the Court had the terms by which to alleviate the concerns of the justices who were worried about the Court's inability to enforce its own ruling, and which, even more egregiously, might discredit the judicial process. Warren, in a later assessment of the draft decree, said the benchmark was chosen because "there were so many blocks preventing an immediate solution of the thing in reality that the best we could look for would be a progression of action."

That action would be slow coming, and the opposition forces in the South had in *Brown II* a convenient way to dodge compliance with *Brown I*. "I had no idea what kind of delaying impact the phrase 'with all deliberate speed' would mean in terms of bringing about desegregation," wrote Patricia Stephens Due in *Freedom in the Family: A Mother–Daughter Memoir on*

Frankfurter's notes on the *Brown* case. The first line of the hand-written paragraph at bottom begins: "with all deliberate speed"

the Fight for Civil Rights. "I also didn't have the wisdom or experience to ask myself what negative changes might take place in the black community as a result of Brown—for example, that a Negro principal at a Negro school could not hope for such a prime assignment at a white school because he would be an outsider, subject to the prejudices of his superiors….Or that the burden of 'busing' students from one neighborhood to another would so often fall on Negro children, since white parents would not want to send their children to Negro neighborhoods."

A more egregious result of the *Brown* decisions was the emergence of the White Citizens' Council, a group that became known as the Klan in suits and not sheets. Beginning in small towns in Mississippi, the Councils were soon as much a part of the southern landscape as cotton and magnolia trees. Typical of the Councils' resolve to hold fast to segregation are these excerpts from a pamphlet from the Association of Citizens' Councils titled "Why Does Your Community Need a Citizens' Council?":

"Maybe your community has had no racial problems! This may be true; however, you may not have a fire, yet you maintain a fire department. You can depend on one thing:

The NAACP (National Association for the Agitation of Colored People), aided by alien influences, bloc vote seeking politicians and left-wing do-gooders, will see that you have a problem in the near future. The Citizens' Council is the South's answer to the mongrelizers. We will not be integrated. We are proud of our white blood and our white heritage of sixty centuries....We are certainly not ashamed of our traditions, our conservative beliefs, nor our segregated way of life."

The virulent reaction to *Brown* was not limited to Klansmen and White Citizens Council members.

A number of elected politicians throughout the South openly identified with the campaign to retain a way of life that was dogged in its determination to "keep the Negroes in their place!" Their aim was to preserve Jim Crow by any means necessary, which meant dragging out every ancient law they could. When these measures failed, they would use whatever illegal means they could get away with. Many knew that when all else failed, they could call on lynch law, nightriders, and other forms of terrorist intimidation.

But now emboldened by the courts and federal government, black Americans stepped up their fight for freedom and equality; they were no longer content to capitulate, to bow and scrape. It might have been this renewed sense of worth and manhood that induced hundreds of young African Americans to test what they felt was a new climate of understanding in the country, even if the testing ground was in Montgomery, Alabama.

5

Rosa Parks and the Montgomery Improvement Association

In the summer of 1955, after ten days at the Highlander Folk School in Monteagle, Tennessee, Rosa Parks was packing to go home and having a last few words with Septima Clark, one of the workshop leaders at a conference on "Racial Desegregation: Implementing the Supreme Court Decision." The decision of the moment was the recent ruling by the Supreme Court on *Brown v. Board of Education*, in which it ruled segregation in schools was unconstitutional. "I could have stayed a while longer," Parks wrote in her autobiography. "It was hard to leave, knowing what I was going back to, but of course I knew I had to leave." It was particularly difficult leaving Clark, whose workshop on citizenship, and other skills needed to register to vote, was so thoroughly enjoyable. A black activist from South Carolina, Clark had been affiliated with Highlander for several years.

Highlander Folk School was started in 1932 by Myles Horton. He had been a student of Reinhold Niebuhr at the Union Theological Seminary and Niebuhr, who also was very influential on Dr. Martin Luther King's life, served on the board at Highlander. Eleanor Roosevelt, socialist Norman Thomas, and the Rev. Harry Emerson Fosdick of Riverside Church were also board members. At the core of Horton's mission was the belief that people could solve their own problems with proper guidance and leadership. They could be the agents of their own liberation. The school began as an institution to assist oppressed white workers in the Appalachian Mountains. But, given the political climate in the country, he had shifted the school's focus to civil rights issues.

People came to the school from every sector of the nation to acquire organizing skills for social change, and desegregating schools was the hot topic of the day.

Parks learned of Highlander from her friend, Virginia Durr, a white woman who was a sponsor of the school. Durr, whose husband Clifford was a lawyer and a dedicated civil rights activist, helped Parks, then forty-two years old, get the scholarship she needed to attend. E.D. Nixon, Parks's boss at the Montgomery branch of the NAACP where she was secretary, had given her the time off. But now the hiatus was over. "So I went back to Montgomery and back to my job as an assistant tailor at Montgomery Fair department store, where you had to be smiling and polite no matter how rudely you were treated. And back to the city buses, with segregation rules." And back to a rendezvous with history.

Many accounts of her decision not to move to the back of the bus on December 1, 1955, have garbled the facts, according to Parks. "When I refused to stand up, on the orders of the bus driver, for a white passenger to take the seat, and I was not sitting in the front of the bus, as many people have said, and neither was my feet hurting, as many people have said; but I made up my mind that I would not give in any longer to legally-imposed racial segregation. No, the only tired I was, was tired of giving in," she explained.

Nor was her act of protest a concocted plan with members of the NAACP. Parks said it was not her intention to get arrested. If she had paid more attention to who the bus driver was that evening, she never would have gotten on that bus in the first place. The driver was James Blake, the same

driver who had put her off a bus in 1943, twelve years earlier. When Blake asked her to move to the back, she refused. "Well, I'm going to have you arrested," he told her. "You may do that," a defiant Parks replied, pushing her wire frame glasses back up her nose.

What Parks did not explain in detail is that all thirty-six seats of the bus were filled, with African Americans from the rear and whites from the front, as was the rule. But whites had priority and were not allowed to share a row with blacks. Blake demanded that the four passengers in the row just behind the whites surrender their seats and move to the back to make room for a white man who had just boarded the bus. When none of them moved, he approached them and spoke more firmly. Three of them responded and moved to stand in the back of the bus. But Parks, insisting she wasn't in the white section, remained seated. Though she was technically right, Blake was the final arbiter of the boundaries. Parks was seated in the section between black and white passengers, the "no-man's land," and that's when Blake announced that she would be arrested. He told her to stay put until he returned with the police. She did.

Eventually two officers in a squad car arrived at the scene. "Two policemen came on the bus and one asked me if the driver had told me to stand and I said yes," Parks said. "And he wanted to know why I didn't stand, and I told him I didn't think I should have to stand up. And then I asked him, why did they push us around? And he said, and I quote him, 'I don't know, but the law is the law and you are under arrest.' And with that, I got off the bus, under arrest."

She was held in jail for several hours before bail was posted for her release. Later that evening, E.D. Nixon asked her if she would be willing to make her experience a test case against segregation. Parks said she would discuss the proposal with her husband and her mother.

Parks is fingerprinted after her arrest

Twice before, Nixon and the NAACP thought they had found a courageous plaintiff who would make a good test case against the segregation laws, but each time the choice was not a good one. Claudette Colvin was fifteen years old, unmarried, and pregnant. Mary Louise Smith was deemed too young and unprepared for the legal ordeal. Parks, Nixon decided, was perfect. "My God, look what segregation has put in my hands," he exclaimed to Parks, who compared to the others possessed no negative factors.

Nixon added, "She was honest, she was clean, she had integrity. The press couldn't go out and dig up something she did last year, or last month, or five years ago. They couldn't hang nothing like that on Rosa Parks." She was attractive and quiet, wrote reporter L. D. Reddick in *Dissent*, "a churchgoer who looks like the symbol of Mother's Day." And she was a devout Methodist, who often taught Sunday school and tutored children of the NAACP

Youth Council at a Lutheran church not too far from her home.

All that remained to test the case was Parks's agreement to be the plaintiff. "I'll have to discuss that with my family," she told Nixon. Both Parks's mother and her husband, Raymond, were horrified by the idea, fearing she would endanger her life. It took a few hours of friendly persuasion before they gave their consent. Parks met with Nixon and told him that she was willing to take part in the case. "If you think it will mean something to Montgomery and do some good," she said, "I'll be happy to go along with it."

Word that Parks had been arrested and would be the test case against segregation in this town of 50,000 African Americans spread like wild fire. "They've messed with the wrong one now," was the phrase repeated throughout the city. Veteran activists such as attorney Fred Gray, one of two black lawyers in town, and Jo Ann Robinson, a college professor at Alabama State College and a member of the Women's Political Council, seized the opportunity to mount a massive boycott of the Montgomery bus system. A meeting was called for December 5, and in the meantime people were asked not to ride the buses. The next move was to get the local ministers involved. Rev. Ralph Abernathy, pastor of First Baptist Church, took the lead. During the days before the planned meeting, the success of the boycott stunned the organizers, as people either walked to where they were going or found other means of transportation. Owners of cars and black-owned cab companies either volunteered to help or reduced fares to transport residents.

In her autobiography, Coretta Scott King recalled the anxiety as they waited to see if people would support the boycott. After a sleepless night, she and Dr. King arose and had some toast and coffee, and then Coretta went to look out her living room window to watch the buses as they passed. "Right on time, the bus came, headlights blazing through the December darkness, all lit up inside," Mrs. King wrote. "I shouted 'Martin! Martin! Come quickly.' He ran in and stood beside me, his face lit with excitement. There was not one person on that usually crowded bus." They stood together and watched other buses go by, and all of them were empty. Dr. King dressed and drove to pick up Rev. Abernathy to observe the impact of the boycott in other parts of the city. It was the same story everywhere they went. Most amazing for Dr. King was the hundreds of people walking to their destinations. Their willingness to sacrifice for freedom moved him.

At her court date Parks was found guilty of violating the segregation laws and given a suspended sentence. She was fined $10, plus $4 in court costs. The crowd inside and outside the court was angered by the decision, but there was no organized protest.

The organization came within days. Rev. Abernathy and the ministers met and formed the

Above: Montgomery citizens walk to work during the bus boycott

Morris Thomas, left, sits in the front seat of a segregated bus after refusing the driver's command to move to the back

E.D. Nixon escorts Rosa Parks to the trial

Montgomery Improvement Association (MIA), and the Rev. Martin Luther King Jr. was elected president. It was commonly believed that King was elected because he was new in town and hadn't made any strong friends or enemies. Placing King in the leadership position helped to quiet the turmoil that was developing between the power struggling ministers and Nixon, who took exception to the secrecy of their tactics, insisting that there was no way they were going to conduct a successful bus boycott without alerting the community and informing them of their goals and objectives. That they had chosen the right man became evident a week after the boycott was launched.

"There comes a time that people get tired," Dr. King said at the first formal meeting of the organization. "We are here this evening to say to those who have mistreated us so long that we are tired—tired of being segregated and humiliated, tired of being kicked about by the brutal feet of oppression." Already there were glimpses of the sterling rhetoric, the creative use of metaphor that would mark his ascension to the upper echelon of the civil rights movement. And the repetition of "tired" must have pleased Mrs. Parks. It must have pleased her as well to hear King intone that he was glad that she was the one since she was of the utmost integrity and a devout Christian. He had finally connected him with his audience, which up to that point was growing listless with his recitation of the city's laws of segregation that had never been completely clarified.

It wasn't long before King and attorney Gray took their demands to the bus company. They sought courteous treatment on the buses; they demanded first come, first served seating; and they asked that black drivers be hired for the black bus routes. All of their requests were rejected. The city commissioners were equally adamant in their rejection of the demands. There was nothing to do but to continue the boycott, though the leaders were doubtful that it could be sustained very long. Weeks later, despite false rumors that it was over, the boycott went on. Even the loss of jobs didn't halt the movement. Both Parks and her husband were soon without employment—he resigned from his barbering position when his wife's name couldn't be mentioned at the shop and Rosa was discharged, but not because of her involvement in the boycott, she was told. Neverthe-

less, she accepted her unemployment as a blessing: she no longer had to worry about how she was going to get to work.

As the boycott gained momentum, a more systematic process was arranged to get people around the city. "There were twenty private cars and fourteen station wagons," Parks noted. "There were thirty-two pickup and transfer sites, and scheduled service from five-thirty in the morning until twelve-thirty at night. About thirty thousand people were transported to and from work every day."

There are a number of ways to measure the effectiveness of the boycott, and some of them were destructive and almost deadly. The homes of both Dr. King and Nixon were bombed. King armed himself, prepared to retaliate, but Bayard Rustin was able to counsel him against such action which he advised

Martin Luther King Jr. speaks to a crowd about the importance of the bus boycott

would be a violation of the principles of nonviolence. Parks and her husband, like the other leaders, received threatening letters and telephone calls. "You're the cause of all this," one caller told her. "You should be killed."

The boycott was registering economically as well. With no customers, the company was soon forced to stop running the buses completely. But the city's lawyers still had one card to play. They dredged up an old law that prohibited boycotts. On February 21, 1956, a grand jury handed down eighty-nine indictments against Dr. King and other members of the MIA. Parks was indicted once more. In March when the court hearings began, Dr. King was the first to be tried. He was found guilty and sentenced to pay a $500 fine or serve a year at hard labor. Later, the conviction was overturned on an appeal. This decision was bolstered by the Southern Manifesto, introduced by one hundred congressmen and senators on March 12, signaling their rejection of the Supreme Court's decision to desegregate the nation's schools. By June, a special three-judge panel in federal District Court ruled in favor of the MIA's segregation suit against the buses. An appeal from the city commissioners threw the case to the Supreme Court, which meant the boycott had to be extended even longer.

On November 13, the boycotters got what they wanted: the Supreme Court had ruled in their favor. Segregation on the Montgomery buses was declared unconstitutional. The decision came just as the mayor's court injunction was issued to stop black people from congregating on street corners while waiting for church cars. "But the MIA did not tell the people to go back to the buses," Parks said. "The written order...would not arrive for another month." It finally arrived on December 20, and on the following day black people were back on the buses, sitting wherever they chose. Remarkably, the boycott had successfully held for more than a year.

The decision was by no means popular with the city commissioners, the bus company, and hundreds

Ralph Abernathy, at left, front seat, and Martin Luther King Jr. ride an integrated bus after the boycott's end

of white residents of Montgomery. Buses were pelted, endured sniper bullets, and there was even an attempt to form a whites-only bus line. But none of the tactics were enough to intimidate or repel a people who had been galvanized to end segregation. And the effects of this victory would soon be felt in other segregated communities across the South. "African Americans in other cities, like Birmingham, Alabama, and Tallahassee, Florida, started their own boycotts of the segregated buses," Parks recalled. "The direct-action civil rights movement had begun."

6

The Little Rock Nine

All the optimism, all the feeling of great cheer from the victory following the bus boycott in Montgomery began to be muffled by forces hostile to the movement. Before 1956 had run its course, the home of Rev. Fred Shuttlesworth, one of Dr. King's most loyal lieutenants, was bombed on Christmas day, but there were no fatalities. To organize against the rising attacks and galvanize the movement, the Southern Christian Leadership Conference was founded in January 1957. The bylaws of the organization were approved shortly after the Supreme Court had ruled in favor of the indicted Montgomery boycotters. Among the board members were Ralph David Abernathy, Joseph Lowery, Jesse Jackson, and John L. Tilley, a minister from Baltimore, Maryland, who was made the first permanent director of the SCLC in 1957. Dr. Martin Luther King was elected president.

While Dr. King and his coterie of ministers were strategizing and nursing a number of incipient boycotts, citizens and officials in Arkansas were mulling over how to best comply with the Supreme Court's desegregation ruling. Although integration was already evident throughout the state, Arkansas still had a long way to go to implement the full intent of the Court's decision to integrate the schools. Only two school districts in the state had attempted to desegregate.

In Little Rock, school superintendent Virgil T. Blossom had concocted a plan that would limit integration and delay it long enough to appease those who opposed its implementation, hoping an appeal at some level would nullify the policy altogether. Only one high school in Little Rock had been included in the plan: Central High School with its two thousand white students.

Throughout a steamy summer the pressure to integrate the Arkansas schools intensified. Seventy-five eager African Americans in Little Rock filled out applications to enter Central High School. In time, that number was shaved to twenty-five hopefuls. One of them was fifteen-year-old Melba Pattillo. When her parents learned what she had done, they were furious, and both her mother and grandmother refused to talk to her for hours. It would have seemed her mother would have been a bit more sympathetic to her daughter's desires since she was one of the first blacks to integrate the University of Arkansas, graduating in 1954.

Soon, Melba Pattillo was attending meetings called by the local NAACP to instruct them on the tactics of integration. The twenty-five aspirants were soon reduced to sixteen students who were prepared to integrate the Little Rock school system, but the threats of violence narrowed the number to nine—Pattillo; Ernest Green, the oldest of the students and a senior; Terrance Roberts, whom Pattillo had known all of her life; Jefferson Thomas, a quiet, unassuming scholar–athlete; the petite, shy Elizabeth Eckford, always serious about her studies; Thelma Mothershed, who, despite a heart condition, was ready for the fray; the ever-singing Minniejean Brown; the energetic and outgoing Carlotta Walls; and the intense but observant Gloria Ray, who attended

EXCERPT FROM THE "SOUTHERN MANIFESTO," MARCH 1956

Declaration of Constitutional Principles

The unwarranted decision of the Supreme Court in the public school cases is now bearing the fruit always produced when men substitute naked power for established law.

The Founding Fathers gave us a Constitution of checks and balances because they realized the inescapable lesson of history that no man or group of men can be safely entrusted with unlimited power. They framed this Constitution with its provisions for change by amendment in order to secure the fundamentals of government against the dangers of temporary popular passion or the personal predilections of public officeholders.

We regard the decisions of the Supreme Court in the school cases as a clear abuse of judicial power. It climaxes a trend in the Federal Judiciary undertaking to legislate, in derogation of the authority of Congress, and to encroach upon the reserved rights of the States and the people.

The original Constitution does not mention education. Neither does the 14th Amendment nor any other amendment. The debates preceding the submission of the 14th Amendment clearly show that there was no intent that it should affect the system of education maintained by the States....

This unwarranted exercise of power by the Court, contrary to the Constitution, is creating chaos and confusion in the States principally affected. It is destroying the amicable relations between the white and Negro races that have been created through 90 years of patient effort by the good people of both races. It has planted hatred and suspicion where there has been heretofore friendship and understanding.

Without regard to the consent of the governed, outside mediators are threatening immediate and revolutionary changes in our public schools systems. If done, this is certain to destroy the system of public education in some of the States.

With the gravest concern for the explosive and dangerous condition created by this decision and inflamed by outside meddlers:

We reaffirm our reliance on the Constitution as the fundamental law of the land.

We decry the Supreme Court's encroachment on the rights reserved to the States and to the people, contrary to established law, and to the Constitution.

We commend the motives of those States which have declared the intention to resist forced integration by any lawful means.

We appeal to the States and people who are not directly affected by these decisions to consider the constitutional principles involved against the time when they too, on issues vital to them may be the victims of judicial encroachment.

Even though we constitute a minority in the present Congress, we have full faith that a majority of the American people believe in the dual system of government which has enabled us to achieve our greatness and will in time demand that the reserved rights of the States and of the people be made secure against judicial usurpation.

We pledge ourselves to use all lawful means to bring about a reversal of this decision which is contrary to the Constitution and to prevent the use of force in its implementation.

In this trying period, as we all seek to right this wrong, we appeal to our people not to be provoked by the agitators and troublemakers invading our States and to scrupulously refrain from disorder and lawless acts.

—Signed by nineteen senators and eighty-one representatives from the South

church with Pattillo. None of them came from families who had originally sued the board for not complying with the desegregation edict fast enough.

"We integrating students shared many things in common," Melba Pattillo-Beals wrote later. "All of our parents were strict, no-nonsense types. Several of them were teachers and preachers, or held well-established positions in other professions. All our folks were hardworking people who had struggled to own their homes, to provide a stable life for their families. We shared many of the same family values traditional to all small-town Americans."

There must have been a collective trepidation among the students and their parents when they heard that a rock had been hurled through the living room window at the home of Daisy Bates, editor-in-

chief of the *Arkansas State Press*, president of the state's NAACP, and coordinator of the efforts to integrate Little Rock schools. It was the same room where the students had met with her on many occasions to map out their plans for the coming school year.

If the Klan or the White Citizens' Council sought to sever the head of the state's civil rights movement then Bates was the target. The incident occurred on the evening of August 22, 1957. "Instinctively, I threw myself to the floor," Bates wrote in her autobiography *The Long Shadow of Little Rock*. "I was covered with shattered glass…I reached for the rock lying in the middle of the floor. A note was tied to it. I broke the string and unfolded a soiled piece of paper. Scrawled in bold print were the words: 'Stone this time. Dynamite next.'"

Just a few days before school was scheduled to start, August 29, 1957, the state court ruled against integration. The segregationists had convinced a judge that armed conflict was brewing, that weapons were being bought and harbored by black and white students. This setback aroused the ever-vigilant NAACP, and they successfully challenged the decree.

As expected, Governor Orval Faubus defied the courts and ordered the National Guard to Central High School. The guardsmen, Faubus announced during a televised broadcast, "will not act as segregationists or integrationists, but as soldiers called to active duty to carry out their assigned tasks." He asserted that "it was not possible to restore or maintain order and protect the lives and property of the citizens if forcible integration is carried tomorrow in the schools of the community." On September 4, despite a ruling to proceed with integration plans from U.S. District Court Judge Ronald N. Davies, the Arkansas National Guard refused to allow the students to enter Central High School.

Elizabeth Eckford recalled those harrowing moments when they were confronted by a phalanx of national guardsmen with their bayoneted rifles. It suddenly dawned on her that the soldiers were not there to protect them. "The crowd was quiet," she related to Daisy Bates. "I guess they were waiting to see what was going to happen. When I was able to steady my knees, I walked up to the guard who had let the white students in. He didn't move. When I tried to squeeze past him, he raised his bayonet and then the other guards closed in and they raised their bayonets.

"They glared at me with a mean look and I was very frightened and didn't know what to do," Eckford continued. "I turned around and the crowd came toward me. They moved closer and closer. Somebody

Two National Guardsmen stand watch at the entrance of Central High School

started yelling, 'Lynch her! Lynch her!' I tried to see a friendly face somewhere in the crowd—someone who maybe would help. I looked into the face of an old woman and it seemed a kind face, but when I looked at her again, she spat on me. They came closer shouting, 'No nigger bitch is going to get in our school. Get out of here!'" **CD**

Faced with menacing taunts, Eckford once more turned to the guards for help, but none was forthcoming. In the distance she saw a bench at a bus stop, and it loomed like an atoll of safety, if she could only get there. "I don't know why the bench seemed a safe place," she related, "but I started walking toward it. I tried to close my mind to what they were shouting, and kept saying to myself, 'If I can only make it to the bench I'll be safe.'

"When I finally got there, I don't think I could have gone another step," she said. "I sat down and the mob crowded up and began shouting all over again. Someone hollered, 'Drag her over to this tree! Let's take care of the nigger.' Just then a white man sat down beside me, put his arm around me and patted my shoulder. He raised my chin and said, 'Don't let them see you cry.'" That man was Benjamin Fine, the education editor for the *New York Times*, who endured similar insults from the mob when he was spat on and called a "dirty Jew."

A little over two weeks later, Judge Davies issued another order to end state interference at the school, and Governor Faubus reluctantly withdrew the troops. By this time, the governor, elected into office for a second term a year before, was symbolic of racial intransigence, inspiring poets, painters, and musicians to excoriate his corrosive behavior. "Tell me someone…who is ridiculous…!" bassist/composer Charlie Mingus shouted to his drummer Dannie Richmond on a recording of Mingus's composition "Fables of Faubus." "Gov…ner…Fau…bus!" Richmond thundered in response.

Governor Orval Faubus

DISC 1
TRACK 5

On September 23, more than a thousand angry whites replaced the National Guard at the school, shouting obscenities and trying to intimidate any black student who dared to cross their encirclement of the site. Avoiding the mob and running a gauntlet of indignities, the students were chaperoned through a side door by school security. This ruse was unintentionally aided by four black men who distracted the mob's attention. These men—all of them reporters, including Jimmy Hicks of the *Amsterdam News*—were chased and beaten, but sustained no serious injuries. "By arrangement the children were to stay at the Bates's home until they received a call from the deputy police chief notifying them that it was safe to come to the school," Hicks wrote. "Mrs. Bates, hoping to slip the children into the school, asked the Negro newsmen not to go along for fear that their cameras would tip the mob off as to what was happening."

The plan was accepted and the newsmen were given a head start in order to arrive in advance of the students. After parking their car a few blocks from Central High, they proceeded toward the school, now and then passing clusters of sullen whites. "When they saw us," Hicks said, "they rushed toward us yelling, 'Here come the niggers.' We stopped and the mob rushed upon us." Hicks; the dour, resourceful L. A. Wilson, editor of the *Tri-State Journal* in Memphis; Moses Newson of the *Baltimore Afro-American* newspaper; and photographer Earl Davy of the *Arkansas State Press* were quickly surrounded and pummeled and kicked by the white mob. It was later speculated by friends and family that the beating Wilson received was directly related to his death in 1960, at age fifty-one.

During their flight from the mob, the journalists encountered several white officers but none of them offered to assist them. Even FBI officers shied away from them, only speaking to them when they were sure no other whites were nearby to witness the exchanges. "After we were safely out of the mob area," Hicks said, "reports came over the radio that we had been sent to the school as 'decoys' to the mob so that they would not notice the Negro children when they slipped in. This is actually what happened but it certainly was not in our plan."

Hours later the entry maneuver was discovered by the crowd outside and the students had to be spirited from the school before the mob again resorted to violence. "Even after the Negroes left the school," an Associated Press story reported, "the crowds remained. Teenagers in two automobiles cruised the outskirts yelling, 'Which way did the niggers go?'" Meanwhile, dozens of white students had already left the school, refusing to "stay in there with the niggers."

As the tension mounted, the crowd continued to hassle and heckle the police. Mayor Woodrow Mann had no recourse but to dispatch a telegram to President Dwight D. Eisenhower requesting federal assistance. At the same time, other civil rights leaders sent letters and telegrams to the White House. Roy Wilkins, executive secretary of the NAACP, was outraged that Eisenhower was not moving with more alacrity to deal with the crisis. For weeks the president and Governor Faubus had debated the issue, both seeking a resolution that wouldn't hurt their political standing. "He has been absolutely and thoroughly disappointing and disillusioning, from beginning to end, " Wilkins observed of Eisenhower. "He has abdicated leadership in a great moral crisis."

Either realizing now that the local law enforcement officers could not maintain order or prompted by the fact that the black community was not going to be cowed by the threat of racial violence, President Eisenhower responded immediately to the mayor's request, deploying 1,200 troops from the 101st Airborne Division and federalizing 10,000 members of the state's national guard to the school to ensure the safety of the children, now dubbed the "Little Rock Nine." Eisenhower's original plan to send U.S. marshals to the school was scuttled. For the first time since the end of the Civil War and Reconstruction, federal troops were on their way to the South to assist the African American community there.

"Under the leadership of demagogic extremists," Eisenhower said in an address to the nation, "disorderly mobs have deliberately prevented the carrying out of proper orders from a federal court. Mob rule cannot be allowed to override the decisions of our courts. If the resistance to the federal court order ceases at once…federal troops will be unnecessary and the city of Little Rock will return to its normal habit of peace and order." 🆑

The presence of soldiers did not stop the mob; in fact, the vociferous white residents became even more rowdy. Now, the courageous Little Rock Nine were experiencing doubts about integration, even though the soldiers were there to escort them to class and took up posts inside the school. Melba Pattillo's little brother, Conrad, mindful of the mob's violent potential, told her "Don't look 'em in the eye. Remember what happened to Emmett Till?"

At the home of each of the students, the phones rang incessantly. Predictably on the other end was a raging voice full of venom and racial epithets. After the federal troops arrived, Pattillo recorded in her diary, "It's Thursday, September 26, 1957. Now I have a bodyguard. I know very well that the President didn't send these soldiers just to protect me but to show support for an idea—the idea that a governor can't ignore federal laws. Still, I feel specially cared about because the guard is there. If he wasn't there, I'd hear more of the voices of those people who say I'm a nigger…that I'm not valuable, that I have no right to live."

A fusillade of whoops and chants of derision ("two, four, six, eight, we ain't gonna integrate!") greeted the black students each day they arrived at the school. They usually came in a station wagon from Mrs. Bates's house accompanied by one Army Jeep in front and one behind, each mounted with a fifty caliber machine gun. Above them, an Army helicopter now and then buzzed the crowd. The six girls wore the flowing skirts and saddle oxford shoes that were the style of the day. Each of them carried several books like shields as they marched toward the school, encircled by a cordon of soldiers, then up the zigzag layer of steps to the front door. For every white student who welcomed the newcomers—several classmates, for example, asked Minniejean

Elizabeth Eckford passes troops on the way to class

DISC 1
TRACK 5

Brown to join the glee club—there were at least a dozen or so who resented them. A few days after the integration process began, Governor Faubus appeared on television to decry what he called "the naked force of the federal government." He held up photos of girls who he said had been roughly man-handled by the soldiers. 🆑

To stem the allegations, the commanding officer of the 101st Airborne ordered his troops out of the city and to barracks at Camp Robinson, about twelve miles from the school. This left the federalized guardsmen to maintain the relative calm that had followed the days of turmoil and rage. Things might have cooled outside, but inside the classrooms and corridors, the black students were the victims of all sorts of insults and abuse. Globs of spit hit them whenever they bumped into a white student. Or they were tripped, slapped, and assaulted so fast that the guards assigned to them couldn't react in time to ward off the blows or to intercept a deliberate trip or kick. Once, when Melba Pattillo was kicked in the shins by another student, she asked the guardsmen why he didn't intervene. "I'm here for one thing," he said, "to keep you alive. I'm not allowed to get into verbal or physical battles with these students."

On more than one occasion the fortitude of the students was challenged. No longer able to endure the harassment, Elizabeth Eckford went to the vice principal's office and told her she could not take it anymore, that she wanted to go home. The vice principal was able to convince her to stay, promising her that she would see to it that things got better. Minniejean Brown dealt with the taunters a different way. Rather than marching teary eyed to the principal's office she dumped a bowl of chili on the head of a white kid who kept calling her a "nigger." Ernest Green witnessed the scene. He said the cafe-

teria was dead silent after the incident. "Then the help, all black, broke into applause," he recalled. "And the white kids there didn't know what to do. It was the first time that anybody [there] had seen somebody black retaliate."

Melba Pattillo was also in the cafeteria when it happened, and she said that Brown dumped chili on two of the white boys. Then, she continued, "a school official showed up, and Minniejean was whisked away, and we were hustled out of the cafe-teria." For this bit of audacity, Brown was promptly suspended. She would be out until the school superintendent said she could return. "One nigger down, and eight to go!" was the new chant that rang in the black students' ears, and that appeared on bulletin boards around the school.

Brown's suspension happened just before Christmas, but she was back in school in January, under the proviso that she not retaliate when badgered and bullied. A few weeks after she was readmitted, a boy doused her with a bucket of soup. She was mortified, stiffened with anger, but did not strike back. Even so, it was only a matter of time before she would wilt under the catcalls, pranks, and physical abuse. When the boy who had dumped the soup on her attacked her again in February, she stood her ground, daring anyone to attack her. Hauled before the principal, she was expelled for good.

Glad to be out of the pressure cooker at Central, Minniejean Brown moved to New York City. She was the recipient of a prestigious scholarship to New Lincoln High School. Moreover, she would live in the house of the famous psychologist Dr. Kenneth Clark, who had played such a vital role in the *Brown v. Board of Education* decision. But she couldn't even board her plane for New York without encountering trouble. A bomb threat had been reported on her flight. The clamor continued when she arrived in

Above: Eisenhower's notes on the Little Rock crisis: "Troops—Not to enforce integration but to prevent opposition by violence to orders of a court"

Above: This draft of an Eisenhower speech begins: "My Fellow Citizens: For a few minutes I want to speak to you about the serious—indeed the sad—situation in Little Rock. In that city, under the leadership of demagogic extremists, disorderly mobs have deliberately prevented the carrying out of proper orders of a Federal Court. Local authorities have not succeeded in eliminating that violent opposition and, under the law, I yesterday issued a proclamation calling upon this mob to disperse. This morning the mob again gathered in front of the Central High School…"

New York City, with a crush of reporters and photographers eager for her to tell her story.

With Brown gone, it meant there was one less black student to assail, which, on the other hand, also meant that somebody would be the recipient of even more belittling and assaults. Later, the NAACP released a report that there had been forty-two instances of harassment of the nine, now eight, black students. But these reports, according to Melba Pattillo, were just the ones reported and did not represent the countless number of times the students just grinned and ignored it. The civil rights group had no idea how many times the students found peanut butter and tacks in their seats; ink stains on their clothes; their lockers rummaged and their books made unreadable.

By the spring of 1958, the circumstances at Central had become almost unbearable for the black students;

still, they endured. Meanwhile, the segregationists were gloating, cheering the fact that Judge Davies was no longer on the bench and overseeing their complaint to halt integration. A judge who loved the traditional ways of the "South like a religion" was slated to replace him. There was very little to be jubilant about for Pattillo and her cohorts. "The experience of walking down that hall to my home-room each morning got so worrisome that I doubled my repetitions of the Lord's Prayer as I walked from the front door up the stairs," Pattillo reminisced. "Inside the home-room class, I was entertained by a whole new series of indignities. I arrived one day to find a doll that resembled me, with a rope around her neck, hanging from a door frame. Another time, someone had provided genuine urine to spray in my seat and on my clothing."

Once more there were appeals from the NAACP to the school board to intervene and provide additional safeguards for the eight students, but there was little to no response to their pleas. With each passing day, the situation got worse as the presence of the guardsmen diminished. It was becoming rarer for Pattillo and the others to get personal escorts. In addition, the school board was seeking a three-year delay in the integration plans. The board wanted all integration suspended until January 1961. Chief among its concerns, as it had been since 1954, was a more precise definition of the Supreme Court's "all deliberate speed" language in the *Brown II* decision. The moves were in accord with Governor Faubus, who declared that racial integration was "not the law of the land—only Congress could make laws."

Many of the white students at Central High, especially a reactionary core of fifty, were determined to block Ernest Green's graduation. Rather than a cap and gown, many proposed a noose for Green, the only senior in what was now called the "Little Rock Eight."

"Let's keep the nigger from graduating" was a recurring mantra among the students, a call to arms that galvanized them in their animosity for the "intruder."

Melba Pattillo's plight was even more disturbing—and perilous. "I had developed a habit of reaching my hand into my locker to find hidden objects before I poked my face in," she explained. "I was searching my locker for my eyeglass case when I reached my hand down deep inside to see whether not or it had fallen. Suddenly there was the sound of popping guns and the smell of smoke just behind me. I quickly turned to see a flaming object flying toward my face. I put my hand up to deflect it. That's when I felt the pain on my first three fingers. I had shielded my eyes from several sparkling hot firecrackers linked together by a wire. My hand hurt, but I could only be grateful it wasn't my eyes that had been burned."

On the Tuesday of May 27, 1958, with more than 4,500 people in attendance to cheer on the 602 graduates at Quigley Stadium, Ernest Green received his diploma, and was thereby the first African American to graduate from Central High in its history. "I figured I was making a statement and helping black people's existence in Little Rock," Green said later. "I kept telling myself, I just can't trip with all those cameras watching me. But I knew once I got as far as the principal and received the diploma, I had cracked the wall." The loud applause for those graduates who preceded him turned to an unbelievable silence when Green's name was called. "Nobody clapped," he said, "but they didn't have to…I had accomplished what I had come there for."

Pattillo and the other black students, as well as the black press, were not allowed to attend the ceremonies. But they listened to it on the radio. When Green's name was followed by silence, Pattillo's mother said, "What the heck. Lots of people in the rest of the world are applauding for Ernie and for all of you who made it through this year."

Indeed, Pattillo's mother was prescient in noting the global implications of Green's graduation and the bravery of the Little Rock Nine. The glaring contradiction between America's might, the rhetoric of democracy and its failure to provide these same rights and measures for the downtrodden at home was evident to millions living abroad. Evident, too, was the racist character of Governor Faubus, who stepped up his campaign against integration as he roared toward the election for a third gubernatorial term, in which he would garner almost seventy percent of the vote in an overwhelming victory. The segregationists cheered their leader.

Cheers were in order for the Little Rock Eight, who at the end of May were making stops in Chicago where they picked up the Robert S. Abbott Award conferred by the Chicago Defender newspaper, then on to Cleveland to receive the NAACP's highest award, the Spingarn Medal, given to a person for his or her achievements in civil rights. At first, when they were told they were selected for this honor, they refused to accept it

Thurgood Marshall sits with Daisy Bates and six of the Little Rock Nine on the Supreme Court Steps

unless it also included their protector and mentor, Daisy Bates. The NAACP agreed and Bates was saluted along with her proteges.

By September 1958, as a new school year dawned, the black students chalked up another court battle and happily packed their bags for still another round of combat at Central. But the relentless governor pulled a coup and instead closed down all the high schools. A large percentage of the city's white students enrolled in private schools. Most black students in Little Rock, including the famed eight at Central, didn't attend school at all that year. It took a year before the Supreme Court ruled the school closings unconstitutional. The decision was too late for two of the families, including Melba Pattillo's, who left the city permanently. After the NAACP forced the doors open again, only Jefferson Thomas and Carlotta Walls were allowed to return and eventually graduate from Central.

But the Little Rock Nine had opened other doors as well. Ministers, who were inspired by their courage and later would commit themselves to the civil rights movement, had a political and biblical motivation, recalling their sermons about "the children shall lead them." James Forman, later a stalwart in the movement, was a graduate student when he watched in awe at developments in Little Rock.

"What was I doing here in graduate school at Boston University, studying African Affairs and government," he questioned in his autobiography *The Making of Black Revolutionaries*, "when down in Little Rock those young students were facing the man? They were agitating. They were together. I should leave this place. I should quit school right now, it just didn't make sense. I should go to Little Rock. There must be some way I can help." A veteran of the Air Force and a bit more mature than his younger colleagues, Forman, like thousands of others, threw himself unflinchingly against the powers of segregation in Little Rock and elsewhere. Inspired by the Little Rock Nine, Forman would make his mark in the movement and earn the respect of all the civil rights leaders, including Dr. Martin Luther King.

7

Rev. Dr. Martin Luther King Jr.

Some years ago I sat in a Harlem department store, surrounded by hundreds of people," Dr. King wrote in *Why We Can't Wait*. "I was autographing copies of *Stride Toward Freedom*, my book about the Montgomery bus boycott of 1955–56. As I signed my name to a page, I felt something sharp plunge forcefully into my chest. I had been stabbed with a letter opener, struck home by a woman who would later be judged insane."

King was rushed to the Harlem Hospital for extraction of the knife. Only later would he learn that the knife's tip had stopped at his aorta. He was a fraction of an inch—or one abrupt movement—from death.

We can only speculate what would have happened to the civil rights movement had we lost Dr. King at that stage of his mission in life. The attack occurred on September 20, 1958, not long after he and wife Coretta had returned from a two-week vacation in Mexico and after he had been arrested for failing to obey an officer in Montgomery when asked to move from a hallway outside a courtroom. King was sentenced to a fine of ten dollars or fourteen days in jail. He said he would serve the time and advised his associates not to pay the money. But when he entered the wagon to be taken to jail they wouldn't let him in—someone had paid the fine, he was told.

Montgomery Police Commissioner Clyde Sellers knew that the city would face a firestorm of bad publicity, not to mention national attention, if they jailed Martin Luther King. Instead, explained King's wife, Coretta, "he paid the fine out of his own pocket and issued a statement that he wanted 'to save the taxpayers the expense of feeding King for fourteen days.'"

Martin Luther King Jr., with wife Coretta, recovers in the hospital after being stabbed

undergraduate studies at Morehouse College, where his father and grandfather had attended, he toyed with the idea of becoming a doctor, but biology didn't appeal to him, nor did the study of law hold his interest. He knew he could always fall back on the ministry, but there were some drawbacks.

"His interest in intellectual matters and his strong social consciousness, together with his normal youthful rebellion against tradition, had decided him against the ministry," his wife observed. "He was strongly motivated toward religion but was opposed to the emotionalism of the church he knew, and he believed in a relevant social gospel which few ministers preached at that time."

After passing the entrance exam at fifteen, King was admitted to Morehouse, where he became a dedicated student and excelled in his classes. He wrote in his autobiography, "When I went to Morehouse as a freshman in 1944, my concern for racial and economic justice was already substantial. During my student days I read Henry David Thoreau's essay 'On Civil Disobedience' for the first time." It was in Thoreau that he came to understand the ideals of nonviolent resistance, and he was inspired by Thoreau's willingness to accept jail time in protest of his government's war.

During the summer breaks, rather than taking some soft, cushy job, he chose manual labor in order to test his physical mettle, alternately working as a baggage handler at the Railway Express Agency and then on the loading platform at the Southern Bedspring Mattress Company. Then, in the summer of 1945, he and a few other Morehouse students labored in the tobacco fields of Connecticut. It was during this experience that he was often called to lead their devotional services; now he heard the whisper of the call to the ministry.

The roar would come through the words of Dr. Benjamin Mays, his mentor and the president of Morehouse. "Listening to Dr. Mays preach, and also hearing another brilliant minister, Dr. George D.

In less than four years, Dr. King had zoomed from an uncertain graduate of Boston University to the headlines of the world's papers, never losing that reserved humbleness and his instinct for finding the nerve center and then articulating the most pressing complaints of the oppressed. By the time he was at the helm of the Montgomery bus boycott, he had wisely chosen a path that had already been traveled by his father and grandfather, though he was at first hesitant, not sure if the ministry was the profession for him. As a child, he often imitated his father's sermons, gesturing and preaching to his congregation of teddy bears. Sitting in the front pews at Ebenezer Baptist Church in Atlanta, he was enthralled by the way his father could make biblical characters come alive during his sermons. Even so, when he entered

Kelsey, head of the theological department, Martin came to see that the ministry could be intellectually respectable as well as emotionally satisfying," Coretta King would later write.

"You are what you aspire to be," Dr. Mays often told his youthful proteges, "and not what you now are; you are what you do with your mind, and you are what you do with your youth. It is not your environment, it is you—the quality of your minds, the integrity of your souls, and the determination of your will—that will decide your future and shape your lives."

At the age of seventeen, King's mind, his will, and his integrity were dedicated to the ministry. His decision pleased his father, and Martin began to plan for his trial sermon. "On the appointed Sunday afternoon, a sizable crowd filed into the church basement,

where trial sermons were traditionally held," Taylor Branch summarized in *Parting the Waters*. "Then others came, and still more, until Rev. King, in his glory, finally shouted, 'It won't hold 'em! It won't hold 'em!' and waved everyone upstairs into the main sanctuary. Young M. L. King did not have the commanding presence of his much larger father in the pulpit, as some noticed, but he already spoke with authority that made people forget his small stature. Although he talked less of Jesus and used more big words than many of his listeners would have like, the trial was a great success." Not yet out of his teens, he had impressed his father enough that he was made assistant pastor of the church.

King's senior year at Morehouse marked his official entry into the fight against racism, or "the Negro

King passes through a picket line after being arrested for protesting lunch counter segregation

The King family in 1962. From left: Martin Luther King III, age four; Yolanda Denise, age six; Coretta; and Dexter Scott, 18 months old.

College and sold watermelons on the campus. For the upstanding deacons this was unacceptable behavior and they asked for and received Johns's resignation.

These encounters at Dexter were occurring while King was matriculating at Crozer Theological Seminary in Chester, Pennsylvania, where he had enrolled in 1948. He began to apply himself seriously in the study of theology at this racially mixed school noted for its high academic standards. He was thrilled to be studying such great thinkers as Rousseau, Hobbes, and most significantly, the Christian theologian Reinhold Niebuhr. The courses were often challenging, but King passed them all, though it does come as a surprise that he barely passed a course in oratory.

Of the eleven students who enrolled that year, King earned the highest grades and was well on his way to becoming the valedictorian of his class. Among the thinkers and scholars who influenced him most was Walter Rauschenbusch, whose emphasis on the social gospel—using one's faith and belief in righteousness to correct social wrongs—was absolutely captivating. As the top student in his class, King set his sights on graduate school at Boston University. He left Crozer armed with a sterling academic record and a passel of recommendations; a brand new car was waiting for him in Atlanta for the long drive to Boston.

On his way to Boston, there was a brief layover in Brooklyn where he was asked to preach a guest sermon at Concord Baptist Church, then under the prestigious leadership of Rev. Dr. Gardner Taylor, a friend of Martin's father. The senior King and Taylor were key members of the National Baptist Convention, and thus Martin was given a special invitation to the pulpit. At twenty-two, it was an opportunity that few young, upcoming ministers ever dreamed of, and he made the most of it with his eloquence and spiritual bearing that kept the congregation in a state of agitation and "Amens."

The excitement of taking the pulpit at Concord stayed with King through his first few days in Boston. An immediate distinction he noticed between

question." He began to consider the notion of civil rights that conceptually had been introduced into the language by a commission appointed by President Harry Truman in its report, "To Secure These Rights." In an article he wrote for the campus newspaper, King assailed the bigotry of Georgia's Governor Eugene Talmadge. The spirit and thrust of his remarks were reminiscent of the Rev. Vernon Johns, another of King's idols who was known for his powerful sermons as the pastor of Dexter Avenue Baptist Church in Montgomery. Johns was an ever-present source of controversy and on several occasions the deacons had sought to remove him from his position. In 1952, the deacons confronted him again after it was disclosed that he had traveled to Alabama State

Boston and Crozer was the size of the student body and the school's bustling rhythm. Soon he was immersed in the gargantuan syllabi on which he spent most of his time studying, so much so that there was hardly anytime to socialize or to become involved in campus activities. His studies even made it impossible for him to join in protests against the Korean War or to push for the inclusion of black clerks at the local Sears. The only thing that occasionally interfered in jaunts to the library was a young lady he had met in 1952. A native of Alabama and a graduate of Antioch College, Coretta Scott was studying voice at the New England Conservatory of Music. They spent as much time together as their class assignments would permit.

It was a mutual attraction between Martin and Coretta, and for the ambitious seminary student she possessed all the things he required of a mate. In due time, he was able to convince his family of their serious affair and plans to marry, which they did on June 18, 1953. Now, he had a marriage to tend and a dissertation to write.

Yet there was one hurdle to overcome: he had been called to pastor the Dexter Avenue Baptist Church. King had won over a congregation populated with zealots devoted to the former pastor Rev. Johns, but Coretta didn't relish the idea of returning to the South with its Jim Crow laws and restrictions on their dreams. Nonetheless, on April 14, 1954, a few weeks before the Supreme Court rendered its decision on *Brown v. Board of Education*, King accepted the offer from Dexter, which temporarily ended the possibility of him succeeding his father at Ebenezer.

At Dexter, King quickly went about the business of rearranging things at the church, much in the same way his father had done upon assuming the leadership at Ebenezer. With the necessary approval from the church's deacons, he formed new committees, boards, and councils. Many of the church's faithful viewed him as a new broom, and he was determined to sweep everything clean.

King was part shepherd, as he oversaw a new flock of worshipers at Dexter, and part student, completing his Ph.D. at Boston University. Then gradually he eased his way into the fight against the discrimination and bigotry that bedeviled his community. An already tension-filled city, charged with racial animosity, Montgomery became even more agitated after fifteen-year-old Claudette Colvin was snatched from a bus and jailed because she refused to surrender her seat to a white passenger. "We need to organize," was Martin's response to the indignity. He told his congregation and others that the time had come for change. Colvin's incident was only the straw that broke the camel's back; the awesome weight of protest against racial injustice was just around the bend.

Martin Luther King Jr., in a St. Augustine, Florida, jail cell after his arrest for attempting to integrate a nearby restaurant.

Nine months later, on December 1, 1955, Rosa Parks refused to move to the back of the bus and the Montgomery Bus Boycott began. King's involvement in the movement elevated him to national and then international prominence. At the beginning of these tumultuous days, King was adjusting to his mission at Dexter, anticipating the arrival of his first born, taking his ministry to numerous churches across the South, and mulling over the idea of running for the presidency of the local NAACP. The latter point was sure to ruffle the feathers of some of the community's elders, who would not take kindly to a newcomer barging in, seeking a leadership role. Ever

DISC 1
TRACK 6

since King had delivered his successful trial sermon there were several who took exception to his overly confident manner, but, thankfully, he had a comrade in the vicinity—Reverend Ralph Abernathy, pastor of First Baptist Church—who had eased his friend's transition from Boston to Montgomery, and now smoothed his entry into the city's movement for social and political change. 🆑

Almost three years older than King, Abernathy seemed to have had an abiding respect and admiration for Martin from the time they first met, despite losing a girl he was courting to his charming friend. Their relationship may have had an unsettling start,

King prepares to enter Mahatma Gandhi's shrine in New Delhi, India

but they soon were inseparable, with Abernathy eventually likening himself to Joshua to Martin's Moses (though some would later call Abernathy "Judas" for disclosing his friend's intimate relations with women other than his wife). They had many religious and cultural interests in common, as well as the social barriers of racism that inhibited them and their people. Years later, Abernathy told Monsignor Noel C. Burtenshaw of the Archdiocese of Atlanta, "The only integration in Montgomery at the time was fifteen minutes each Sunday. A black preacher was allowed to enter the all white Jefferson Davis Hotel, go through the lobby and climb the back stairs to a radio station. I remember it was March and it was my turn. I preached on hope. Dr. King heard it and called me. He wanted to get together. We did and we never really were apart after that until he died."

As a student at Alabama State University, Abernathy had organized several protests against the barracks-like dormitories and the atrocious food. Later, he and E.D. Nixon, the city's NAACP stalwart, paved the way for King to be elected president of the Montgomery Improvement Association (MIA), formed after Rosa Parks's bold defiance. King, according to cynics, acquired the position because he was new in town, and thus had not accumulated a lot of personal baggage. He possessed no skeletons in the closet, no coterie of friends, nor had he been in Montgomery long enough to have any longstanding enemies who might have challenged his meteoric ascension.

"Dr. King was new to Montgomery, and Dr. Abernathy had been trying to get him active in civil rights work," Rosa Parks wrote in her autobiography. "Rufus Lewis attended Dexter Avenue Baptist Church and had a very good opinion of Dr. King. Rufus Lewis had an exclusive night club—only registered voters could go there. It was Rufus Lewis who nominated Dr. King to be president of the MIA."

While King welcomed his new appointment as the leader of the MIA, he was ever mindful of its demands and the toll it would take on his family, his ministry,

Time Magazine declares Martin Luther King Jr. Man of the Year, 1964

and members of his church. He was a bit nervous when he delivered his first speech before the MIA. He put that matter in the hands of God.

And on this occasion and many thereafter, King would let the Lord speak for him. He praised his people and their relentless struggle for freedom and justice.

The bus boycott grew day-by-day as more and more citizens became involved, many of them moved to action by King's organizational and oratory skills. A white resident, upset by the boycott, cornered King one day and berated him for leading a disturbance of the peaceful coexistence between blacks and whites in Montgomery. "You have never had a real peace in Montgomery," King retorted. "You have had a sort of negative peace in which the Negro too often accepted his state of subordination. But this is not

DISC 1
TRACK 6

true peace. True peace is not merely the absence of tension; it is the presence of justice. The tension we see in Montgomery today is necessary tension that comes when the oppressed rise up and start to move toward permanent, positive peace." 🄲🄳

To break the boycott, the bus company tried all sorts of misinformation and deception. Even more troubling was the harassment of black residents by various city agencies, exacerbated by endless taunts and death threats to members of the MIA. The epitome of malevolence came on January 30 when the Kings' house was bombed. The destruction of parts of his home that endangered his family combined with the skein of speaking engagements and coordinating of the boycott to jeopardize King's physical and mental health. To continue at such a rapid pace, he was told by his doctor, might be hazardous.

But it was not possible to slow down—the city's legal counsel were prepared to slap the MIA and its car pool with charges of public nuisance charge and operating without a license. On November 13, almost a year after the boycott began, King was in court listening as the city demanded $15,000 in damages. He was in the process of conferring with his colleagues when a reporter approached King and handed him a press release. With each line he read his expression grew more jubilant: "The United States Supreme Court today affirmed a decision of a special three-judge U.S. District Court in declaring Alabama's state and local laws requiring segregation on buses unconstitutional." God almighty had spoken from the nation's capital, King told his astonished but delighted friends.

A little over a month later, the decree from the Supreme Court arrived in Montgomery. King, Abernathy, E.D. Nixon, and Glenn Smiley, a white minister and a member of the pioneering civil rights group, the Fellowship of Reconciliation, took a ride on the city's first integrated bus. Far less symbolic were thousands of black passengers who boarded the integrated buses in the days that followed, much to the chagrin of the Ku Klux Klan which held several demonstra-

tions protesting the new integrationists. Several parades of men in white, pointy top sheets did not delay the wave of residents gleefully testing the new policy. What the detractors could not deter with rallies they did with dynamite. The celebration halted when news came that a bomb had been planted at Abernathy's home, destroying his front porch. Then black churches were targeted. None of those arrested and arraigned were ever convicted of the crimes.

One reaction to the spree of bombings was the further consolidation of the civil rights movement with the founding of the Southern Christian Leadership Conference. King was elected to head the new organization. The position provided him with another forum from which to make his call for peace and justice. It was also a platform that gave him international cachet. In March 1957, he and Coretta, along with such notables as Ralph Bunche, Congressman Adam Clayton Powell, and A. Philip Randolph traveled to Ghana to witness the independence of the new nation. The trip abroad was also an opportunity to tour several major European cities, including Rome, Geneva, London and Paris. But all the celebrity and global respect he had garnered could not deflect a mean-spirited municipality, still reeling from the MIA victory. Ways were being devised to bring "that uppity Negro" down. They would have to bring him down from an even loftier standing after he was awarded the NAACP's Spingarn Medal for his "inspired leadership" of the bus boycott.

In the spring of 1958, King spoke at a black college in Pine Bluff, Arkansas. Since he was in the area, he thought he would pay a visit to Little Rock. He arrived just in time to attend the graduation ceremonies of Ernest Green, "and he came up to sit with my mother and Mrs. (Daisy) Bates and a couple of other friends in the audience," Green remembered.

A few weeks later King had a more important rendezvous. He, along with other civil rights leaders, had been invited to the White House to meet with President Eisenhower. Selecting those who would join him evolved into a political skirmish. It was finally decided that King would be accompanied by A. Philip Randolph, Roy Wilkins of the NAACP, and Lester Granger of the National Urban League. Congressman Powell's name had been bandied about as a potential visitor, but it was scrubbed at the last moment by members of Eisenhower's cabinet for undisclosed reasons. Missing that meeting was of no significance to Powell or to the others in the long run. Eisenhower maintained his consistently neutral involvement in civil rights issues, with the one notable exception of sending troops to Little Rock.

In late 1958, King continued to review lessons on nonviolence and the importance of enduring hardships for your beliefs. He studied and reflected on the teachings of Mahatma Gandhi, India's great spiritual leader and martyr. Like Gandhi, King often dreamed of leading his people to freedom and prosperity.

Early the next year, he visited India and person-ally experienced the impact of Gandhian philosophy. He recalled how much the trip convinced him to pursue the path of nonviolence.

"It was a marvelous thing to see the amazing results of a nonviolent campaign," King wrote. "India won her independence, but without violence on the part of Indians. The aftermath of hatred and bitterness that usually follows a violent campaign was found nowhere in India.

"The way of nonviolence," he explained, "leads to redemption and the creation of the beloved community."

It was the latter strategy that would inform the rest of King's days as a civil rights leader, although he certainly could not envision then the heights to which he would rise as a "drum major for peace" in the coming dramas of Albany, Selma, Birmingham, Chicago, Harlem, and Memphis.

King delivers his acceptance speech for the Nobel Peace Prize

8

Sit Down for Your Rights

Although there were minor sit-in demonstrations in the 1950s, the protest tactic as a major movement didn't gather momentum until February 1, 1960, when Ezell Blair Jr. (Jibreel Khazan), David Richmond, Joseph McNeil, and Franklin McCain—all of them freshmen at North Carolina Agricultural and Technical College in Greensboro—occupied stools at the Woolworth store and refused to move until they were served. They gave notice to all that a new breed of students had emerged in the South and they were ready to confront the inequities that for too long had smothered their opportunities and stifled their dreams.

After they stopped by Ralph Johns' clothing store on Market Street, the four freshmen entered Woolworth's Five & Dime at approximately 4 pm and purchased some school supplies and other items. They then approached the lunch counter and ordered coffee. As was the custom and practice of the store, they were promptly refused service at the counter, though they had been allowed to make purchases in other parts of the store. "We don't serve coloreds here," the waitress told them. Undaunted, the quartet, like Rosa Parks had done in Montgomery, remained seated. While they waited for the waitress to return from the other end of the counter, a black woman who worked at the store yelled at them, "You are stupid, ignorant! You're dumb! That's why we can't get anywhere today. You know you are supposed to eat at the other end."

After being assailed by the black employee, policemen came in the store and stared at the young men, but said nothing. It was clearly an attempt to intimidate them. The four appeared unperturbed. When the store closed at 5:30 pm, they got up and left, not sure what their next move would be.

DISC I
TRACK 7

"It all started out as a personal thing," Franklin McCain later said. "Personal from the standpoint that we didn't like the idea of not having dignity and respect, and our feeling of self-worth. We decided it was up to us to find some relief. So, something that started out very personal ended up being very public." Blair, at that time only seventeen, recalled how the four of them began to plot their move without violating some of the state laws. "I told Joseph McNeil that we couldn't say boycott in North Carolina because if you do they take you to court or put you in jail. So, we looked to the models of Dr. King and Rosa Parks and what took place in Montgomery, Alabama. We wanted to find out if what they said in the Bill of Rights in the Constitution was true…we wanted equal rights for all Americans." McNeil viewed the action as a "down payment on our manhood, to take on something that might have enormous risks and implications, and it turned out to be something we all can be very proud of." 🆑

For James Farmer, a founder of the Congress of Racial Equality (CORE), the four symbolized a change in the mood of African Americans. "Up until then," he asserted, "we had accepted segregation, begrudgingly, but we had accepted it. We had spoken against it…but no one had defied segregation…but these four freshmen sat in at the lunch counter…and refused to leave. This sparked a movement throughout the South."

For the next several days the sit-in movement simmered in Greensboro, but the number of demonstrators swelled. On Tuesday, February 3, the four initiators returned to the counter, this time as part of a group of about twenty students. They entered at mid-morning and stayed the entire day. They were not served.

Protesters sit at a whites-only lunch counter. From left: Joseph McNeil, Franklin McCain, Billy Smith, and Clarence Henderson

White residents of Greensboro gawked at the demonstrators, hoping that these were college students merely indulging a spontaneous whim. Others felt a more ominous intrusion and deemed it the work of outside agitators or even communists who were poisoning the minds of young black men. Realizing they were treading on precarious legal ground, the students decided to take their plight to the local chapter of the NAACP. By now they numbered in the hundreds which presented a problem for Dr. George C. Simkins, the chapter's president. He was aware of the situation right from the beginning, because he had received a phone call from Ralph Johns, who had given the four money to make the purchases at Woolworth's. "He had been trying to get me to do the same thing, but...I had just finished with a jail sentence, so I told him I'd have to get straight on that one before I started on any other."

Dr. Simkins advised them that the gravity of the situation required someone with a better understanding and more experience. He wrote to the New York office of CORE requesting assistance. CORE's field secretary, Gordon R. Carey, who had previously helped some North Carolina students through their protests, arrived from New York on February 7.

Hoping to stymie the demonstrations, managers at Woolworth's and S. H. Kress, the other five-and-dime in Greensboro targeted by the students, began closing down sections of the counters or the entire store in cases where there were rumors of violence and bomb threats. On more than one occasion the students were harassed and heckled by gangs of whites, who sometimes followed their hoots by hurling bottles and cans, dousing them with catsup and pelting them with eggs. But Greensboro wasn't the only city where the sit-ins were occurring. In Raleigh, forty-three blacks were charged with trespassing on what the manager of Woolworth's contended was "private property."

Northerners protest a New York department store for practicing discrimination in its southern chains

In Greensboro, the four who had triggered the spreading sit-ins found it difficult to get a good night's sleep. "There were nightly threats," Blair remembered. "They said 'We'll get you niggers if you go down there the next day.' What could we do? We didn't have any protection, no bodyguards."

As the protests increased, the already uneasy race relations in North Carolina cities became even more strained. Many white North Carolinians were baffled by the protests, believing they had made considerable concessions since the Supreme Court's *Brown v. Board of Education* decision of 1954. There had already been desegregation of some of the schools and public facilities, some pleaded. "We don't want token freedom," the fearless Rev. Fred Shuttlesworth of Birmingham, Alabama, roared to a meeting of black citizens in

Greensboro. "We want full freedom. What would a token dollar be worth?"

Rev. Shuttlesworth's rhetorical question was answered and seconded at another meeting, this one comprising mostly whites. Harold C. Fleming, executive director of the Southern Regional Council, an interracial group of Southern leaders with headquarters in Atlanta, declared, "Those who hoped that token legal adjustments to school desegregation would dispose of the racial issues are on notice to the contrary. We may expect more, not less, protests of this kind against enforced segregation in public facilities and services of all types."

Fleming's words proved prophetic. Farther south in Florida, the young people were catching the infectious spirit of spontaneous rebellion, and in too many instances they didn't have to get their inspiration from the evening news. In Tallahassee, in the spring of 1959, a nineteen-year-old black woman, a student at Florida A&M University (FAMU) had been forced from her car by four white men and savagely raped seven times. And though the men were convicted of the crime—a rarity in a place and time when white men committed such acts of atrocity with impunity—the incident lingered in the minds of many African Americans as the sit-in movement stirred more and more people to action.

Patricia Stephens Due, 21, and her sister, Priscilla, 22, didn't need any further provocation, since they had been thoroughly indoctrinated by CORE and were poised to join the fight to end segregation. "A regional 'sympathy sit-in' day [in tribute to the action in Greensboro] was scheduled for Saturday, February 13, and Tallahassee CORE took part," Due noted in her autobiography. "About ten of us—students from FAMU and two Negro high school students, dressed in neat school attire—carried our schoolbooks and calmly walked inside the Woolworth store on Monroe Street. In 1960, signs above the lunch counter at Woolworth advertised sundaes for a quarter and an entire roast turkey dinner for sixty-five cents. We sat at the cushioned, straight-back counter stools and asked for slices of cake. The surprised waitress refused, but we remained at the counter."

A segregated lunch counter in Virginia. Moments later a fight broke out when African Americans came in seeking service

They held their positions despite being baited and insulted by white hoodlums circling near them, trying to provoke them into a fight. "What are you niggers doing in here?" one of them bellowed in their faces.

Tallahassee's first sit-in attracted a number of local reporters but it failed to resonate beyond the immediate vicinity of the protests. Something had to be done to propel the demonstrations, to make the whole city pay attention. The next move not only aroused city residents, it catapulted to the national media. On February 20, nineteen days after the Greensboro sit-ins began, the Tallahassee demonstrations got underway. The plan this time was to include whites in the demonstration.

"Seventeen of us—mostly FAMU students, with two high school students and a local forty-three-year old resident, Mary Ola Gaines—arrived at Woolworth at approximately 2 pm," Due wrote. "None of us knew Mrs. Gaines, who was the only legal-age adult in our group that day. She'd heard about the planned sit-in through the Inter-Civil Council and had decided to join us after work." Gaines was a long-time resident of Georgia and worked as a housekeeper. She knew nothing about CORE and was only there because she believed in doing the right thing. Now the group had someone in their ranks who couldn't be accused of being an outside agitator.

Amid shouts and threats, the group, along with their white observers, took seats at the counter and gave the waitress their orders. Each protester had a book or a newspaper and they tried to read while surrounded by an increasingly large and noisy crowd with mayhem on its mind. Out of the side of her eye, Due saw one young white thug approach them with a baseball bat. Then another one began tugging on her clothes, trying to unseat her. This tug of war went on for nearly an hour, but the students maintained their seats and their cool.

By this time the two white observers were gone, and on the heels of their departure the mayor of Tallahassee arrived. After a few moments of dialogue

with the mayor and other city officials, the knot of demonstrators dwindled to eleven, including Due and her sister. They were obstinate in their demand to be served. "So that was that," Due said. "All eleven of us were arrested for disturbing the peace by 'engaging in riotous conduct.'" As they were marched off to jail, they were forced to walk a gauntlet of cheering and applauding white residents, all of them glad to see the troublemakers behind bars.

At the police precinct the protesters were booked, fingerprinted, and processed. Bail was set at $500 each. "I do not remember how we paid our bail," Due recalled. "We couldn't find any local attorneys willing to represent us, so CORE asked the American Civil Liberties Union (ACLU) in Miami to provide attorneys." Tobias Simon and Howard Dixon, both white, defended them, and the NAACP assigned Gratten Graves Jr., a black attorney. The protesters pled not guilty, and when the word got out about the forthcoming trial, fellow students at FAMU voted not to go to school. Their plan to attend the trial forced the judge to postpone it for two weeks, hoping that would be enough time to allow things to cool off.

But with the fires of protest ignited, it wasn't long before the city was a raging inferno of resistance. Almost daily people were being arrested for demonstrating without a permit and carted off to jail. But the arrests didn't stop the growing unity between black and white demonstrators, and as the protests intensified, the students and their supporters were beginning to feel optimistic about ending segregation at Woolworth's and McCrory's, the other large department store in the area.

But the relative peace they had established amidst the protests wouldn't last, as the arrest of many student protesters galvanized an even larger contingent to march. They were more than a thousand strong as they marched peacefully toward downtown Tallahassee. But they never made it. They were confronted by a battalion of police officers at the railroad tracks that divided the city. "The tear gas bombs began to fly,"

James Farmer, director of CORE, sits at a newly integrated lunch counter

Due recounted. "Officials later maintained that we had a three-minute warning, but I remember no such warning. All I remember is that what had begun as a peaceful march turned to havoc."

One officer who remembered Due from other demonstrations lobbed a teargas canister directly in her face. "The thick, bitter chemicals filled my eyes, nose, and mouth," she said. "I coughed and choked, flailing and blinded, as other students around me screamed and fled. For a terrifying instant, I could not breathe at all. My eyes were afire."

Patricia Due was led to safety by a stranger with military experience who told her not to rub her eyes, that the burning would soon go away. The burning eventually subsided but the gassing scarred her vision, making it necessary for her to wear dark glasses, even at night. She had them on when she showed up for

her court date from the previous demonstration and was sentenced to $300 or sixty days in jail. Due and several others decided to go to jail rather than pay the fine. It was the first time any activists in the student sit-in movement had chosen to remain in jail. It was a tactic that would surface again and again during the civil rights movement.

"I would not pay to maintain a segregated system," Due said later. "In addition to that, people had to know what was happening in America. I decided I would serve the sixty days. Three of those who were arrested and sentenced got out of jail and immediately began the appeal process. Initially, eight of us went to jail, then three more got out, and five of us spent forty-nine days in the Leon County jail in Tallahassee. We were given five days off each month for good behavior, and the extra day to avoid publicity.

"While we were in jail, we received support from Jackie Robinson, a telegram from Dr. Martin Luther King Jr., and received hundreds of letters from citizens who couldn't understand why, in America, we were jail for asking for 'service at a Woolworth lunch counter.'"

In his letter to Due on March 19, Dr. King expressed his concern for the young activists who chose to serve time: "As you suffer the inconvenience of remaining in jail, please remember that unearned suffering is redemptive. Going to jail for a righteous cause is a badge of honor and a symbol of dignity. I assure you that your valiant witness is one of the glowing epics of our time and you are bringing all of America nearer [to] the threshold of the world's bright tomorrows."

Five hundred miles from the campus of FAMU, students at Fisk University were in the midst of their own uprising. The sit-in demonstrations begun in Greensboro had spread to activists at the Nashville, Tennessee, campus, particularly Diane Nash and John Lewis, who had already received lessons in nonviolent protest from that estimable tactician James Lawson, a member of the Fellowship of Reconciliation (FOR).

Tall, bespectacled, and with a mild demeanor, Lawson was only in his thirties, but had already accumulated an impressive record of service as a pacifist, spending more than a year in jail as a conscientious objector to the Korean War. After being released from jail, he traveled to India as a Methodist missionary and studied the teachings of Mahatma Gandhi. He studied theology at Oberlin College where he first heard Dr. King speak and was a divinity student at Vanderbilt when he began conducting his nonviolent workshops as a member of the Fellowship of Reconciliation.

When the demonstrations against segregation began in Nashville, it was Lawson who set them in motion. John Lewis wrote in *Walking with the Wind*, his autobiography, "More than five hundred students filled the seats and spilled into the aisles [in the chemistry building] to hear Jim Lawson announce that we would be staging sit-ins at all of Nashville's major department stores and that volunteers would be needed."

On Saturday morning, February 13, 1960, the same day students in Tallahassee staged their "sympathy sit-in," one hundred and twenty four protesters filed out of First Baptist Church on their way to downtown Nashville. All of the five-and-dime stores were on Fifth Avenue, and Lewis led his delegation to Woolworth's. Except for a horde of screaming whites, chanting "Niggers go home!" the demonstration was without incident. Nor was there any violence the following Thursday. Diane Nash, age twenty, a native of Chicago who had transferred from Howard University to Fisk, recalled how nervous the waitresses were at one of the stores. "They must have dropped $2,000 worth of dishes that day," she said.

Within a week, the physical attacks the students feared came when a gang of whites stormed into Woolworth's and began snatching the students from the stools, burning them with cigarettes and pounding them from head to toe. When the police arrived, they arrested eighty-one of the protesters, allowing all the white aggressors to go free.

Alarmed by what had happened, black residents came together and raised $50,000 to bail the students out of jail. They were represented in court by Z. Alexander Looby, a prominent black lawyer, and his partners. But the protesters fared no better in court than they had in the streets; they were given the option of paying a $50 fine or spending thirty days in the county workhouse. "We feel that if we pay these fines," charged Nash, saying and doing what Patricia Stephens Due would later do in Tallahassee, "we would be contributing to and supporting the injustice and immoral practices that have been performed in the arrest and conviction of the defendants."

Millions across the nation were privy to the tumult in Nashville. With each attempt to offset the movement, the city only incurred more embarrassment and outrage. Telegrams of support for the students came from such luminaries as Harry Belafonte, Ralph Bunche, and Eleanor Roosevelt. Given the stepped up pressure of the continuing sit-ins and the flurry of letters from people all over the country, the city's fathers began to waiver and buckle. So did the businesses. In the middle of March, the nation had its first sit-in victory when four blacks were served at the Greyhound bus terminal, where a demonstration had occurred two weeks before. The victory didn't come without a strong reaction—the students were beaten while they ate and two unexploded bombs were found at the terminal the next day.

Reporter David Halberstam observed that a biracial citizens' committee was formed with the hope of curbing the hostility between blacks and whites. "A temporary cease fire has been announced," Halberstam wrote, "but damage is already staggering."

From the standpoint of the black community, even more effective than the sit-ins was the well-organized boycott of downtown Nashville. Suddenly—and no one knew for certain the origins of the tactic—blacks stopped shopping in the stores where in a good year it was estimated they spent more than $60 million. Not having these black dollars in the till was a devastating blow to the financial well-being of white businessmen and women, who were already reeling from the loss of dollars from white flight to the suburbs.

"By the beginning of April, those stores stood virtually empty," Lewis wrote. "One leader of a local black Baptist church asked every person in the congregation who had not spent a penny downtown in the previous two weeks to stand. Everyone in the room rose."

Although the boycott had a dramatic impact, that didn't mean the sit-ins were halted; in fact, they increased, and even more so as Easter approached. Meanwhile at Shaw University in Raleigh, North Carolina, another significant development took

place. Ella Baker, a board member of the Southern Christian Leadership Conference, had convened a meeting of students to assess where the sit-in movement was headed and to what extent existing civil rights organizations might help. Lewis, busy with his studies, couldn't attend, but Nash and a couple other Fisk students did. When they returned from the meeting, they informed Lewis and their colleagues that a new organization had been founded—on April, 17, 1960, the Student Nonviolent Coordinating Committee was birthed.

But the feeling of a new beginning was broken just a day after the students returned from Raleigh when attorney Looby's house was firebombed. Half of his house was blown away, but he and his wife miraculously survived. It was clearly a cowardly act to scare the students, but it had an opposite effect. By noon of that day, two thousand students, faculty and towns-

Police inspect Z. Alexander Looby's bombed home

people locked arms and marched toward city hall with Nash and the Rev. C. T. Vivian leading the way. At the time it was the largest civil rights march in the nation's history. Lewis estimated the total crowd at five thousand.

At city hall, the protesters encountered Mayor Ben West, wearing his traditional bow-tie. When Nash asked him if he favored integrating the lunch counters, he said he did, though his qualification that the decision be left to the store owners and managers was muffled by the roar of the crowd.

The next morning's paper pounced, with headlines announcing: "Integrate Counters—Mayor." Now the store owners could began the process of integration without taking the blame since the mayor had decreed it.

Almost a month went by before city officials and the store owners agreed to a period of calm in which the contending forces would set aside their grievances and conduct some "carefully orchestrated" test servings in the downtown sector. Lewis wrote that on the afternoon of May 10, 1960, "six downtown Nashville stores we had marched on, sat in and been arrested at during the previous three months served food to black customers for the first time in the city's history."

While the protesters played down the fact that they had achieved a relative victory, it was a major breakthrough in the battle for civil rights and it would be celebrated from coast to coast. If the celebrations were tempered in Nashville and other hot spots in the South, it was because the activists on those fronts knew that they may have won a battle, but the war was far from over.

"We still had miles to go before Nashville could be called a desegregated city," Lewis would write. "Sit-ins, marches, arrests, and beatings would continue for the next four years as our student movement turned to hotels, movie theaters, and fast-food restaurants across the town. I would be part of many of those demonstrations, but there was something else waiting in my immediate future, something that would carry me far beyond Nashville and even deeper into the movement. That something else was a bus."

9

Riders in the Storm

A relative calm settled over Nashville, Tennessee, during the summer of 1960. The turmoil caused by the sit-ins of the preceding months had taken its toll on both the students and the store owners. But as soon as school opened in the fall, the sit-ins resumed. By the middle of October, the movement received a powerful boost when Dr. Martin Luther King entered the fray. King had gone to Atlanta to attend the first national meeting of the Student Nonviolent Coordinating Committee (SNCC), which by this time was rapidly becoming two bickering factions of students and representatives from Atlanta and Nashville. One group, the Nashville activists, insisted on keeping the sit-ins as the central focus; the organizers in Atlanta wanted to stress voter registration. The split within SNCC itself was almost as wide as the breach between SNCC and the Southern Christian Leadership Conference (SCLC), of which King was president. Although the two organizations fought the same war, their tactics and choice of battles left them frequently at odds.

So, King's appearance had a dual purpose: to close the gap between SNCC and SCLC and to help calm the internal rift in SNCC, though none of this was clearly stated at the time. Surely, King was aware of the criticism from the members of SNCC regarding his campaign for voter registration and his non-commitment to their sit-ins. Whatever might have been the final nudge, by October 19, 1960, he joined a contingent of students as they moved en masse on a local Atlanta department store.

"I took part in the lunch counter sit-ins at Rich's department store as a follower, not a leader," King wrote in his autobiography. "[The students] wanted me to be in it, and I felt a moral obligation to be in it with them."

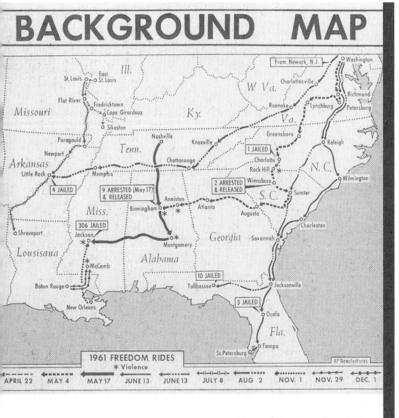

BACKGROUND MAP

1961 FREEDOM RIDES
★ Violence

APRIL 22   MAY 4   MAY 17   JUNE 13   JUNE 13   JULY 8   AUG 2   NOV. 1   NOV. 29   DEC. 1

Map of the Freedom Rides

He was arrested along with 280 students. Right away King made it clear that he was prepared to stay in the Fulton County Jail no matter how long the sentence. There would be no payment of bail. After nearly a week, officials realized that King and the students were serious about their resolve. To offset an increasingly aroused community, the merchants agreed to drop charges and King and the students were released immediately. However, because he had violated his probation, stemming from a bogus traffic arrest charge in May 1960, King was held and then transferred to the DeKalb County Jail to await trial.

At the end of the trial, King was stunned to be sentenced to six months hard labor. He was shackled in chains and taken to a prison two hundred and thirty miles from Atlanta. "And all over a traffic violation," King sighed.

When the news spread of King's arrest and imprisonment, a collective resentment swept the land. Some of King's associates, including his wife, Coretta Scott King, quickly appealed to Senator John Kennedy and Vice President Richard Nixon, who were in the midst of a bruising battle for the White House. Informed of the situation, Kennedy put a call in to Coretta and then dispatched his brother, Robert, who was managing his presidential campaign, to intercede. Robert phoned a judge, a bond was arranged, and King was released the next day. All of this happened two weeks before the presidential elections, and the Kennedy forces used the incident and their involvement to curry decisive votes from black Americans. They seized the moment, printing a couple million pamphlets emblazoned with the words "No Comment," Nixon's response when asked his feelings about the jailed King.

Kennedy defeated Nixon handily in the electoral college vote, but by less than one percent of the popular vote. The new president had garnered seventy percent of the black vote, which many concluded helped him edge out Nixon. The association with King had helped deliver Kennedy, but that didn't mean the minister would be invited to the inauguration to hear the new president's remarks on the "celebration of freedom."

Meanwhile, the sit-in movement had reached more than one hundred cities by November 1960, jumping like a raging wildfire from one county to the next. And in Nashville, John Lewis was back on the front line. Much to the chagrin of his family, he was arrested for the third time, well on his way to an eventual forty arrests before his crusading days were over. Despite the arrest, Lewis's spirits were lifted two weeks later when he learned that a decision had come from the Supreme Court extending the federal ban on segregation to all terminals for interstate travel. *Boynton v. Virginia* was the official name of the ruling, and it was a welcome early Christmas present for activists in the movement, as well as for the thousands of black patrons who utilized the interstate bus system throughout the South. Even so, the decision, like *Brown v. Board of Education*, was merely a decree; it had to be put into practice.

But before testing *Boynton v. Virginia*, Lewis, assisted most loyally by James Bevel and Bernard Lafayette, both fellow students at the American Baptist Theological seminary, began orchestrating demonstrations against the segregated movie theaters of Nashville.

The issue was finally brought to a head when they placed their bodies directly in front of the doors of the movie theater. By March, just about the time

EXCERPT FROM SUPREME COURT'S DECISION IN *BOYNTON V. VIRGINIA*, DECEMBER 5, 1960

The basic question presented in this case is whether an interstate bus passenger is denied a federal statutory or constitutional right when a restaurant in a bus terminal used by the carrier along its route discriminates in serving food to the passenger solely because of his color.

Petitioner, a Negro law student, bought a Trailways bus ticket from Washington, D.C., to Montgomery, Alabama. He boarded a bus at 8 pm which arrived at Richmond, Virginia, about 10:40 pm. When the bus pulled up at the Richmond "Trailways Bus Terminal" the bus driver announced a forty-minute stopover there. Petitioner got off the bus and went into the bus terminal to get something to eat. In the station he found a restaurant in which one part was used to serve white people and one to serve Negroes. Disregarding this division, petitioner sat down on a stool in the white section. A waitress asked him to move over to the other section where there were "facilities" to serve colored people. Petitioner told her he was an interstate bus passenger, refused to move and ordered a sandwich and tea. The waitress then brought the Assistant Manager, who "instructed" petitioner to "leave the white portion of the restaurant and advised him he could be served in the colored portion." Upon petitioner's refusal to leave an officer was called and petitioner was arrested and later tried, convicted and fined ten dollars in the Police Justice's Court of Richmond on a charge that he "unlawfully did remain on the premises of the Bus Terminal Restaurant of Richmond, Inc. after having been forbidden to do so" by the Assistant Manager....

Interstate passengers have to eat, and the very terms of the lease of the built-in restaurant space in this terminal constitute a recognition of the essential need of interstate passengers to be able to get food conveniently on their journey and an undertaking by the restaurant to fulfill that need. Such passengers in transit on a paid interstate Trailways journey had a right to expect that this essential transportation food service voluntarily provided for them under such circumstances would be rendered without discrimination prohibited by the Interstate Commerce Act. Under the circumstances of this case, therefore, petitioner had a federal right to remain in the white portion of the restaurant. He was there under "authority of law"—the Interstate Commerce Act—and it was error for the Supreme Court of Virginia to affirm his conviction.

Lewis was delivering his senior sermon at American Baptist Theological seminary, the city's theaters were at last opened to interracial seating. This hopeful sign of progress might have appeased some residents, but it only inspired Lewis to seek more barriers to defy and then scale.

By the spring of 1961, Lewis, along with Bernard Lafayette, who would later become one of Dr. King's most reliable lieutenants, had written a letter to Rev. Fred Shuttlesworth in Birmingham, Alabama, expressing an interest in desegregating that city's rigid Jim Crow policy, especially in the bus terminals. Shuttlesworth wrote back and told Lewis that while he appreciated his spunk, the proposal was much too dangerous. Furthermore, their arrival from Ten-

nessee would be viewed by local whites as an invasion of "outside agitators."

Within a few days of the rejection by Shuttlesworth, Lewis saw an ad in *The Student Voice*, SNCC's monthly newsletter, placed by the Congress of Racial Equality (CORE). The organization was looking for volunteers to test the recently passed *Boynton* decision by integrating interstate transportation facilities. The campaign was called "Freedom Ride 1961." The native of Alabama couldn't believe his eyes. "I immediately wrote for an application," Lewis recalled. "When it arrived, it contained detailed warnings about violence and arrests, which were nothing I hadn't faced already in Nashville. This would be more dangerous, no doubt. This was the

Freedom Riders from Tennessee wait to board a Greyhound in Birmingham, Alabama. Drivers refused to let the racially mixed group board

A busload of Freedom Riders encounter police and National Guard in Montgomery, Alabama

Deep South we were talking about, the belly of the segregated beast. But I wasn't frightened. On the contrary, I was elated. And eager."

A few days later, Lewis, brimming with anticipation, received a reply from CORE. Alone in his dorm room, he opened the letter apprehensively and slowly a smile spread across his face. He had been accepted. Inside the letter was a one-way bus ticket from Nashville to Washington, D.C. "No graduation present could be sweeter than this," he wrote. Rather than hearing the thrilling sounds of "Pomp and Circumstance" and marching down the aisle to receive his diploma, Lewis would begin a career of activism instead. His aisle would be on a bus humming down the highway into the heart of Dixie.

There was nothing new about taking on the segregated transportation system in the South. The first "Freedom Rides" occurred in 1947 and were organized by the Fellowship of Reconciliation (FOR). Sixteen men rode at risk to test the merits of the Supreme Court decision in the Irene Morgan case of 1946, which declared that segregated seating of interstate passengers was unconstitu-

tional. With this failed effort as a precedent, James Farmer, the head of CORE, decided he would launch a second attempt on May 4, 1961, from the nation's capital.

At first, Farmer was reluctant to make the trip, since he was saddled with coordinating other activities. He told the press that they planned to complete the journey to New Orleans by May 17, in time to celebrate the anniversary of *Brown v. Board of Education*. Ten days later, having encountered few hostile incidents beyond a mob attack in Rock Hill, South Carolina, the team of brave souls split into two groups for the ride from Atlanta to Birmingham. One racially-mixed group would travel in the first bus, a Greyhound, and the second group would make the journey in a Trailways bus. Their itinerary was westward on U.S. 78, with Anniston, Alabama, the only planned stop.

The lead group's worst fears greeted them when they arrived at the Anniston bus depot. More than two hundred angry white people surrounded the bus, some of them banging on the doors and windows with iron pipes and slashing the bus's tires. Only the presence of Alabama state investigators, who were traveling incognito with the protesters, kept the mob from pushing open the doors. Though the tires were ripped, the driver sped away with the mob in pursuit. When they stopped outside of town to repair the tires, someone hurled a firebomb through the bus's rear door. Passengers fled from the bus, escaping as it became a roaring inferno.

Jim Peck wrote in his autobiography, *Freedom Rider*, "All the passengers managed to escape before the bus burst into flames and was totally destroyed. Policemen, who had been standing by, belatedly came on the scene. A couple of them fired into the air. The mob dispersed and the injured were taken to a local hospital." But Peck, a middle class white man, a graduate of Harvard, and heir to a clothing company, was not on this bus. He was on the one traveling an hour behind—the one whose passengers faced now nearly certain physical danger.

A highly aroused mob awaited the arrival of the Trailways bus, the second vehicle, at the terminal in Anniston. The passengers, including Peck, who days earlier had taken over as group leader when Farmer had to leave to attend his father's funeral, were aware of what had happened to the bus ahead of them. That violence made them all the more apprehensive.

Gripped with fear, the passengers sat anxiously, waiting to see if the police would provide protection from the hundreds of angry whites milling around the bus. By now, both groups—the passengers and the mob—waited to see who would make the next move. When members of the mob stormed aboard the bus, they attacked two students—Herbert Harris, a Morris Brown sophomore, and Charles Person, a freshman at Morehouse. Somewhat surprised by the blows, the students hadn't recovered when several of the white men began dragging them from the bus.

"As they did, group leader Peck and Walter Bergman, a sixty-year-old retired professor from Michigan, jumped out of their seats at the back and ran forward, horrified, to protest," Taylor Branch

related in his Pulitzer Prize winning history, *Parting the Waters*. "They did not get very far. One of the white men turned from the two students and hit Peck with a blow that knocked him backward over two seatbacks. Another fist dropped Bergman to the floor. Suddenly, the fury of the mob turned on the two downed white Freedom Riders. Some lifted Peck from the seat to rain blows on his bloodied face, while others stomped on the chest of the prostrate Bergman." Now, in addition to a ravaged, practically destroyed bus, the media had a bloody face to put on the front page and display on the evening news. Ⓒ

The Trailways bus, with several toughs from the mob commanding the front seats to make sure the Freedom Riders remained in the rear, pulled out for Birmingham. The Riders thought they had endured the worst, but they were mistaken.

Although it was Mother's Day when the Freedom Riders, battered and bruised but unbowed, pulled into the Birmingham bus terminal, there was no portent of a peaceful holiday. They had no idea of the trap that had been set for them, that Birmingham Public Safety Commissioner Bull Connor had promised the Ku Klux Klan fifteen minutes to commit whatever mayhem they wanted on the passengers. And this they did without mercy. Moreover, Connor used the holiday as an excuse not to have police assigned at the terminal.

Already caked with blood, Peck, Bergman, and Person were once more targets for the mob. They and others were relentlessly pummeled. Dr. Bergman was beaten to his knees, and when he tried to crawl away he was kicked repeatedly in the ribs. He was attacked so savagely that he sustained permanent brain damage and had a stroke that would leave him paralyzed for the rest of his life. It took more than fifty stitches to close the wound to Peck's head. "One passenger," reported CBS correspondent Howard K. Smith, "was knocked down at my feet by twelve of the hoodlums, and his face was beaten and kicked until it was a bloody pulp."

DISC 1
TRACK 8

Meanwhile, the Greyhound bus survivors were being turned out of the hospital in Anniston because of a threatening white mob. The Rev. Fred Shuttlesworth devised a plan to rescue the Riders: he asked for volunteers to drive a caravan of cars to pick them up and transport them to Birmingham. Soon, there were eight cars, with shotguns and rifles protruding from the windows, on the way to get the freedom fighters in Anniston. After all the Freedom Riders were together at Shuttlesworth's home, Simeon Booker, a reporter for *Jet* magazine, was finally able to make contact with Attorney General Robert Kennedy. CD

All the Freedom Riders wanted from Kennedy was safe passage out of Birmingham and on to Montgomery. To complicate matters, a busload of students were on the way to Birmingham from Nashville. James Bevel, the nominal leader among the Nashville students, selected the ten Freedom Riders' "reinforcements." They were determined to make the trip. John Lewis was the only veteran civil rights activist in the group that included two whites. "When we got to the Birmingham city limits, the bus was stopped, and a member of the police department got on," Lewis remembered. "We told them we were Freedom Riders…and they took us into custody and took us to the Birmingham city jail."

Almost immediately Lewis and his companions went on a hunger strike. Several days of non-cooperation from the singing, starving Freedom Riders frustrated Connor and his minions. Connor and his men put seven of them into three cars in the dead of night and they took off for what the Riders thought was a

DISC 1
TRACK 8

George Lincoln Rockwell, center, and members of the American Nazi party refuel their hate bus on the way to Mobile, Alabama

ride back to Nashville. But they never made it that far. When Connor and his crew reached the border between Alabama and Tennessee, they put their passengers out, leaving them in the middle of Klan territory. The Riders' instincts guided them away from the white residences, across railroad tracks, to what they believed to be an area where blacks lived. They were right, and after some pleading they were able to convince an elderly couple to allow them to use the telephone and put them up for the night. The next morning one of their comrades drove a hundred miles to pick them up and they crammed into the car for a return trip to Birmingham.

It was not until May 20 that a bus and a driver were secured for the next leg of the journey. Jim Peck was in the hospital recuperating when a reporter asked him about his future plans and whether the Freedom Rides had been worth the cost. Without hesitation and demonstrating unflinching courage, Jim Peck remarked: "The going is getting rougher, but I'll be on that bus tomorrow headed for Montgomery."

"We finally got a Greyhound bus to take us from Birmingham to Montgomery," Lewis said. "There was no one on the bus but us, and during the one hundred miles from Birmingham to Montgomery, every fifteen miles a state patrol was stationed for our protection."

By the time they reached the Montgomery city limits, some two hours later, the police escort, including a plane, peeled away and the Riders were

Blood-splattered Freedom Riders John Lewis, left, and James Zwerg after being beaten by segregationists

A Freedom Rider bus burns after being firebombed near Anniston, Alabama

once again on their own. At first, when they arrived at the bus terminal, there were only a few people sitting around, along with several newsmen. An eerie silence pervaded the place, and Lewis felt something was not right. Suddenly, from out of nowhere, came hundreds of people, brandishing every conceivable weapon. Lewis ordered his team not to run, but stand together. "Git them niggers, git them niggers," the angry white mob yelled. Before they assailed the Riders, the mob attacked the press. Cameras were taken from the photographers by members of the onrushing crowd, and then used to beat them unmercifully. Next in line was one of the Riders, Jim Zwerg. "Nigger lover," the mob shouted. There was nothing his comrades could do but watch him disappear into the frenzied mob.

While the mob was beating Zwerg with his own suitcase, Lewis moved quickly and secured a cab that spirited the five black women riders from the scene. Because of the segregation laws, the taxi driver refused to take the two white women, Susan Wilbur and Sue Harmann. Zwerg was knocked unconscious. Lying in a writhing heap not far from him was

William Barbee, a classmate of Lewis's. A sea of people descended on him as he tried to protect himself from more punches and stomps. The beating he received was so severe that, like Dr. Bergman, he was left paralyzed for the rest of his life. Lewis, too, was knocked unconscious when someone wielding a Coca-Cola crate hit him on the head

"By the time I regained consciousness," Lewis said, "the scene was relatively under control. Floyd Mann, Alabama's state public safety director, had pushed his way into the mob, tried pulling some men off of William Barbee's body, then raised a pistol and fired in the air, warning the crowd away."

The mob was so inflamed that even John Seigenthaler, a white Justice Department official, was not spared its wrath. Some of the Freedom Riders sought shelter at a local church. Lewis and Barbee were taken to a nearby doctor's office to get patched up; it took several stitches to close the wound to Lewis's head. From there, Lewis was taken to the home of Rev. Solomon Seay, who like Shuttlesworth, was a stalwart among Montgomery's civil rights activists. Word about the altercation in the city spread fast, reaching

Diane Nash in Nashville, Dr. King in Chicago, and the Kennedys in the White House. "Dr. King and Rev. Abernathy were out of the city [Montgomery], but they returned and organized a mass rally," Lewis said later. "Several hundred people attended."

Just as the meeting was called to order, rocks began banging against the walls and windows of First Baptist Church. Then there was a report that a car had been set afire. Reverend Solomon Seay hurried to the pulpit and told the hundreds gathered there not to panic, that everything was going to be all right. His optimism was based on a phone call between Dr. King and Robert Kennedy that was taking place in the church's basement. But the minister's calming words were shattered when a brick smashed through the church's large stained glass window. Still, the people remained calm, even as they began ushering children downstairs to safety.

Within seconds, tear gas intended to disperse the white mob outside began seeping into the church, and people were covering their faces with handkerchiefs and coughing. Hysteria seemed imminent, particularly when a loud noise erupted from outside.

What they had heard, though, as many of them cowered under the pews and in the church's corners, was the sound of the Alabama National Guard moving in and taking positions outside the church. Kennedy's promise to do something had been fulfilled. However, the arrival of the soldiers to put down the incipient riot also provided a bulwark blocking the people inside from getting out. Not until early the next morning were the 1,500 people crammed in the church escorted out by the troops. No longer in imminent danger, the Freedom Riders began to discuss plans to move on to Mississippi, which, as they had been told, could be even more treacherous than Alabama. "We thought it was important to keep the Freedom Rides going," Lewis explained. "Some of the people wanted to call the rides off. We decided to travel through Alabama…our purpose was to arouse black people

all over the South that segregation was not over."

On May 24, despite Robert Kennedy's call for a "cooling off" period, twenty-seven Freedom Riders, including Lewis, Jim Lawson, and James Farmer, left Montgomery for Mississippi on two buses. To curb their anxiety and because they were now under the protection of the Mississippi National Guard, as they crossed the state line into Mississippi, the riders began singing:

> "I'm taking a ride on the Greyhound bus line.
> I'm riding the front seat to Jackson this time.
> Hallelujah, I'm a-traveling,
> Hallelujah, ain't it fine.
> Hallelujah, I'm a-traveling
> Down freedom's main line."

"Upon our arrival at the Jackson bus station," Lewis recounted, "we learned that the first busload of riders had already been arrested and taken to jail. Now would be our turn."

"First we were taken to the city jail and then transferred to the Hinds County Jail," Lewis continued. "From here we were sent on to Parchman Farm."

The dreaded Parchman Farm was about a hundred miles northwest of Jackson and was completely surrounded by a barbed wire fence. In effect, the penitentiary was nothing more than a modern slave plantation that was known to be the worst prison in the state, if not the country. "'We have some niggers here who will eat you up, if you continue singing those freedom songs,'" Lewis said of the greeting they received by the prison's superintendent, Fred Jones. "We were led into a cement building and forced to take off all our clothes…for more than two hours we stood there strip naked…this was an attempt to dehumanize us. Then they led us two by two, two blacks, two whites—segregation started as soon as we were inside the jail. They demanded we take a shower with an armed guard standing by. If you had a beard or a mustache, you had to shave it off…After taking a shower you were taken to your cell and given a Mississippi undershirt and a pair of shorts."

Behind bars at Parchman Farm, where they each had a metal frame bed and a mattress made by the inmates, the Freedom Riders were beyond the legal reach of the federal government. They were at the mercy of diabolically creative guards who found all sorts of ways to punish the riders without leaving any physical evidence. On one occasion, Lewis remembered, a fire hose was brought in and they were blasted with jets of water. Doused with cold water, the riders were then exposed to giant fans, freezing them in flooded cells. Then, when the weather was hot, they were not allowed any ventilation and the ceiling lights were never turned off, making it difficult to sleep.

To protest the mistreatment, the riders sang chorus after chorus of freedom songs. The guards threatened them, demanding they stop the singing. When the threats failed, they told them they were going to take their mattresses. And they did.

"So now we were left with the cold steel bunks and the thin shorts and singlets," Stokely Carmichael wrote in *Ready for Revolution*, his autobiography. "But it's midday in Mississippi. The cell block is warm enough, hot even. After lunch, the preachers decide to praise their God with prayer and hymn singing. I think they thought that since the jailers professed to be good Christians, they'd not interfere with their worship." Unappreciative of this ploy, the guards next promised to spray them with hoses, if they didn't stop their prayers. The hosing was followed by the hum of the giant fans, which sent, literally and figuratively, a most uncomfortable chilling effect from cell to cell.

Finally, on July 7, after little over three weeks at Parchman—and three days after America's Independence Day—the riders were free to go. "On the trip back to Jackson," Lewis recalled, "I thought about

Julia Aaron, left, and David Dennis sit on a Freedom Bus next to their escorts

the fact that we had just about literally been through hell, first in Anniston, then in Birmingham, then in Montgomery, and now here at Parchman. Freedom Riders were flooding the South now, scores of buses would pass through Georgia and Alabama and Mississippi and Louisiana, carrying riders who would continue the work we began in May.

"But the work was just beginning," Lewis continued. "I knew that now. As I boarded a train in Jackson to carry me to Nashville, I knew that my calling was not to go on to India. If there was anything I learned on that long, bloody bus trip of 1961, it was this—that we were in for a long, bloody fight here in the American South. And I intended to be in the middle of it."

10

The Student Nonviolent Coordinating Committee (SNCC)

The Student Nonviolent Coordinating Committee (SNCC) or "Snick," as it was popularly known, was an outgrowth of the sit-in movement. It was founded in 1960, at Shaw University in Raleigh, North Carolina. Ella Baker, a board member of the Southern Christian Leadership Conference (SCLC), was largely responsible for convening the meeting of young people that would lead to the founding of the direct-action organization. While it was the sit-in demonstrations that gave rise to SNCC, it was the voter registration drives in some of the most dangerous parts of the South that would give it lasting acclaim.

Baker was a veteran activist whose radical roots began while she attended Shaw University in the 1920s, long before any of her young charges were even born. Her ever-evolving political perspective had taken her through a number of organizations with often opposing ideologies before she found her niche at the Southern Christian Leadership Conference in the late fifties. By 1959, she had surrendered her executive position at SCLC to Rev. Dr. Wyatt Tee Walker with an eye toward unifying the various youth factions that were rapidly spreading throughout the South. Her intentions, said Barbara Ransby in her biography *Ella Baker and the Black Freedom Movement*, was "to help the students consolidate their initial victories and make linkages with one another." According to Ransby, she also wanted to coax them in a politically leftward direction.

Baker set the historic first meeting at Shaw University for April 16–18, 1960. It was rather propitious that the meeting, under the unwieldy rubric of the Southwide Student Leadership Conference on Non-violent Resistance to Segregation, was held on an Easter weekend. When the call went out to black college campuses and community organizations for such a gathering, she anticipated attracting a hundred or so participants. But she should have known that with

her sense of organization and thorough pre-planning that more than double that number would appear. The idea was not to impose her own ideas on the group, but to allow them to be independent of the elders, especially those she was familiar with at SCLC.

What became evident among those who assembled at Raleigh was the division of thought and purpose from a faction of students from Atlanta and the comparatively more seasoned civil rights activists from Nashville. "About a dozen of us drove down from Nashville," John Lewis wrote in his autobiography. "Over two hundred students were there, from Northern college campuses as well as from the South. But the two groups who had the most influence and respect were our Nashville contingent and the

Ella Baker

Atlanta chapter....Although a founding principle of SNCC had been a mistrust of concentrated leadership, a rivalry of sorts had grown between our two groups. It's human nature, I guess. We did our best to control it, but there was a bit of a power struggle from the beginning between Nashville and Atlanta."

At the helm of the Atlanta faction stood Julian Bond, the slender son of aristocratic lineage with schoolboy good looks, who aspired to be a poet when he wasn't totally immersed as an activist. Bond was a graduate of Morehouse College. His father, Horace Mann Bond, was a past president of several universities, so his pedigree was diametrically opposite of Lewis's sharecropping background. But Bond seemed more concerned about the presence of SCLC and Congress of Racial Equality (CORE) members than he was about the wedge being driven between the students. Bond, like many of the students, was fearful of being overwhelmed by the older organizations, of their voices being muffled by veteran preachers and leaders.

"We were suspicious of SCLC, very suspicious of CORE," Bond said years later. "We were trying to form a temporary Student Nonviolent Coordinating Committee with another conference planned for Atlanta in October to make it a permanent organization."

But the "temporary" tag was dropped long before the fall meeting in Atlanta, when the first official meeting was held in Atlanta in May. "That Atlanta meeting," noted future SNCC chairman Stokely Carmichael, "voted to remain independent as the Student Nonviolent Coordinating Committee, elected Marion Barry of Nashville to the chair, and affirmed its commitment to nonviolence."

That fall the Committee met again and elected Charles McDew chairman. "Thus in about nine months, thanks to Ms. Baker, an isolated and impulsive act of defiance, a tentative gesture coming out of a dormitory room bull session, had evolved into an organization, or at least the bare bones of one. To have called it a national organization then would have been a big stretch, but I and my new community at

John R. Lewis

Howard were members of a beginning student organization that would profoundly affect this nation," wrote Carmichael, by then a member of NAG (Nonviolent Action Group) at Howard University.

It was out of the Atlanta meeting that SNCC drafted its statement of purpose, bearing all the earmarks of Gandhian philosophy and *satyagraha*, the Hindi word for "holding onto truth," as well as Dr. King's notion of passive nonviolence. "What was remarkable about SNCC," remembered Mary King, one of the group's charter white members, "is that it came together and despite almost anti-ideological position, particularly in the early years, it developed a framework for social change that spark plugged and catalyzed a whole series of other movements."

Until September 1961, SNCC functioned primarily as a coordinating agency for the Southern protest groups which met every two months to discuss strategy and tactics. Among the actions it initiated or supported was the call to fill the jails at Rock Hill, South Carolina, in February 1961 and continuing the Freedom Rides after CORE abandoned them in the spring of 1961, following the attacks by white mobs. Its next big campaign was voter registration, and the urban centers and rural towns of Mississippi were the areas targeted.

In his memoir, SNCC member James Forman summarized why Mississippi was chosen as the place to launch the campaign: "The state which had led the Southern drive to take back from black people the vote and other civil rights won during Reconstruction, the state which had reduced the number of registered black voters from 190,000 in 1890 to 8,600 in 1892, through a combination of new laws, tricks, and murder. It was Mississippi, with a larger proportion of blacks than any other state and the lowest proportion—only 5 percent—of eligible blacks registered to vote." It was also a state that gladly welcomed and sanctioned the nefarious activities of the Ku Klux Klan and the White Citizens' Council.

In the spring of 1960, Bob Moses was visiting a relative in Hampton, Virginia, when he saw a sit-in demonstration on television. Within hours he was part of it, and it was his introduction to the movement. When the Harvard graduate with a master's degree in philosophy returned to his home in Harlem, he made up his mind to join the movement officially and headed for SCLC's offices in Atlanta; he had not been told about SNCC at that time. His objective had been facilitated by Bayard Rustin, who ran the SCLC office in Harlem and who wrote a letter endorsing Moses's intention to be a summer volunteer. Before long the bespectacled Moses had shifted his allegiance to SNCC and

SNCC STATEMENT OF PURPOSE

"We affirm the philosophical or religious ideal of nonviolence as the foundation of our purpose, the presupposition of our faith, and the manner of our action. Nonviolence as it grows from Judaic-Christian tradition seeks a social order of justice permeated by love. Integration of human endeavor represents the crucial first step toward such a society.

"Through nonviolence, courage displaces fear; love transforms hate. Acceptance dissipates prejudice; hope ends despair. Peace dominates war; faith reconciles doubt. Mutual regard cancels enmity. Justice for all overthrows injustice. The redemptive community supersedes systems of gross social immorality.

"Love is the central motif of nonviolence. Love is the force by which God binds man to Himself and man to man. Such love goes to the extreme; it remains loving and forgiving even in the midst of hostility. It matches the capacity of evil to inflict suffering with an even more enduring capacity to absorb evil, all the while persisting in love.

"By appealing to conscience and standing on the moral nature of human existence, nonviolence nurtures the atmosphere in which reconciliation and justice become actual possibilities."

was soon meeting with forty-nine-year-old Amzie Moore, a local NAACP chairman in Mississippi. They began plotting ways to increase the number of registered black voters in the state.

In the summer of 1961, Moses arrived in McComb, Mississippi, an urban center in the southwest section of the state. Rather than Cleveland, Mississippi, where he had hoped to be dispatched, Moore sent him to McComb. "Just 250 of the Black residents were registered to vote but that put it way ahead of the surrounding counties," Moses reported in his memoir *Radical Equations: Math, Literacy and Civil Rights*. He wasted little time in his appointed task and began holding voter registration workshops in a church that belonged to E.W. Steptoe, a small, wiry man who was the head of the Amite County NAACP, which he largely kept afloat out of his own pockets.

That August, Moses got his real introduction to the violence he would endure for more than four years as a SNCC organizer. He and several other local residents were on their way to register to vote when they were accosted by a group of white men. Their trek had been interrupted by a passing funeral that temporarily delayed them. "We paused at another corner for a moment," Moses recalled, "then suddenly some white men walked up, and without a word, one of them swung, hitting me in the temple with the handle of a knife. It was Billy Jack Caston, the sheriff's cousin and the son-in-law of then state representative E. H. Hurst. He swung again and again, hitting me in the head as I tried to shield myself by stooping with my head between my knees."

The beating left Moses in a semi-conscious state, and it might have been even worse had not his companions bravely intervened. Helped to his feet, Moses said he didn't recall what he said or did, but he was told that he commanded the men to move on to the registrar's office and register. With his white T-shirt now a bloody red, he was taken to a black doc-tor in the county, needing nine stitches to close the gash. The doctor then offered Moses his car to use in the project.

Because Moses had been relatively successful in getting blacks to register, his reputation put him in the limelight and in the cross hairs of white residents who didn't appreciate him "stirring things up" among the local blacks. Before the beating, he had already been to jail and encountered daily harassment from the sheriff and other white officials.

The assault on Moses was a prelude to what quickly evolved into an epidemic of beatings. John Hardy, a SNCC field secretary, was hammered across the head by white registrar when he persisted in bringing blacks to his office to register. After the battering, Hardy was arrested. And when rumors spread that a lynch mob was forming, the sheriff spirited Hardy off to a jail in Pike County for his own safety.

The violent upheaval culminated one evening in September 1961. Herbert Lee, a longtime friend and associate of Steptoe, pulled into a local cotton gin. Behind him, driving a pick-up truck, was E. H. Hurst, the state representative whose son-in-law, Billy Caston, had assaulted Moses. Hurst jumped from the truck brandishing a .38 pistol and pointed it at Lee. He was angry at his childhood friend for participating in the voter registration campaign. Lee refused to acknowledge Hurst until he put the gun down. At first it appeared that Hurst would put the gun away. Then the enraged white man turned and shot Lee just above the ear. "There were a dozen people at the gin but Lee's body, dying and then finally dead, lay on the ground for two hours with Blacks afraid to touch it and whites refusing to," Moses wrote. "Hurst claimed that Lee attacked him with a tire iron and was never charged with the murder."

At Lee's funeral, Medgar Evers, one of the speakers, did what he could to comfort a distraught widow, who blamed Moses and Chuck McDew for her husband's death. Lee's death all but brought the voter registration drive to a lamentable halt. Moses himself was for a moment immobilized, pondering if the project was worth getting people killed and risking his own life. But he had to continue, he concluded, if for no more reason than to honor Lee's sacrifice and death.

By the winter of 1961–62, Moses's resumption of organizing the branch had proven effective. He was able to recruit seventeen native Mississippians to the SNCC staff. With this accomplished, Amzie Moore decided it was time for Moses to open up the registration front deeper in the Delta. If Mississippi was a closed society, as some sociologists concluded, then the Delta was the bolted door. This region, in Indianola, the county seat of Sunflower County, was the home base of racist U.S. Senator James O. Eastland and the malevolent White Citizens' Council. Moses was so effective in developing his branch that he even impressed such local NAACP leaders such as Aaron Henry and Medgar Evers. He also renewed a working unity with the Council of Federated Organizations, the year-old body forged by SNCC and CORE that for the most part had been inactive.

The unity made them a more dangerous foe to their enemies, who began to resort to even deadlier forms of retaliation for the upsurge in voter mobilization. Terror struck on February 28, 1963, on a lonely stretch of highway between Greenville and Greenwood. Moses, Randolph Blackwell of the Voter Education Project, and the trio's driver, Jimmy Travis, were on their way to a staff meeting in Greenwood when they noticed a Buick following them. Since they were traveling on a country road, it was not easy to elude the pursuers.

"The car continued to follow until there were no other cars in sight, and then it pulled up alongside us as if to pass," Travis said. "At that time, I thought they were going to throw something at us or try to run us off the road. I felt something burn my ear and

I knew what they were doing. They had opened fire on us…it sounded like a machine gun. I yelled out that I had been shot, as I let go of the wheel. Moses grabbed hold of the wheel and brought the car to a stop on the shoulder of the highway. I was scared. I didn't know what was happening."

Travis had been shot once in the head and another bullet ripped through his shoulder. He was admitted to a hospital in Greenwood where his wound was cleaned but the bullet was still lodged in his head. Later, in Jackson, Mississippi, the bullet was finally removed and Travis miraculously survived.

The shooting of Travis marked the beginning of the third phase of the voter registration campaign in Greenwood. Samuel Block was at the center of the first phase in the summer of 1962. Block was the area's field secretary for SNCC and he was later joined by Willie Peacock from Charleston, Mississippi. For the next several months they engineered an intense and fearless voter registration campaign, defying the insults and threats of white residents. Block and Peacock's diligence amazed the town's black people, who believed the activists would only be there for a brief spell and then move on since they had nowhere to stay. As a result, they received little cooperation and were repeatedly arrested. But they remained, undaunted, going from door to door, from one lonely farm house to the next.

A breakthrough occurred in the winter of 1962–63. "A food and clothing drive was organized around the country and shipped into Greenwood and thousands of people turned out from the plantations and in town to stand in line, to wait in the cold to get a box of food to take home to a family of eight to ten children who were literally starving," Moses explained. "You have to understand that Leflore County didn't have a bad cotton crop that year. In the first place they had a bumper crop, turned in more cotton and made more money than they had the year before."

Because the cotton was long that year, the white farmers were able to use machines to pick it, thereby depriving the black laborers an opportunity to share in the bounty. This left many black families destitute. SNCC seized the opening and began a food drive at the courthouse, where the black residents could also register to vote.

Despite the taunts from the white farmers who drove by the long lines outside the courthouse, the blacks refused to leave and were glad to get relief from SNCC and other leaders, such as Dick Gregory, who chartered a plane and flew down from Chicago with food for the hungry residents of Greenwood.

It was this humanitarian act that prompted the whites in the county to resort to violence, including the burning of buildings and the shooting of Travis, to stop the increasingly successful registration drive. But rather than cower in fear, SNCC workers stepped up their campaign. "We gathered our people from around the various towns in the Delta where they were working, moved into Greenwood to see if we couldn't have a crash program to try to get as many Negroes as we could to go to register to vote," Moses said. "This seemed to be the only way to answer this kind of violence. Instead of letting up, we poured it on. Instead of backing out, we moved more people in. Instead of showing any kind of fear, we would show them for once the Negro was not going to turn around…and if anything was going to happen at all, it was going to be increased activity."

As many of the SNCC workers expected, their increased activity was met with increased violence. On March 4, the windows of Aaron Henry's drugstore in Clarksdale were smashed. Two days later, Samuel Block and Willie Peacock were sitting in a car in front of the SNCC office with two young ladies from Greenwood when a shotgun blast shattered the windows of the car. Fortunately, no one was hurt. On March 24, the SNCC office was set on fire. Witnesses reported that two white men were seen running from the building as smoke poured out through the broken windows. Inside, the place had been ransacked, with phones ripped from the walls and the furniture demolished. Two days later, the home of Dewey Greene was blasted with shotgun pellets.

With each new round of violence, the activists and the black residents assembled and protested. Soon, they were so outraged and emboldened that hundreds of them assembled and marched down to the Greenwood courthouse. "We never made it to the courthouse," Moses related. "The police met us with dogs near city hall. They threatened to turn the dogs loose if we didn't turn around. We left city hall and started toward the courthouse. We walked about two blocks and the police met us again. They were carrying guns, and some were on motorcycles and some were in cars. Finally Jim Forman and Lawrence Guyot were arrested, so we turned back and walked to the church."

When they refused to disburse, the police followed them and began arresting the leaders, including Moses and seven others. They were placed in the county jail on charges of disorderly conduct. They remained in jail for a week, refusing to pay the bail, as they had done before.

Jim Forman's diary tells the mood during the week in jail: "April 2, 1963: We have been in jail a week today. Our morale is good, although there are serious undertones of a desire to be free among some members of the group. Now and then, the jokes of one or two turn to the outside. John Doar and the Justice Department received some sharp but still humorous comments from some of the fellows. They actually believed the Justice Department would have them out by last Monday. When we received news that the temporary injunction had been denied, Lafayette Surney and Charles McLaurin, in particular, were somewhat disappointed. Some of us tried to explain that we must prepare ourselves psychologically to spend six months in this jail."

On April 4, they were finally released from jail. An apparent agreement had been arranged between the Justice Department and Greenwood officials. Within a week or so, Forman was on his way to Atlanta where a full meeting of the SNCC staff was scheduled for April 12–14. It would be another Easter weekend affair, as it had been with the founding of the organization three years earlier. More than 350 students and some sixty SNCC staff were present, including Bob Moses, who offered a thorough analysis of the turmoil in Greenwood. "We are trying to get workers and train them," he told the assembly, "and most of them are out of high school or college and they need to go back, or we think they need to go back. In the meantime, it's hard to get other people and train them in time so that they carry on the work. This is the big dilemma."

How to educate the general population while they struggled for the right the vote was indeed a dilemma, and there were a number of proposals offered, including one of mass education for all those involved in the movement. "SNCC has struggled merely to exist in the early days of political activity—now its survival was no longer in question," Forman wrote. "The 'Freedom Singers' led by Ber-

SNCC press conference

nice Johnson Reagon, were singing the tales of the student movement across the country and helping to raise necessary funds. Bill Maloney was working hard in the New York office, which had opened at last to raise funds and to create political support. But we had achieved more than a certain sense of organizational security. The meeting was permeated by an intense comradeship, born out of sacrifice and suffering and a commitment to the future, and out of knowledge that we were indeed challenging the political structure of the country, and out of a feeling that our basic strength rested in the energy, love, and warmth of the group. The band of sisters and brothers, in a circle of trust, felt complete at last."

And they would need all the love and trust they could muster in Georgia and Alabama as new fronts opened and others overlapped with the campaign in Mississippi.

11

Ain't Gonna Let Nobody Turn Me 'Round

Charles Sherrod was a slender twenty-two-year-old with glasses and a short Afro hairstyle in 1961 when he arrived in Albany, Georgia. He had the appearance of a scholarly choir boy, which in fact he had been as a child growing up in Petersburg, Virginia, and as a member of Mount Olivet Baptist Church. But behind his quiet demeanor was a committed activist, a field director who was on a mission for SNCC, which he had joined a few months before. His mission, as it had been when he participated in the sit-in movement in Richmond, Virginia, and Rock Hill, South Carolina, was to challenge the segregation laws.

Located in the southwest region of Georgia, Albany had 56,000 residents, just under half of them African Americans. The reason this tiny city had been targeted may have stemmed from an earlier incident that winter at Albany State, a black college, where women students had been attacked by white men who had sneaked in their dormitories and pelted them with eggs. Other than that, the city was comparatively peaceful with a number of prominent black entrepreneurs operating their own businesses. The community afforded opportunities to African Americans that did not exist in many other southern cities. Still, the specter of discrimination hovered at every turn: there was no evidence that *Brown v. Board of Education* had in any way altered the segregated school system; the library and public facilities had racial restrictions; and large numbers of blacks were not allowed to vote.

After the incident at Albany State, the NAACP's Youth Council staged a rally protesting the attacks. Several members of the student government were suspended when the school's administrators heard about the rally, which only incensed the more active students. They were very much aware of the civil rights demonstrations occurring in Mississippi, Alabama, and other places. Possibly spurred by these developments, Sherrod and his SNCC cohorts arrived in Albany with the hope of organizing the whole city, something they had never attempted before. On November 1, Sherrod and another SNCC member, Cordell Reagon, who was just eighteen years old, led a group of black students to Albany's Trailways bus terminal. They had decided to test a recent ruling by the Interstate Commerce Commission, which was merely following the Supreme Court's decision outlawing segregation in interstate travel facilities.

DISC 1
TRACK 9

King speaks at a church rally in Albany, Georgia

The SNCC leaders and the students occupied seats in the all-white section. When the police arrived and asked them to leave, they did so obediently. But they had achieved their purpose. They proved that the same old segregation practices of the past were still in place.

The members of SNCC had made a bold move and it disturbed the local branch of the NAACP, which had its own agenda for ending segregation. Dissension flared up between the two civil rights groups that would not subside until the Albany Movement, consisting of several groups, was forged by the middle of November. Dr. William Anderson, an osteopath and owner of a drug store, was elected to head the new formation and Slater King, member of a prestigious Albany family, was elected vice president.

Dr. Anderson, a native of Americus, Georgia, had come to Albany to begin his practice and had no intentions of getting involved in the civil rights movement. "That was not in my long-range plans," Anderson said. But when he went to Albany to practice, he was segregated twice. "First," he said, "because I was black and second, because I was a DO (doctor of osteopathy). Because there was a city hospital in Albany, there were no private hospitals. There were no black hospitals in Albany, although it was bigger than Americus. So, I was denied hospital privileges, as were the other two black doctors in Albany. No black doctor had ever had any hospital privileges in Albany." **CD**

The segregated treatment in the medical profession and then in society at large might have served to push him into the movement. Because he was a doctor, many believed he would be the best mediator to allay the heated differences.

"Despite the new partnership," Juan Williams observed in *Eyes on the Prize*, "the Albany NAACP planned to recapture the initiative from SNCC. They hoped to have one of their members arrested in the illegally segregated bus terminal. The NAACP could then bail that person out and go to court asking that the federal government's desegregation ruling be enforced."

But the innovative SNCC members were not about to be outflanked. Rather than accept bail, as the members of the NAACP had done after being arrested for sitting in the bus terminal, the SNCC members chose to remain in jail. It was a creative tactic that was emulated throughout the movement. Equally shrewd was the move by Albany Police Chief Laurie Pritchett, who realized that by arresting the students for a sit-in he would violate a federal law. Instead he said they had been arrested for failing to obey the police. "It had nothing to do with interstate commerce," Pritchett lied, just the first of his strategies to out-maneuver his civil rights adversaries.

The police chief's tactic may have been a good one in the short term, but by jailing the students he further aroused a city that was gradually shedding the restrictions of Jim Crow. Within a few days, the Albany Movement convened its first mass meeting. "The church was packed before eight o'clock," Sherrod recalled. "People were everywhere in the aisles, sitting and standing in the choir stands, hanging over the railing of the balcony upstairs, sitting in trees outside near windows…And when we rose to sing 'We Shall Overcome,' nobody knew what kept the top of the church on its four walls…I saw standing beside me a dentist of the city, a man of the streets singing and smiling with joyful tears in his eyes, and beside a mailman with whom I had become acquainted along with people from all walks of life. It was then that I felt, deep down within where it really counts a warm feeling, and all I could do was laugh out loud in the swelling of the singing."

Bernice Johnson, later to marry Cordell Reagon, was a student activist at Albany State who was moved by the singing. "When I opened my mouth and began to sing, there was a force and power within myself I had never heard before. Somehow this music…released a kind of power and required a level

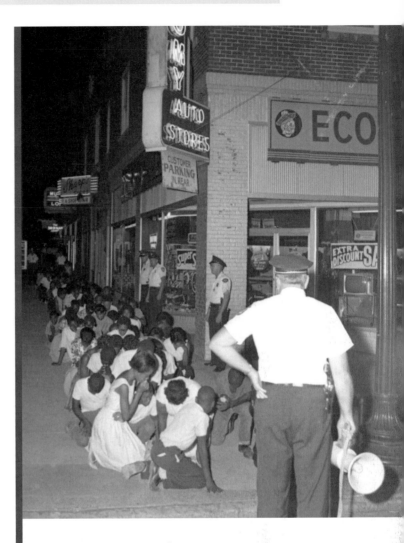

Pray-in demonstration in Albany

of concentrated energy I did not know I had." The experience was so affecting that she would later see the power of freedom songs in the civil rights movement, which subsequently influenced her to found the group Sweet Honey in the Rock.

Motivated by the meeting and the songs, the movement quickly intensified, gathering additional impetus when a small band of Freedom Riders, both white and black, arrived in town on an integrated train from Atlanta. Almost all of them were arrested for trespassing, disorderly conduct, and obstructing traffic before they could get out of the station. Once again local law enforcement officials had taken the

Pritchett arrests King for peacefully protesting at City Hall

bait. Now, the city was in the national spotlight. With each massive protest that followed, the jails in the city were soon filled to capacity. By the middle of December, more than five hundred demonstrators were behind bars. 🆑

The critical mass had been attained—the leaders of Albany Movement decided. They could now bring in the heavy guns. Dr. Anderson sent for Dr. Martin Luther King Jr., his former Morehouse College classmate. Addressing a rally, King told the activists in Albany, "They can put you in a dungeon and transform you to glory. If they try to kill you, develop a willingness to die....We will win with the power of our capacity to endure."

The next day Anderson prevailed on King to lead a march. King had planned to come only for a day

and then drive back to Atlanta with Rev. Abernathy and his chief of staff, Dr. Wyatt Tee Walker. That plan was scuttled upon hearing the entreaties of Dr. Anderson. King, Abernathy, and Anderson led more than 250 people as they marched on city hall. They were all arrested for parading without a permit, disturbing the peace, and obstructing the sidewalk. King refused to pay the fine, assuming he'd spend the Christmas holiday behind bars. He knew that he needed to stay locked up to bring light to the ongoing problems and breakdown in negotiations.

Dr. King had vowed to stay in jail until segregation no longer existed in Albany. Police Chief Pritchett wasn't about to wait the minister out, instead arranging a deal with the protesters whereby the city would desegregate the bus and train terminals and release

King and hundreds of others if the movement promised to end demonstrations. After two days in jail, King was set free on property bonds posted by local residents. He had nothing to do with the agreement between the police chief and the Albany Movement. But he felt it imperative that he not block the peaceful settlement. He was back in Atlanta when he learned they had been duped. For the SNCC activists, learning that none of the promises made by the city would be fulfilled proved a terrible setback, defusing the momentum they had obtained during the few months of protest demonstrations.

It didn't take long before the Albany Movement was back in action and more determined than ever to uproot the vestiges of discrimination. The new year, 1962, was hardly a week old when a teenager was arrested for using "vulgar language," when in fact what she had done was sit in the white section of a bus. When Sherrod took a seat in the white section of the lunchroom at the bus terminal, he was charged with loitering. Chief Pritchett was determined to end the protests and somehow remain within the law.

By summer, Dr. King was back in the city to stand trial for the charges brought against him in December. He was there in time to witness courtroom guards manhandle several SNCC members, including Bob Zellner, Tom and Casey Hayden, and Per Laursen, for aiding and abetting Sherrod when he refused to sit in the court's colored section. Meanwhile, King had his own moment to stand before a judge. King, Rev. Abernathy, and two others were ordered to pay $78 fines or face forty-five days in jail. King and Abernathy chose not to pay their fines and remained in the filthy basement jail.

Dr. King and Abernathy weren't in jail an hour before a mass rally was held that evening. Before the rally, protesters marched on Albany's city hall. More than two dozen people were arrested. Later that evening, there were violent clashes between brick-throwing black teens and the police outside the church where the rally was held.

After spending three days in jail, King and Abernathy were informed that Chief Pritchett wanted to see them. They were told that their fine had been paid and they were free to go. "I've been thrown out of lots of places in my day," Abernathy later quipped, "but never before have I have been thrown out of jail."

Back on the streets, Dr. King and Abernathy were once more caught in the throes of the protests, which by now had taken on an angrier mood. Besides the marches and rallies, there were increased incidents of rock throwing and violence, resulting in still more arrests. Near the end of July, King and others were arrested while they conducted a prayer pilgrimage to city hall. Once more, the jails in Albany were jammed to capacity. Chief Pritchett had to secure jail space outside the city to accommodate the hundreds arrested. Compounding the disturbances in the streets, there was mayhem in the jails. Slater King's pregnant wife, Marion, was knocked unconscious by a deputy sheriff during a visit to see her husband. King's brother, C. B., was severely beaten by a sheriff in a nearby county because he was "a nigger."

Although Albany was now in the national spotlight because of Dr. King's involvement, Washington, D.C. paid only scant attention. Finally, at a

Four African Americans are loaded into a paddy wagon after attempting to integrate Albany lunch counters

press conference in August, President Kennedy made a statement on the issue, saying, "I find it wholly inexplicable why the City Council of Albany will not sit down with the citizens of Albany, who may be Negroes, and attempt to secure them in a peaceful way, their rights. The United States government is involved in sitting down at Geneva with the Soviet Union. I can't understand why the government of Albany, City Council of Albany, cannot do the same for American citizens." These sentiments might have ameliorated the sentencing of King and his cohorts a week or so later; their sentences were suspended. King sent a telegram to the president to express gratitude for the directness of his statement on the Albany crisis, writing, "Rev. Abernathy and I earnestly hope you will continue to use the great moral influence of your office to help this critical situation."

There may have been some concessions from the court, but city officials, including Mayor Asa Kelley, were less than enthusiastic about the president's remarks. In fact, those words from Washington only made Albany's white leaders more obstinate. Where they were beginning to bend a little before, they now refused to negotiate with the movement. As views calcified, both sides of the struggle began to assess where they stood and what had been gained. They also weighed their losses. Clearly, the demonstrations had hurt the commercial activity of Albany, particularly the bus system. A boycott of the buses by black residents had all but relegated those vehicles to the garages. Even major retailers

Ralph Abernathy and Wyatt Tee Walker inspect a bombed church in Leesburg, Georgia, about 20 miles from Albany

with plans to enter Albany's market changed their minds because of the general instability of the city. "To thwart us," Dr. King recounted in his autobiography, "the opposition had closed parks and libraries, but in the process, they closed them for white people as well, thus they had made their modern city a little better than a rural village without recreational and cultural facilities."

King left Albany in a deep depression, feeling that other than a moral victory, very little had changed. All the rallies, protests, marches, arrests, and violence had done nothing to shake the determination of the segregationists. People whose lives had been drastically altered believed they had struggled in vain. From his perspective, the Albany Movement was a failure.

But hundreds of African Americans in Albany were of another opinion. King may have believed he failed, but that sense of futility did not necessarily pervade the residents of Albany who had marched and went to jail with him. Sherrod, who years later became a city commissioner in Albany, said, "Now I can't help how Dr. King might have felt, or...any of the rest of them in SCLC, NAACP, CORE, any of the groups, but as far as we were concerned, things moved on. We didn't skip one beat." Part of that beat included the success of black voter registration a few months after King's departure that led to African American businessman Thomas Chatmon securing enough votes in his election for a city commission seat to force a run-off election. And the following spring, the city commission removed all the segregation statutes from its books. But the most important victory went to the SNCC volunteers who worked diligently in and around Albany to topple the bulwarks of segregation. King had talked about the enduring power of suffering to bring about change, but it had proved to be insufficient in Albany. What was beneficial for the SNCC members was the lessons they learned—Albany was a training ground that gave them a deeper understanding of the movement, what tactics and strategies to use in future battles. They learned how to keep a movement of many people together for a long time. Their experiences would serve as a model for the battles in other cities in the South.

Another unplanned valuable lesson emerged— the role of freedom songs in the movement. The activists discovered the songs' uplifting power, even in the face of often flagging morale and spirit. In fact, the Albany Movement has often been characterized as the "singing movement." Bernice Johnson Reagon, later to become a leading musicologist and performer, put in context the inspiration music provided for marchers and mass meetings. "After the song," she said, "the differences among us would not be as great. Somehow, making a song required an expression of that which was common to us all....This music was like an instrument, like holding a tool in your hand."

After Albany, the freedom songs served as a vital part of the civil rights movement. They became a required element in the organizational plans of SNCC, and the songs, many of them old spirituals, were even more effective when the ingenuity of the activists provided different words, making them fit a particular time, place, and circumstance. The traditional "Oh, Freedom," was given new urgency when the words were changed:

> "No segregation, no segregation, no segregation over me
> And before I'll be a slave, I'll be buried in my grave
> And go home to my Lord and be free."

Like much of the civil rights movement, Albany was part victory, part defeat. Yes, the schools and lunch counters were for the most part still segregated, but now hundreds of blacks were registered to vote. More than anything, it was a testing ground, a place where movement activists could assay what they'd done, measure the advances and setbacks, and properly plot the next move—in Birmingham. Even Dr. King recovered from the morose feelings that stayed with him weeks after he left Albany.

King was satisfied that the movement had taken the high moral ground and he believed that the precedent had been set to wage long and difficult battles in the name of freedom.

"The people of Albany had straightened their backs, and, as Gandhi had said, no one can ride on the back of all unless it is bent. The atmosphere of despair and defeat was replaced by the surging sense of strength of people who had dared to defy tyrants, and had discovered that tyrants could be defeated."

Or, in the words of the famous freedom song:

> "Ain't gonna let nobody turn me 'round
> Turn me 'round, turn me 'round.
> Ain't gonna let nobody turn me 'round
> I'm gonna keep on walkin', keep on talkin',
> Marching up to freedom land."

12

Meredith in Mississippi

Political change appeared to have stalled in Albany. But in Africa, European colonialism was gradually being swept away by freedom fighters in their respective countries. Twenty-nine-year-old James Meredith was too busy trying to transfer from one college to another to notice these international developments. In a letter to Thurgood Marshall, then chief counsel to the NAACP, Meredith stated his intent to transfer from Jackson State College to the University of Mississippi at Oxford. "My academic qualifications, I believe, are adequate," Meredith wrote, hoping to allay Marshall's fears that he might not have the qualifications for such an undertaking. "While in the Air Force, I successfully completed courses at four different schools conducting night classes. As an example, I completed thirty-four semester hours of work with the University of Maryland's Overseas Program. Of the twelve courses completed I made three As and nine Bs.

"I am presently enrolled at Jackson State College, here in Jackson," Meredith continued. "I have completed one quarter of work and I am now enrolled in a second quarter at Jackson. For the work completed I received one A, three Bs and one C. Finally, I am making this move in what I consider the interest of and for the benefit of: (1) my country, (2) my race, (3) my family, and (4) myself. I am familiar with the probable difficulties involved in such a move as I am undertaking and I am fully prepared to pursue it all the way to a degree from the University of Mississippi."

Jackson State College and the University of Mississippi were just a four-hour drive apart on Highway 55, but a galaxy apart racially. Jackson State was one of several historically black colleges and universities in the state; the 114-year-old University of Mississippi was all-white, and

Mississippi Governor Ross Barnett was determined to keep it that way.

James Meredith was backed by a strong legal team in his fight to enroll in the University of Mississippi. He was supported by Marshall, Medgar Evers, Mississippi's state field secretary for the NAACP who had been rejected by the university's law school in 1954, and the NAACP's attorney, Constance Baker Motley. Other African Americans had applied to the university, but the NAACP felt that Meredith was the best candidate. According to William Doyle in his

An effigy of Meredith hangs from a University of Mississippi dormitory

book, *An American Insurrection: The Battle of Oxford, Mississippi, 1962,* Meredith had been planning to enroll at the university right after Kennedy's inauguration, forcing the president to live up to the promises he made during his campaign.

After being turned down twice in 1961, Meredith took his complaint to the district court. He charged that he had been denied admission because of his color. The district court ruled against him. But, on an appeal, this decision was reversed by the Fifth Judicial Circuit Court on September 3, 1962. By a 2 to 1 decision, the judges ruled that Meredith had indeed been denied admission solely because of his race and that Mississippi was maintaining a policy of educational segregation.

The showdown Meredith had anticipated with Governor Barnett arrived on September 20. Accompanied by two federal marshals and a department of justice attorney, Meredith, a nine-year Air Force veteran, marched onto the campus and up to the registrar's desk. Barnett, who had appointed himself the university's registrar, invoked the powers of his office and refused to allow Meredith to register. When told he was in contempt of court, Barnett angrily retorted, "Who are you to say that I am in contempt?"

For the next four days, negotiations continued between Governor Barnett and the White House, though these conversations were then unknown to the public. President Kennedy had agreed to such private discussions in order not to embarrass the governor, whose political popularity had experienced a recent decline. Barnett and his inner circle of advisors felt this issue was a perfect opportunity for him to regain his stature and a chance to strongly restate his opposition to integration. On Saturday, September 29, Barnett found his moment to boldly announce his stance. "I love Mississippi," Barnett boomed at halftime of a college football game between Mississippi and Kentucky. "I love her people…her customs!" The stadium rocked with the response of "Never, Never!" They cheered their governor, chanting, "Never shall our emblem go, from Colonel Reb to Old Black Joe!"

The rebel yell was probably still resounding across Ole' Miss's gridiron when Governor Barnett left the stadium to take a call from President Kennedy. "I understand Governor that you will do everything you can to maintain order," Kennedy began, and was quickly interrupted by Barnett who repeated those same words, and then went on to say, "we don't want any shooting down here."

"Governor, can you maintain this order?" Kennedy asked.

"I don't know," the governor responded. "That's what I'm worried about. I don't know whether I can or not."

Barnett explained to the President that there were quite a few armed men in and around campus and they presented a danger.

In response, the President declared, "The only thing is…I've got my responsibility to carry out and I just want to get with you in a way that is the most satisfactory and causing the least chance of damage of people in Mississippi." **CD**

Come Sunday, it was Barnett's turn to call the president. He wanted Kennedy to know that he was willing to go along with a plan that had been devised by Attorney General Robert Kennedy that would allow the governor to save face, yet still comply with the court order. Under arrangement, the army troops would escort Meredith to the campus and draw their guns, thereby "forcing" the state to admit him. Such a gambit would make it appear that Barnett had no choice but to accede in order to avert the possibility of violence and bloodshed. Kennedy rejected the scheme, fearing that it would later be revealed and embarrass him. As a counter move, the President threatened the governor, promising to disclose to the world that they had been conducting private discussions on the matter.

While Kennedy dangled this threat, he had already authorized federal troops to go to Oxford.

James Meredith is escorted to registration by federal marshals

They would be joined by Mississippi National Guard units, state troopers, and more than one hundred deputy marshals. That Sunday evening Meredith arrived on campus and was secretly hustled to Baxter Hall, not too far from the Lyceum, where troops and law enforcement officials were assembled. They had to stare down hundreds of students who were becoming rowdier by the moment, eager to vent their disgust on the men blocking the entrance to the building. If they had known Meredith had already been spirited past them, they probably would have pushed through the door, stampeding the men on guard.

Within an hour of Meredith's arrival, an incident occurred that triggered an upheaval.

DISC I
TRACK 10

Burned cars and rubble in the aftermath of the violence on campus

One of the white students, incensed by the presence of a black man driving a military vehicle, attacked the driver, spraying him in the face with a fire extinguisher. This incident was followed by a shower of cans, rocks, and bottles hurled at the state troopers. Seeking safety, the troopers fled the scene, as the students overturned cars and lit bonfires. "We were inside Old Miss' administration building," Rick Tuttle of the *Miami Herald* reported. "Outside, in the darkness, the mob howled. And the shotgun roared from beyond the screen of tear gas set down by white-helmeted marshals who hid behind parked autos."

For two hours, the Lyceum building was under siege, and the marshals had all but depleted their supply of tear gas, the only weapon at their disposal. When sixty Oxford National Guardsmen arrived there was a temporary lull, but soon they were pinned down by a sniper from a nearby building.

With each flash of rifle fire, shotgun burst, or blast from a Molotov cocktail the mayhem increased. Meanwhile, the governor and the President were broadcasting their pleas for the violence to cease. But it was to no avail—the riot had become an armed insurrection. At its peak, the disturbance was so hostile that very few photographs of the battle survived. "Photographers were being attacked and beaten, and literally wandering the streets begging for their lives with smashed cameras," wrote author William Doyle.

As the night wore on, the violence claimed its first fatalities. French reporter Paul Guihard and photographer Sammy Schulman had just arrived in Oxford, shortly after President Kennedy's call for calm. They had come all the way from Jackson, passing cars and trucks festooned with Barnett bumper stickers and Confederate flags, most of them headed north to the battleground. When they pulled into Oxford and parked their car, the turmoil was still raging. Students warned them to hide their cameras, lest they get smashed. Guihard, eager to enter the fray to get the story, left Schulman, suggesting they meet at the car in an hour.

"At that moment, the mob suddenly rushed toward them, away from the marshals," a team of reporters from *Look* magazine reported. "Guihard walked straight into the crowd. Some ten minutes later, he stood near a girls' dormitory, diagonally across the grove. An assassin stood close behind him and fired a .38 pistol. The bullet pierced Paul Guihard's back and entered his heart." Later, a little before midnight, Ray Gunter, a young Oxford jukebox repairman, was watching the exchange of gunfire and the burning cars when a bullet from a .38 struck him in the forehead, killing him before he reached the hospital.

Deciding it was pointless to appeal any longer to Governor Barnett, President Kennedy ordered Army Secretary Cyrus Vance to deploy some 20,000 troops immediately from their location in Tennessee. "No man, however prominent or powerful, and no mob, however unruly or boisterous, is entitled to defy a court of law," the president had announced on national television. Soon, the president was on the telephone with the governor once more, upset that the incident had gotten out of control and that his federal marshals were endangered. 🆑

Under orders from Deputy Attorney General Nicholas Katzenbach, Lt. Henry Gallagher's unit of 650 troops and 120 Jeeps and trucks were quickly dispatched from Memphis. But it would not be an easy trip. Ordinarily the drive would have taken only a couple of hours, but with Mississippi residents intentionally blocking or slowing the route, it became a six-hour trip. On the outskirts of town the convoy was further slowed when the mob hurled huge logs and railroad ties onto the highway. Finally, after several tension-filled minutes, the troops were able to disperse the mob.

An order was released for the local National Guard to enter the campus. Captain Murray Falkner was in charge of the Oxford unit. Because of the situation at the Lyceum, Katzenbach ordered Falkner to take his soldiers there to protect the marshals who were down to their last few canisters of tear gas. To get through the mob, the guardsmen revved up their vehicles and plowed straight ahead. "We had rifles and bayonets, but no bullets," said Falkner. Many of the Army troops were also ordered by the Kennedy administration to put away their bullets the night of the riot in an attempt to minimize the violence.

Falkner and his men arrived at the Lyceum Building just in time. "They had about ten minutes supply of tear gas left," Falkner said of the marshals when he arrived at the building. "If I hadn't moved my units

DISC 1
TRACK 10

Ross Barnett

to the campus when I did, the marshals would have been overrun and the rioters would have burned that part of campus." Somehow a man from the mob was able to secure a bulldozer, which he drove straight into the line of troops. The troops created a diversion and grabbed control of the bulldozer and the driver, whom they forcibly removed.

It was early in the morning before the troops were able to quell the riot. Sunrise revealed a campus overrun with debris, smoke was still swirling from the hulks of overturned cars, shattered glass from Molotov cocktails was strewn in the streets and sidewalks, the lawns were marked with tire tracks from Jeeps, and ambulances continued to cart away the wounded.

One hundred and sixty marshals were injured; twenty-eight of them shot. Two men had been shot and killed. Two hundred people had been arrested, fewer than a fourth of them students at the university.

The mob's resistance had been for naught. It was nearly eight o'clock when James Meredith, who maintained remarkable calm through the ordeal, walked across the battle-scarred campus to the registrar's office. "I was engaged in a war," he told a CNN reporter some years later. "I considered myself engaged in a war from day one. And my objective was to force the federal government—the Kennedy administration at that time—into a position where they would have to use the United States military force to enforce my rights as a citizen."

An hour later he was on his way to a course in Colonial American History, no doubt aware of his own place in history. That first day was not without its tension, however. There were catcalls as he was escorted to class by Chief U.S. Marshal James P. McShane and Justice Department attorney John Doar. When he entered the dining hall he was met

James Meredith receives his degree

Meredith lays across Highway 51 after being shot

with a barrage of boos from a circle of students, shout-ing all sorts of insults. But Meredith ignored them, refusing to react to their taunts. Soon, there were sev-eral students by his side, as they would be during the course of the year, willing to forsake their other friends in order to protect him from their more enraged classmates.

Among his visitors on campus was Medgar Evers, who had been a steady and reliable counselor throughout the clamor. Evers often came to give Meredith the moral support he needed, particularly when the stress threatened to break his usual reserve. He was there to remind Meredith that for thousands, if not millions of black Americans, he was a hero, and that his act of courage should not be overlooked in the fight against segregation.

Another man who spent some time with Mered-ith was his temporary roommate, Harrison Goldin, chosen to be Meredith's roommate for his first two weeks on campus. Goldin recounted those days: "The campus had a surreal quality: Before the week

was out, more than 25,000 troops would be commit-ted to the operation. I quickly settled into a routine with Meredith. Each morning as we dressed he would outline his schedule: say, breakfast in the cam-pus cafeteria, his first class, a visit to the campus bookstore, a stop at the library, a second class, lunch, etc. I would brief Katzenbach, and he would gather the commanders of the various security forces and plan that day's protection strategy.

"After dinner Meredith and I would sit in the dormitory room while he studied and I read the newspaper," Goldin remembered. "On Wednesday evening, my third day on the campus, Meredith looked up from his books and casually mentioned that the next morning he was planning to pick up tickets for the opening football game that Saturday.

"I was stunned: 'Oh, Meredith,' I said, addressing him as he preferred, 'you can't do that. The football stadium will be a disaster for you. Thousands of fans will be in a fever pitch; by halftime a lot of them will be drunk. You'll be the only black face in the whole arena. There's no way to protect you in an enclosed space like that.'

"Meredith dismissed me quietly and firmly: 'Look,' he said, 'I'm here because a U.S. District Court judge said I have the right to be here and do what every other student does on this campus. Saturday, they'll all be at the football game, and I will, too. The job of the government is to protect me.'"

When Goldin told Katzenbach of Meredith's intentions, Katzenbach called and tried to convince Meredith of the gravity of the situation and the uproar he would certainly cause once the students had a few beers in them. But Meredith insisted he was going, citing the same reason he had given Goldin about exercising his rights as a student and that it was the government's job to protect him.

Meredith would repeat the same reply to Attorney General Robert Kennedy, to Rev. Martin Luther King Jr., and to President Kennedy himself. The only thing to be done, the president determined, was to move the game to another part of the state, thus preserving the sanctity of the law.

During his entire year on campus, Meredith was under constant federal protection. U.S. marshals took up residence next to Baxter Hall where he stayed and accompanied him to all of his classes. Lt. Henry Gallagher was put in charge of a sixteen-man sharpshooter unit that could instantly be by Meredith's side if needed. Still, Meredith remained an inviting target for any sniper with a high-powered rifle who wanted to take his life.

Along with the daily insults he endured, Meredith received hundreds of letters threatening his life.

"I used to sit up in his dormitory room with him and read the letters," Gallagher recalled. "There were death threats to him and his family…letters saying they were going to kill his mother and his father." Meredith shrugged them off. Nothing would distract him from his studies.

In the summer of 1963, while most civil rights activists were preparing for the March on Washington, Meredith was once more in the spotlight when he graduated with a bachelor's degree in political science. Other than his own singular involvement in the fight against segregation, he did not participate in the marches and protests led by the Student Nonviolent Coordinating Committee (SNCC) or the Southern Christian Leadership Conference (SCLC). Three years later he would write his autobiography, and then, to prove that things had changed for the better in Mississippi and to draw publicity to voter registration efforts, he would embark on a solo March against Fear, walking from Memphis to Jackson, Mississippi. It was almost a fatal mistake. At Hernando, Mississippi, just thirty miles from his starting point, Meredith saw an armed man aim at him from some bushes alongside the road. He dove to the ground, but not fast enough. Three shotgun blasts ripped toward him, two finding their mark. FBI agents and reporters who were following the march witnessed the ambush. An ambulance took him to hospital where doctors later said his wounds were not life-threatening. His audacious walk had proven that white violence was still very much a part of Mississippi society.

"OXFORD TOWN," BY BOB DYLAN

Oxford Town, Oxford Town
Ev'rybody's got their heads bowed down
The sun don't shine above the ground
Ain't a-goin' down to Oxford Town

He went down to Oxford Town
Guns and clubs followed him down
All because his face was brown
Better get away from Oxford Town

Oxford Town around the bend
He come in to the door, he couldn't get in
All because of the color of his skin
What do you think about that, my frien'?

Me and my gal, my gal's son
We got met with a tear gas bomb
I don't even know why we come
Goin' back where we come from

Oxford Town in the afternoon
Ev'rybody singin' a sorrowful tune
Two men died 'neath the Mississippi moon
Somebody better investigate soon

Oxford Town, Oxford Town
Ev'rybody's got their heads bowed down
The sun don't shine above the ground
Ain't a-goin' down to Oxford Town.

Reverend Fred L. Shuttlesworth

DISC 1
TRACK 12

concluded that it was "worst big city in America." "Volunteer watchmen stand guard twenty-four hours a day over some Negro churches," *New York Times* reporter Harrison Salisbury observed in the spring of 1960. "Jewish synagogues have floodlights for the night and caretakers. Dynamite attempts have been made against the two principal Jewish temples in the last eighteen months. In eleven years there have been twenty-two reported bombings of Negro churches and homes. A number were never reported officially."

It was against this violent background that the board of the Southern Christian Leadership Conference decided in May 1962 to give serious attention to segregation in the steel town of Birmingham. They discussed the possibility of aligning their forces with those of Shuttlesworth's Alabama Christian Movement for Human Rights. Dr. Martin Luther King knew that Birmingham would be a real testing ground, and a civil rights victory here could signal a change in the entire course of the struggle

for freedom and justice. "Because we were convinced of the significance of the job to be done in Birmingham, we decided that the most thorough planning and prayerful preparation must go into the effort," King remembered.

A three-day retreat was called by King and the board members of the SCLC in January 1963 to outline the strategy for Project C. Even while they were shaping their attack, Alabama Governor George Wallace delivered his salvo during his inaugural speech in Montgomery, bellowing, "In the name of the greatest people that have ever trod this earth, I draw the line in the dust and toss the gauntlet before the feet of tyranny, and I say, segregation now, segregation tomorrow, segregation forever!" **CD**

The stubborn governor let them know how difficult the struggle was going to be, but Albany had taught them some vital lessons about how they might conduct the battle in Birmingham. Most critically, they would not spread their forces too thin. Moreover, rather than a general attack on segregation, the focus would be on the business sector of the city. Black consumer power in Birmingham was quite substantial, so a boycott of the stores would have a tremendous impact on business. After the retreat, King and the board met with Shuttlesworth and his organization at the Gaston Motel. The Gaston would be the temporary headquarters of the movement, and later in May, on the eve of Mother's Day, it would be ripped apart by a bomb.

If the campaign in Birmingham was to be successful, it would require funds to be keep it going, to pay the bails, and no one was better at raising money than Dr. King. Since Easter was a key time of the year for merchants, King and his colleagues decided to launch the protests in early April. One thing they had to consider was the coming mayoral election in March. To avoid their demonstrations being used as a political football, the group agreed to begin the campaign two weeks after the elections. However, there was no decisive winner in the initial balloting, so a runoff was scheduled for the first week in April.

King and other leaders feared that Connor would use the protestors' activities to his advantage with white voters. As the staunchest and seemingly loudest segregationist, Connor could surge ahead. "We might actually have had the effect of helping Connor win," King related in his autobiography, "Reluctantly, we decided to postpone the demonstrations until the day after the runoff."

Postponing the demonstrations left hundreds of volunteers wondering what to do next. They were disappointed that all their plans had gone awry, but King felt that, given the circumstances, a better opportunity would soon present itself. Meanwhile, he resumed his speaking engagements around the country, accepting an invitation from Harry Belafonte in New York City to meet with a large contingent of lib-

erals with their checkbooks open. King and Shuttlesworth, who had accompanied him to New York to help make their plea for funds, returned to Birmingham on April 2, the same evening of the election. They quickly alerted volunteers that the demonstrations were on again—set for the following day.

King and his supporters arose with the sun to discover that Boutwell had defeated Connor. There was little to cheer, Shuttlesworth lamented, because Boutwell was nothing more than "a dignified Connor." This meant that Connor, Chief of Public Safety, would resume his seat as one the city commissioners, a position he and the other commissioners had promised not to relinquish until 1965, almost three years later. Despite the elections, the city controversially sat under two forms of government—sitting commissioners and an elected city council—which might have some impact on the impending demonstrations.

Above: Abernathy and King are confronted by policemen for leading a demonstration in the Birmingham Business District

Right: Eugene "Bull" Connor

Given the situation, the demonstrators limited their initial activity to sit-ins. The plan was to have a modest beginning and then gradually step up the campaign. A number of weekly meetings were planned in order to provide cohesion and momentum. King and Shuttlesworth were among the speakers at each of the forums. **CD**

DISC 1
TRACK 11

One thing King and the movement learned from Albany was the important role of music, particularly the freedom songs. These songs—"We Shall Overcome," "Oh, Freedom," and "Come By Me, Lord, Come By Me" among them—were vitally inspirational and never failed to lift spirits. The music, King mused, helped them to "dip down into wells of a deeply pessimistic situation and danger-fraught circumstances and to bring forth a marvelous, sparkling fluid of optimism." So, there was no need for weapons, no knives, no guns, not even a toothpick,

he told the volunteers. The conviction that they were right would be the only weapon they would need against Bull Connor's vicious dogs.

After lunch counter sit-ins led to multiple arrests, King felt it was time to move to the next stage of nonviolent protest. They had tried to get permits for the protest but Bull Connor told them the only permit they were going to get was one to go to jail. On April 6, thirty protesters, including Rev. Shuttlesworth, marched on Birmingham city hall. All of them were arrested. Connor turned loose his dogs on Palm Sunday, and their sharp teeth ripped into the legs of the protesters led by King's brother, A. D. In addition to the dogs and nightsticks, Connor secured a court injunction forbidding any further picketing. A number of civil rights leaders listed on the order were forbidden to demonstrate in Birmingham, including King. Faced with the dilemma of diminished funds to

A patrolman and a police dog lunge after a demonstrator

Policemen lead school children to jail for protesting against discrimination

bail volunteers from jail and the need to have him free to orchestrate the campaign, King decided that it was time for him to go to jail. "Not knowing how it was going to work out," recalled Andrew Young, "he walked out of the room and went down to the church and led a demonstration and went to jail. That was, I think, the beginning of his true leadership."

It was Good Friday and Dr. King was on his way to jail, along with Rev. Abernathy and fifty others. King was in solitary confinement for a full day, worrying about the status of everything about the movement, from its finances to its mood.

The morale of the black community was surprisingly upbeat as many of them gathered on the steps of the Sixteenth Street Baptist Church and sang the songs that carried them through the struggle. There were a number of encounters between demonstrators and the police, but they never boiled over into melees. Meanwhile, the local white clergy began their offensive, hoping to nullify King's incarceration. They took a full-page ad in one of the city's top papers

denouncing King and calling him a "troublemaker."

In response, King began by writing in the margins of the paper in which the ad appeared and continued it on scraps of paper to draft what became his famous "Letter from a Birmingham Jail." Most of the 6,800-word letter was addressed to the ministers who felt that his act was "unwise and untimely." And they criticized his tactic of direct action. Addressing his accusers, King explained that actions like sit-ins and marches were indeed their own form of negotiation. "Nonviolent direct action seeks to create such a crisis and foster such a tension that a community which has constantly refused to negotiate is forced to confront the issue," he wrote. "It seeks to dramatize the issue that it can no longer be ignored."

Nor could King's incarceration be ignored. He had written the letter on April 16, while the demonstrations persisted, though not with the intensity of previous days. Four days later he and Abernathy accepted the bail and they proceeded straight to the Room 30 at the Gaston Motel to map out the next

Teenagers wait in custody as wards of the court after participating in civil rights demonstrations

phase of Project C. While in jail, a number of letters from students praying for his safety had arrived. Somehow, he thought, they had to find a way to involve the students in the campaign. He was aware of the criticism that would come if young people were brought into the fray, but the movement needed something dramatically fresh. Plus, he told his board members, it would let the children know they had a stake in the fight to end segregation.

While King was in court where he was found guilty of civil contempt and then freed pending an appeal, his staff—James Bevel, Andy Young, Dorothy Cotton, and Bernard Lee—was busy talking to young adults all over the city, conveying to them the purpose of the movement and what role they could play. By May 2, the staff had recruited hundreds of young people who were ready to launch their own demonstration in front of the jail. Soon the jails were overflowing with youngsters and the national media were there to witness each confrontation and arrest. Near city hall a skirmish broke out between a group of protesters and

the police. Twenty-three people were arrested, including A. D. King, Dr. King's younger brother.

On May 3, Connor's patience ended. There would be no more meeting nonviolence with nonviolence—the police waded into the throng of protesters and savagely attacked, beating them with batons and allowing their snarling dogs to rip whatever part of a protester they could grab. Those were the visual images that were transmitted all over the world. Birmingham was living up to its reputation as the "worst city in America for race relations."

The clamor finally subsided, but the next few days had continued turmoil. By May 6 back at the Gaston Motel there were moments when the protesters believed they had the upper hand because there were no signs of dogs and the police had retreated to some extent. The celebration was short lived when it was reported that the one thousand students arrested were without proper shelter and food. Led by James Forman and Dorothy Cotton, dozens of protesters gathered at the jail and began tossing candy bars over the wire fence to the inmates. Then the rains came and still there was no protection for the arrested students. That evening it would get even worse when the chilly night winds wailed across the compound. Now the protesters returned with more food and blankets for the shivering students.

Forman and the others retired to the hotel to plan the next day's demonstrations. Rather than starting them at 1 pm as they had done on previous days, the leaders rounded up the students for earlier rallies outside Sixteenth Street Baptist Church. When Connor was informed of the move, he was furious.

But there was little he could do about the various violations because there was no more room in the jails. This situation emboldened the protesters and more than a thousand of them rushed downtown, where they had failed to get in earlier demonstrations. They were joined by hundreds of others, all of

them marching down the streets singing "We Shall Overcome."

But May 7 would be scarred by a massive assault on the protesters by the police and the firemen. "Four fire engines arrived at the intersections and set themselves up for 'business,'" reported Len Holt of the *National Guardian*, a radical weekly newspaper out of New York City. "Each disgorged its high-pressure hoses and nozzle-mounts were set up in the street. I was to learn the reason for the mounts later, when I watched the powerful water stripping bark off of trees and tearing bricks from the walls as the firemen knocked Negroes down.

"The hoses were directed at everyone with a black skin, demonstrators, and non-demonstrators," Holt reported. "A stream of water slammed the Rev. Fred Shuttlesworth against the church wall, causing internal injuries. Mrs. Colia LaFayette, a twenty-five-year-

Firefighters turn their hoses on demonstrators

Deputy attorney general Nicholas Katzenbach, right, listens as Governor George C. Wallace speaks against integration of the University of Alabama at Tuscaloosa

old SNCC field secretary from Selma, Alabama, was knocked down and two hoses were brought to bear on her to wash her along the sidewalk. A youth ran toward the firemen screaming oaths to direct their attention from the sprawling woman."

All while the streets were being soaked and black people flung hither and thither by propulsion of water, Burke Marshall from the U.S. attorney general's office was trying to call a truce and reach a settlement between the warring factions. It seemed the discussions were fruitless until on that Tuesday evening one hundred or more white Birmingham businessmen felt enough was enough. This was, King noted, the beginning of the end.

On Wednesday, President Kennedy devoted the opening of his press conference to Birmingham, expressing his gratitude that the opposing sides had agreed to a settlement. "Even while the President spoke," King observed, "the truce was briefly threatened when Ralph and I were suddenly clapped into jail on an old charge. Some of my associates, feeling

that we had again been betrayed, put on their walking shoes and prepared to march. They were restrained, however; we were swiftly bailed out, and negotiations were resumed."

A real "good" Friday arrived on May 10. An accord was announced between the protesters and the business community, much to Connor's chagrin. To counter the agreement, he went on radio and denounced the "weak-kneed" businessmen who had capitulated to the "rabble-rousers." He then called for a boycott of all the stores that had agreed to the integration plan, which included:

1) The desegregation of lunch counters, rest rooms, fitting rooms, and drinking fountains, in planned stages within ninety days after signing.

2) The upgrading and hiring of Negroes on a nondiscriminatory basis throughout the industrial community of Birmingham, to include hiring of Negroes as clerks and salesmen within sixty days after signing the agreement—and the immediate appointment of a committee of business, industrial,

and professional leaders to implement an area-wide program for the acceleration of upgrading and employment of Negroes in job categories previously denied them.

3) Official cooperation with the movement's legal representatives in working out the release of all jailed persons on bond or on their personal recognizance.

4) Through the Senior Citizens' Committee or Chamber of Commerce, communications between Negro and white to be publicly established within two weeks after signing, in order to prevent the necessity of further demonstrations and protests.

An immediate and violent response to the agreement came the next night. Following a Ku Klux Klan rally on the outskirts of town, the home of A. D. King was bombed. Then another bomb was planted just outside the door where King and his board members usually met. Thankfully he was not in town at that time. Incensed by the craven audacity, blacks took to the streets again, this time abandoning King's nonviolent tactics. Stones were hurled at police cars. Now the Klan or whoever planted the bombs had what they wanted—a renewed battle between the black community and the law enforcement officers and their allies in the white mob. "The

TELEGRAM FROM GOVERNOR GEORGE WALLACE OF ALABAMA TO PRESIDENT KENNEDY, MAY 13, 1963

The statute you cite as authority for sending troops to the city of Birmingham even though invoked previously by you is in direct conflict with Art. 4, Section 4 of the Constitution of the United States which states that the U.S. shall guarantee to every state of the Union a republican form of government and which also provides that the U.S. can use its National Military forces to quell domestic violence only when requested to do so by the Legislature of that State or the Governor if the Legislature cannot be convened. Neither the Legislature or I, as Governor, has requested you to send troops into the state to quell domestic violence....

Each of the lawfully constituted officials of the City of Birmingham, Jefferson County, and State of Alabama has publicly denied having any knowledge of any so-called agreement and has equivocally denied the authority of any group of white citizens to negotiate with the lawless mobsters who had been leading the Negroes of Birmingham in weeks of violence and law breaking until this violence was put down by local and state law enforcement officers.

There is no precedent for the use of federal National Military troops to enforce an alleged agreement by unauthorized, anonymous individuals working in the secrecy without authority of any duly constituted officials.

In my judgment your duty is to guarantee the right of this State and the City of Birmingham to handle their own domestic affairs, and any intervention into the affairs of this State or the City of Birmingham, whether by the use of National Military troops or otherwise, is in direct violation of your constitutional obligation.

slaughter in Birmingham," author James Baldwin observed, "was not merely the action of a mob. That blood is on the hands of the state of Alabama, which sent those mobs into the streets to execute the will of the state."

By May 22, King was back in town; he was joined by three thousand federal troops, dispatched by the president to halt any further eruptions. Adding to the problems, the Birmingham board of education had earlier decided to either suspend or expel all the students involved in the protests. But the day King returned, Judge Elbert Tuttle of the Fifth Circuit Court of Appeals reversed a lower court decision that had supported the board, and the students would be reinstated. Once more it was time to jump for joy in the black community, and they would jump even higher the next day when they learned that the Alabama Supreme Court had ruled that the recently elected city council was the city's legal government, thus ousting Bull Connor and his fellow commissioners, permanently.

Much of the remainder of the summer of 1963 in Birmingham was spent adjusting to the realization that something had been accomplished in toppling the walls of segregation. Even so, there was much to

be done before the city would become, as Dr. King said, "a model in Southern race relations." King, though, could not tarry too long here. He had a date with destiny in the nation's capital.

Connor may have been officially pushed aside, but he was soon working with Governor George Wallace, who by June 11 was standing, his feet firmly planted, at the entrance of the University of Alabama blocking James Hood and Vivian Malone, two black students, from breaking the school's color barrier. But the U.S. Justice Department was equally adamant about getting the students registered. Deputy Attorney General Nicholas Katzenbach, who had such a powerful presence during the riot the year before at the University of Mississippi in Oxford, informed Wallace that he was in violation of federal court order, demanding he step aside. Later, when the head of the state's national guard made the same request, Wallace begrudgingly left the campus, and Hood and Malone became the first black students at the University of Alabama. The breakthrough was a prelude to President Kennedy's new civil rights bill which he sent to Congress on June 19, just one week after an activist named Medgar Evers had been assassinated in Mississippi. **CD**

DISC 1
TRACK 12

14

Medgar Evers

By the summer of 1963, the civil rights movement had become a daily item in the media. Millions in America and around the world were glued to their televisions, many of them cringing, as snarling dogs ripped at the legs of children and as water shot from hoses knocked protesters off their feet in Birmingham. The movement had clearly escalated, and more and more young people were traveling from all over the country to participate in the campaign against segregation. From the sit-ins to the Freedom Rides to the boycotts to massive demonstrations, the civil rights activists—in Alabama, Georgia, Mississippi, and even in the North—reflected the songs that inspired them: nothing was going to turn them around.

A crop of remarkable leaders stood in front of the bands of courageous marchers against racism and discrimination. Among them was Medgar Evers, who since 1952 had been an active member of the National Association for the Advancement of Colored People (NAACP). In 1954, when *Brown v. Board of Education* had become the burning issue in the struggle for civil rights, Evers was promoted to field secretary in charge of the Mississippi NAACP.

Evers was born in Decatur, Mississippi, in 1925 to a working class family. His father, a farmer, also worked at a sawmill; his mother, of mixed heritage, served as a domestic, doing laundry and ironing for white families. As a child, Evers had few educational opportunities. Attending an elementary school required a round-trip of nearly twenty-five miles. After spending one year in the segregated Army during World War II, he returned home and almost immediately tried to assert his democratic rights. He and his brother, Charles, who would also

become a distinguished civil rights leader, caused quite a disturbance in Decatur in 1946 when they tried to vote. The death threats they received were the first of many.

But Evers was not about to allow the threats, no matter the source, to keep him from doing what he thought was right. If Mississippi was wrong, he was determined to make it right, and not for a moment did he entertain the notion of settling elsewhere. "It may sound funny, but I love the South," he wrote in his essay, "Why I Live in Mississippi."

"I don't choose to live anywhere else. There's land here, where a man can raise cattle, and I'm going to do it some day. There are lakes where a man can sink a hook and fight the bass. There is room here for my children to play and grow, and become good citizens—if the white man will let them."

One thing the white man was not going to let

black people do was get a decent education. Evers set out to change this. He attended Alcorn A&M College in Lorman, Mississippi, graduating in 1952, a year after marrying Myrlie Beasley. In September 1954, a few days after the birth of their second child, Evers learned his application to enter the law school at the University of Mississippi had been rejected. Ole Miss, he was informed, had turned him down on the basis of some vague technicalities.

"It really started when Medgar wanted to go to Ole Miss," his brother, Charles, recalled. "I was his financier, more or less, and people never could figure where in the world he was getting the money from. And that did cost a lot of money, just to even get an application because you had to have, I think, five alumni to sign saying it was all right with them; this was back before [James] Meredith even thought about going to Ole Miss. And it cost a lot of money to get around all this [that] Medgar was doing. I was advocating voter registration and advocating rights for blacks."

In effect, Evers' attempt to enroll at Ole Miss constituted one of the state's first tests of the recent mandate from the Supreme Court that it was no longer legal to operate segregated schools. One door closed and another one opened for Evers as he gladly accepted the leadership position with the NAACP. He was officially charged with the responsibility of registering more blacks to vote, fighting the white store owners who persisted in discriminating against black patrons, and ending the barriers that denied blacks in Mississippi equality in education. It wasn't long before he was being heralded as the next prominent force in the civil rights movement. This was not good news to members of the Ku Klux Klan and the White Citizens' Council.

As the new head of the state's NAACP, Evers rejuvenated the crusade for justice, which was by now evident in most of the major cities in the South. He was among the first members of the newly formed Southern Christian Leadership Conference (SCLC), a coalition of ministers who helped organize protests in various states. No state needed the organization as badly as Mississippi. Police brutality, among other things, was rampant in the late fifties and early sixties when Evers established a youth chapter of the NAACP in McComb, a small city in the southwestern part of the state.

Evers also made frequent visits to Greenwood and he was proud of what the Student Nonviolent Coordinating Committee (SNCC) members had done there to intensify the voter registration campaign, which the NAACP had been trying to do for years. "When Medgar Evers came up from Jackson to speak," Bob Moses recalled, "he had gotten fired up by what he saw. I remember, Greenwood made him feel he needed to go back to Jackson and really start working there." If the residents of Greenwood were aroused and demonstrating for their rights, Evers

concluded, then it was time for the people in Jackson to increase their mobilization.

All the enthusiasm Evers had garnered from his leadership around the state was dampened on September 25, 1961, when he was told that Herbert Lee, a founding member of the Amite County NAACP, had been shot and killed by E. H. Hurst, a white state legislator. This wasn't the typical case of white violence and black victim. "They had grown up across the road from each other," said Michael Sayer, a white New Yorker who was on the SNCC staff in the early 1960s. "They were friends. They broke bread together…their children played together." But when Lee became active in the civil rights movement, things changed between the old friends. "When Herbert Lee got involved in the voter registration in 1961, he stepped across this cultural divide. And E. H. Hurst invited Herbert Lee to see him down at the cotton gin, and he assassinated Herbert Lee."

Hurst claimed he shot Lee in self-defense; he was never charged for the crime. Angered by the murder, Evers nonetheless appealed for peace during his remarks at Lee's funeral. Despite his praise of Lee's dedication to the movement, he was assailed by the dead man's widow, who blamed Evers and other activists for her husband's murder. It would take months before Evers got over this moment of anguish. He knew the only way to avenge Lee's murder was to work even harder to prevent such a tragedy from happening again. 🄲

In addition to his duties at the NAACP, Evers also spent time counseling James Meredith, who was summoning advice and support in his attempt to register as a student at Ole Miss. Having gone through this routine several years before, he was prepared to assist Meredith, particularly as it pertained to developing the legal briefs necessary to contend in the state and district courts. After the turmoil subsided and Meredith registered as the first black student at the college, Evers continued to offer moral support

Disc 1
Track 13

through weekly visits, assuring Meredith that there were thousands in Mississippi wishing him luck and praying for his safety.

With Meredith protected around-the-clock by federal marshals from the U.S. Attorney General's office, Evers felt he could focus his attention on other pressing matters. Of increasing urgency was his organization's role in a movement that with each day witnessed the arrival of fresh forces under the aegis of the SNCC, the SCLC, and the Congress of Racial Equality (CORE). Rather than vie against one another, Evers and a few of the other leaders, especially Bob Moses, believed unity was the only recipe against white reaction. To this end, in February 1962, Evers had been a significant player in forging a united Council of Federated Organizations (COFO). Oddly, the national NAACP refused to join the coalition, a decision probably related to its quarrel with the local officers over the direction of the organization.

In May 1963, three students at Tougaloo College, near Jackson, organized a sit-in at a Woolworth's. What began as a nonviolent protest became another violent encounter of the civil rights movement. "A huge mob gathered, with open police support and, while the three of us sat there for three hours, I was attacked with fists, brass knuckles and the broken portions of glass sugar containers, and was burned with cigarettes," wrote John Salter in his memoir. Salter, who had talked Evers out of participating in the sit-in, was covered with as much blood as he was with salt, sugar, mustard, catsup, and an assortment of other condiments. His associates, Joan Trumpauer and Anne Moody, were also completely covered with whatever the white mob could dispense from the lunch counter. Dr. Martin Luther King arrived at the scene, hustled them into a car, and sped away. The shepherd of nonviolence had come just as another round of assault was beginning.

The violence at Tougaloo was an omen for even worse tragedy to come. Most vulnerable were leaders such as Evers and the highly emotional but resource-

The bloody trail left by Evers

ful Dave Dennis of CORE. After one meeting, at Dennis's request, the two men switched cars. Dennis felt that his white station wagon was becoming too recognizable in Canton. But his car was no more recognizable than Evers' because later that evening Dennis was stopped by two or three carloads of white men who forced him out of the car and told him they knew who he was. When two truckloads of field hands returning from work drove by, they provided enough of a distraction for Dennis to hurry to his car and rush back to Jackson.

For the next several weeks, Dennis and Evers were followed, sometimes by white segregationists, sometimes by the police. On Tuesday, June 11, Evers finally ended a long meeting that may have been extended because they had heard about Governor Wallace's defiance at the entrance to the University of Alabama. He was driving home when he once again noticed a police car behind him. He stopped and placed a call to the FBI to report that he was being followed by the police and that earlier he had almost been run down by a police patrol car while crossing the street. In his report to the police, Evers noted that the officers were laughing as he hurried out of harm's way. The FBI told him they would look into matter and pass on the information.

Knowing his life was in danger, Evers phoned his wife several times that day. As he had done that morning before he left for work, he told her how much he loved her and the children. They would be his last phone calls.

Evers made several stops after leaving a NAACP meeting, including dropping off a friend who needed a ride. His wife, Myrlie, heard Evers pull into the driveway a little after midnight. Two of the children were waiting for their daddy to come home, while the third, the baby, was sleeping. "I was asleep across the bed and we heard the motor of the car coming in and pulling into the driveway," Mrs. Evers said later. "We heard him get out the car and the car door slam, and in the same instant, we heard the loud gunfire. The

A hole from the bullet that pierced Evers' back

children fell to the floor, as we had taught them to do, and I made a run for the front door, and turned on the light and there he was. The bullet had pushed him forward…he had the keys in his hand, and had pulled his body around the rest of the way to the door. There he lay. I screamed, and people came out. Our next door neighbor fired a gun, as he said, to try to frighten anyone away, and I knew then that that was it."

Evers, bringing home an armful of "Jim Crow Must Go" T-shirts, had been shot in the back just below the right shoulder blade. That he was able to crawl some forty feet is indicative of his strength. He was rushed to the University Hospital. The shot had gone through his body, a window, an interior wall, off the refrigerator, and finally struck a coffee pot. In a neighbor's station wagon on the way to the hospital, Evers tried to sit up, asking the attendants to help him. Evers had lost a considerable amount of blood and suffered internal injuries. He died an hour later at the hospital.

Myrlie Evers said she was outraged by her husband's assassination. "I don't think I have ever hated as much in my life as I did at that moment," she said. "I can recall wanting a machine gun in my hands and to stand there and mow them (white people) all down. I can't explain the depth of my hatred at that point." But at this moment, and over the succeeding years, she would recall her husband's admonishments about curbing her rage and hostility. "Medgar would say, 'Myrlie, don't allow yourself to drop to the level of those who hate you. You are the only one to suffer as a result of it. Those you hate, most of them don't know it and those who do could care less. So you end up being the injured party. Let it go.'" **CD**

DISC 1
TRACK 13

The sniper's bullet ignited a large demonstration in Jackson in which 158 black residents were arrested. A white man had been picked up, questioned, and then released. Police could not connect him to the rifle with a telescopic sight that was found near the bush where the sniper had fired the shot. Almost immediately, the NAACP offered a $10,000 reward for information leading to the arrest and conviction of the killer.

That night after the arrests, Myrlie Evers spoke at rally at the Pearl Street Church. Though tired, she appeared composed. "It was his wish that this [Jackson] movement would be one of the most successful that this nation has ever known," Evers said of her husband's dreams. She told the rapt audience how her husband had spoken of death, and that he was ready to go. "I am left with the strong determination to try to take up where he left off," she continued. "I hope that by his death that all here and those who are not here will be able to draw some of his strength, some of his courage and some of his determination to finish the fight."

Myrlie Louise Evers kisses her late husband's forehead

Mourners pass the casket prior to Evers' funeral

Anne Moody, one of the Tougaloo students who had been mercilessly roughed up at Woolworth's back in the spring, found herself among the 158 people arrested after Evers' murder. She got out of jail that Saturday, the day before Evers' funeral. She had lost about fifteen pounds and she was glad to be going home to a decent meal. Despite her exhaustion and illness due to her time in jail, she pulled herself together the next morning and attended Evers' funeral at the Masonic Temple. "Just before the funeral services were over, I went outside," she remembered. "There was a hill opposite the Masonic Temple, I went up there to watch the procession. I wanted to see every moment of it."

Moody watched the changing mood of the crowd. The dismay and bitterness were gradually changed to anger. The procession was about a mile long and it seemed to stretch all the way from the Temple to the funeral home. When the mourners reached Capitol Street, they tried to break through a phalanx of police officers. Even after Evers' body was taken inside the funeral home, there were still some participants who refused to disperse. Goaded on by members of SNCC, a small group of protesters broke out in freedom songs. Soon, the size of the crowd had increased to more than a thousand as they marched back toward Capitol Street where they had been stopped before. Once more they came to halt when faced with a heavily armed police force. While they debated their next move, several melees had erupted on the periphery of the main body. "Along the sidewalks and on the fringes of the crowd," Moody recounted, "the cops knocked heads, set dogs on some marchers, and made about thirty arrests, but the main body of people in the middle of the street was just stopped."

For a while neither side blinked. "Shoot, shoot!" the protesters dared the police. A sudden shift in mood occurred when the fire trucks arrived. The crowd began to move back, no longer inching forward.

Angered by the show of force, some of the protesters or bystanders began throwing rocks and bottles at the police. Slowly, a no-man's land, littered with glass and debris, existed between the police and protesters. Now, stuff was flying out of nearby windows, imperiling all below. Into the fray, from behind the police lines, came John Doar of the U.S. Justice Department. With bottles sailing around him, Doar walked fearlessly into the crowd, pleading with them to stop throwing objects. Within a few minutes, Dave Dennis, a leader of CORE, was by his side, gathering bottles, rocks, and cans from the hands of would-be throwers.

As days and weeks passed, there was a relative calm after Evers' death; a calm followed by confusion, according to Moody. "Each Negro leader and organization in Jackson received threats," she wrote. "They were all told they were 'next on the list.'

Things began to fall apart. The ministers, in particular, didn't want to be the 'next'; a number of them took that long-promised vacation to Africa or elsewhere. Meanwhile, SNCC and CORE became more militant and began to press for more demonstrations. A lot of the young Negroes wanted to let the whites of Jackson know that even by killing off Medgar they hadn't touched the real core of the Movement. For the NAACP and the older, more conservative groups, however, voter registration had now become number one on the agenda. After the NAACP exerted its influence at a number of strategy meetings, the militants lost."

The assassination of Medgar Evers rocked a nation already reeling from the power and expanse of the civil rights movement. He was barely known outside of Mississippi, but now Evers' name could be heard everywhere. White folk singer Bob Dylan seemed to

Above: A prayer meeting at the Meridian train station before Evers' casket is sent to Arlington National Cemetery

Right: Byron de la Beckwith, left, is escorted to the police station in Jackson, Mississippi

have a song for every major episode in the movement. He had memorialized Emmett Till in song and now he was pouring his heart and soul out to Evers. "Only a Pawn in Their Game" was the title Dylan gave to his ode to a fallen hero, which called out the cowardly murderer as a poor white man merely used as a "tool" taught "to protect his white skin." **CD**

Later, Phil Ochs and Nina Simone would weigh in with their folk and blues laments to Evers, who was buried in Arlington National Cemetery. "You can kill a man but you can't kill an idea," Evers had said on many occasions. The day after the burial, his wife and children were invited to the White House by President Kennedy. Instead of telling him about her pent-up emotions and how her husband had devoted his life to making America better, she merely told the president that she was doing all right.

But Myrlie Evers wouldn't be doing all right until the killer of her husband was brought to justice. It would take two mistrials and three decades before Byron De La Beckwith was convicted of murdering Evers. Upon hearing of the verdict in 1994, Mrs. Evers said that "now he faces the ultimate judge…Beckwith was the epitome of evil, who forever embraced racism and hatred, and who caused so much pain and suffering of so many people." De La Beckwith spent seven years in prison before his death at the age of eighty.

After Evers' death, his brother, Charles, replaced him as field secretary for the NAACP in Jackson. Just days after Evers' murder, President Kennedy called a meeting with civil rights leaders to discuss his proposal for a new civil rights bill. It was a strong proposal and the president had promised to put it at the top of the Congressional calendar. Included in the proposal was an end to segregation on interstate public accommodations; the attorney general would be in charge of integrating the nation's schools; and he would possess the power to eliminate federal funds for any program not in compliance.

Leaders of the civil rights movement applauded the president's plan, but believed pressure was still needed in order to make sure it made it through Congress. There seemed to be only one way to guarantee that the bill was passed and enforced: get the nation and world's attention with a mass march on Washington. Once more A. Philip Randolph was at the helm. In 1941, he threatened a march that forced President Roosevelt to capitulate. Could the same tactic work again to guarantee the passage of the Civil Rights Bill? Randolph and his allies believed it was worth a try.

DISC 1
TRACK 13

15

The March on Washington

Almost ten years after *Brown v. Board of Education* and following a decade filled with sit-ins, freedom rides, demonstrations, and protests against segregation, the nation's civil rights leaders were still not satisfied with the pace of their progress. They had every reason to be disappointed in the state of Black America, particularly in the economic realm, where blacks were hard-pressed to find a decent job. An appreciable dent had been made in the political arena, but unemployment continued to plague black Americans. In 1963, black unemployment was at 11 percent, while white unemployment was at 5 percent. An alarming disparity existed between black and white wealth and family income. White Americans earned on average almost twice as much as a black family.

Gradually, as the impact of the civil rights movement escalated with each encounter, the various organizations began to think more and more about the economic plight, which was the point of many of the boycotts against discriminating white merchants. From the Albany, Georgia, protests the leaders learned a number of ways to improve their fight for justice, and Birmingham had taught them even more. Now, it was time to really apply the pressure, since there was a possibility that Congress might table the proposed Civil Rights Bill sponsored by President Kennedy.

Fresh from battles in Alabama, Mississippi, Arkansas, Georgia, and elsewhere, the movement leaders, guided by the venerable A. Philip Randolph, agreed that the next major demonstration ought to be brought to the nation's capital. "Birmingham had made it clear that the fight of the Negro could be won if he moved that fight out to the sidewalks and the streets, down to the city halls and the city jails and—if necessary—into the martyred heroism of a Medgar Evers," Dr. Martin Luther

King declared in his autobiography. "The Negro revolution in the South had come of age." Moreover, King believed that the fight was in the tradition of America's greatest statements, including the Constitution and the Bill of Rights.

King and others concluded that the struggle had now been expanded on a broad front and had earned the right to an emotional peak.

When Randolph suggested a unification of the movement in a march on Washington, he struck a chord that resonated from the Great Lakes to Stone Mountain, Georgia. The idea was a stroke of genius because the march would galvanize the disparate forces with their differing tactics and would bring the leaders from the various fronts together for a combined attack at the very apex of domestic policy. It was Randolph, among the most highly respected

activists and founder of the Brotherhood of Sleeping Car Porters, who twenty-one years earlier had thought of the first march on Washington. The march never materialized, but the mere threat compelled President Franklin Delano Roosevelt to sign an executive order prohibiting discrimination in the munition plants.

In 1962, Randolph believed it was time to dust off the old tactic and to see if it still had some relevance. At first there was only lukewarm response from other civil rights leaders. Without their full support and cooperation, the march would not be effective. To get the other members of the so-called "Big Six" to the table required all the cunning Randolph could muster. Each of them—Roy Wilkins of the National Association for the Advancement of Colored People (NAACP); Whitney Young Jr. of

An Appeal to You from

MATHEW AHMANN   ISAIAH MINKOFF
EUGENE CARSON BLAKE   A. PHILIP RANDOLPH
JAMES FARMER   WALTER REUTHER
MARTIN LUTHER KING, JR.   ROY WILKINS
JOHN LEWIS   WHITNEY YOUNG

to MARCH on WASHINGTON

WEDNESDAY AUGUST 28, 1963

America faces a crisis . . .
Millions of Negroes are denied freedom . . .
Millions of citizens, black and white, are unemployed . . .

We demand: — Meaningful Civil Rights Laws
— Full and Fair Employment
— Massive Federal Works Program
— Decent Housing
— The Right to Vote
— Adequate Integrated Education

In your community, groups are mobilizing for the March. You can get information on how to go to Washington by calling civil rights organizations, religious organizations, trade unions, fraternal organizations and youth groups.

National Office —

MARCH ON WASHINGTON FOR JOBS AND FREEDOM

170 West 130 Street   •   New York 27   •   PI 8-1900
Cleveland Robinson   Bayard Rustin
Chairman, Administrative Committee   *Deputy Director*

Above: A flyer for the March on Washington: "America faces a crisis…Millions of Negroes are denied freedom…Millions of citizens, black and white, are unemployed…We demand: meaningful Civil Rights Laws; full and fair employment; massive Federal Works Program; decent housing; the right to vote; adequate integrated education…"

Right: The official program for the March on Washington lists performers Marian Anderson and Mahalia Jackson and speakers including A. Philip Randolph, Myrlie Evers, and the Rev. Dr. Martin Luther King Jr.

MARCH ON WASHINGTON FOR JOBS AND FREEDOM
AUGUST 28, 1963

LINCOLN MEMORIAL PROGRAM

1.	The National Anthem	Led by Marian Anderson.
2.	Invocation	The Very Rev. Patrick O'Boyle, *Archbishop of Washington.*
3.	Opening Remarks	A. Philip Randolph, *Director March on Washington for Jobs and Freedom.*
4.	Remarks	Dr. Eugene Carson Blake, *Stated Clerk, United Presbyterian Church of the U.S.A.; Vice Chairman, Commission on Race Relations of the National Council of Churches of Christ in America.*
5.	Tribute to Negro Women Fighters for Freedom Daisy Bates Diane Nash Bevel Mrs. Medgar Evers Mrs. Herbert Lee Rosa Parks Gloria Richardson	Mrs. Medgar Evers
6.	Remarks	John Lewis, *National Chairman, Student Nonviolent Coordinating Committee.*
7.	Remarks	Walter Reuther, *President, United Automobile, Aerospace and Agricultural Implement Workers of America, AFL-CIO; Chairman, Industrial Union Department, AFL-CIO.*
8.	Remarks	James Farmer, *National Director, Congress of Racial Equality.*
9.	Selection	Eva Jessye Choir
10.	Prayer	Rabbi Uri Miller, *President Synagogue Council of America.*
11.	Remarks	Whitney M. Young, Jr., *Executive Director, National Urban League.*
12.	Remarks	Mathew Ahmann, *Executive Director, National Catholic Conference for Interracial Justice.*
13.	Remarks	Roy Wilkins, *Executive Secretary, National Association for the Advancement of Colored People.*
14.	Selection	Miss Mahalia Jackson
15.	Remarks	Rabbi Joachim Prinz, *President American Jewish Congress.*
16.	Remarks	The Rev. Dr. Martin Luther King, Jr., *President, Southern Christian Leadership Conference.*
17.	The Pledge	A. Philip Randolph
18.	Benediction	Dr. Benjamin E. Mays, *President, Morehouse College.*

"WE SHALL OVERCOME"

the National Urban League; Rev. Martin Luther King Jr. of the Southern Christian Leadership Conference (SCLC); James Farmer of the Conference of Racial Equality (CORE); and John Lewis of the Student Nonviolent Coordinating Committee (SNCC)—utilized different tactics and had his own separate agenda to achieve the organization's goals and objectives. Plus, the leaders were deeply competitive, eager to push aside the other in order to command the bank of microphones at a press conference. Most of the resistance came from Wilkins, who stated that the NAACP would not participate in an event if civil disobedience was planned, and from John Lewis, representing a younger, more militant generation who were not afraid to stage protests and boycotts in Washington, D.C. It took some coaxing to get all of them to agree. Beyond the Big Six, there was the Big One—President Kennedy.

On June 22, the president agreed to meet with the Big Six. The black men were on one side of the table in the cabinet room of the White House, and the white men—President Kennedy, his brother, Robert, vice president Lyndon Johnson, and special assistant Arthur Schlesinger Jr.—sat on the other side. Kennedy's opening gambit was to ask the leaders to call off the march. His main reason for canceling the event was his fear that it would seriously compromise the pending Civil Rights Bill, which would put an end to racial discrimination and segregation in the eyes of the law. "We want success in Congress," Kennedy stressed, "not just a big show at the Capitol. Some of these people [in Congress] are looking for an excuse to be against us. I don't want to give them a chance to say 'Yes, I'm for the bill, but I'm damned if I'll vote for it at the point of a gun.' It seemed to me a great mistake to announce a March on Washington before the bill was even in committee. The only effect is to create an atmosphere of intimidation, and this may give some members of Congress an out." 🆒

The leaders were sympathetic to the President's plight, but they told him they too were caught in an untenable position. Randolph explained that it was

A. Philip Randolph speaks to the press

almost impossible to control angry protesters if the march were to be postponed. To do so, Randolph told Kennedy, would be to surrender the streets to the proponents of violence. The reference was clearly to Malcolm X, whose fiery speeches not only assailed the current White House administration but excoriated the Big Six. Kennedy had Congress; the Big Six had Malcolm X. The meeting concluded without any clear resolution; there was only the promise to stay in touch.

Among themselves, the Big Six made the same promise and honored it that July 2 at New York's

DISC 2
TRACK 1

President Kennedy with the leaders of the March

Roosevelt Hotel. One of the pressing concerns raised by Wilkins was who would organize and direct the march. For Randolph there was only one man: Bayard Rustin. Roy Wilkins firmly objected. Three things about Rustin bothered the NAACP leader: his association with the white Left; his imprisonment as a conscientious objector during World War II; and his sexual orientation. Though it was not widely known, Rustin's homosexuality was a nettlesome issue for most of the black leaders as well as among many in the rank and file. John Lewis of SNCC, however, quickly voiced his support for Rustin.

"The consensus was that he be involved, and Wilkins relented," Lewis noted in his autobiography. "That was probably the most important decision made that day—to name Randolph the march director and Rustin his deputy." The often rancorous

meeting concluded on a high note as they voted to add four white co-chairmen to the march leadership: Matthew Ahmann, of the National Catholic Conference for Interracial Justice; the Reverend Eugene Carson Blake, of the National Council of Churches of Christ in America; Rabbi Joachim Prinz, of the American Jewish Congress; and Walter Reuther, of the United Automobile Workers. The date for the march was set for Wednesday, August 28, 1963.

Randolph may have conceived the march, but his trusted lieutenant, Bayard Rustin, was responsible for making all the pieces fit smoothly together. It was an awesome task, and no one but Rustin possessed the ensemble of skills needed to pull it off. A seasoned activist with extensive experience in organizing mass protests, Rustin was by Randolph's side in 1941, so he knew the mechanics of the march and how to conduct it. With only two months to organize a massive protest, he wasted no time once the word was given. Among the first things he did was to set up headquarters in Harlem at Reverend Thomas Kilgore's Baptist Church, with a smaller office in Washington. His core staff of two hundred volunteers quickly set about coordinating the daunting details, all of which Rustin delivered with precision and alacrity.

Still, there was a multitude of detractors who believed that even as resourceful as Rustin could be, he would need a miracle to organize a march in six weeks in which more than 100,000 people were expected to participate. The optimistic Rustin felt it was indeed a challenge, but one that could be done if he had the proper team and funds. "I am a technician," he told a reporter. "My job is to carry out policy as established by top leadership."

Rustin also had to deal with the press, coordinate travel arrangements from towns all over the country, massage the sponsors, and fight off the critics. One of the most vociferous opponents of the march was Senator Strom Thurmond of South Carolina. He centered his venom on Rustin, calling him a draft dodger, a communist, and a pervert. This was the kind of attack Wilkins had anticipated, but rather than point the finger at Randolph and remind him of his warning, he stood up for Rustin, adding that he "was a man of exceptional ability."

While fending off naysayers and southern racist politicians, Rustin kept his eyes on the number of balls he had in the air: marshals had to be trained to help maintain order; thousands of people had to be fed; sanitation measures were an absolute necessity; buses had be parked; the program had to start on time and end promptly to meet district regulations; and there had to be security for all the notables who had been invited and agreed to attend. It was a huge undertaking and Rustin, lighting one cigarette with another, worked around the clock, the phone like an appendage to his head.

Above: Marchers crowd Constitution Avenue

Left: The crowd at the Lincoln Memorial

King waves to the waiting crowd

Getting the word out to the people was essential if the march was going to live up to the goal of bringing 100,000 or more to Washington, D.C. The black press, the pulpit, and word of mouth complemented the thousands of fliers mailed by Rustin and his crew. Organizing the passage of folks by train, buses, and caravans of cars was coordinated meticulously, and when all was said and done, more than thirty special trains, two thousand chartered buses, and three air-

lines were involved in conveying a quarter of a million participants to the historic event.

Two days before the march, August 26, 1963, Rustin and leading members of his organizing team moved their headquarters from Harlem to the Statler Hilton Hotel in Washington, D.C. On the next day, eight of the ten co-chairs of the march arrived at the hotel. Dr. King, registered at the Willard Hotel, wasn't there. He was in his room working on his speech. Nor was CORE's James Farmer present. He had been jailed in Plaquemine, Louisiana, for leading a civil rights demonstration. "A number of his colleagues in the North felt that Farmer had refused bail, and elected to stay in jail, so as to dramatize his heroic plight while other leaders were basking in the spotlight of the great March on Washington," Rustin wrote.

On the eve of the march, Rustin and his crew received a surprise visit from Malcolm X, who had widely condemned the march, calling it the "farce on Washington." Malcolm said he had come because he "belonged there." He said nothing about this visitation in his autobiography. It was a time in Malcolm's life when he was deeply troubled by the revelations of Elijah Muhammad's adultery. When told of Malcolm's presence at the hotel, Wilkins brushed it off, saying he was not surprised, and that there was much work to be done and little time to be concerned about Malcolm or anyone else's visit.

Rustin later remembered that on the morning of August 28 the streets were almost deserted. But within a couple of hours after daybreak, thousands began to stream into the city. By 9:30 am, about forty thousand demonstrators had gathered around the Washington Monument. Most of the 250,000 who finally assembled there were common and ordinary working people, people who had taken three days off from their jobs and probably spending money they didn't have so they might lift their voices for the cause. Dr. King was awed by the crowd. He swelled with pride over what he considered to be an army. It carried no weapons and was entirely volunteer, but its strength was unrivaled. "It was white, and Negro, and of all ages," he said. "It had adherents of every faith, members of every class, every profession, every political party, united by a single ideal. It was a fighting army, but no one could mistake that its most powerful weapon was love."

Love may have provided the connective tissue of the march, but it was the church and the unions that had done the most to rally people to the event. Only the AFL–CIO's national leadership body was among the missing labor unions. Because of Walter Reuther's position as one of the co-chairs of the event, the United Auto Workers and their banners were scattered throughout the throng. "We Demand Voting Rights!" "We March for Jobs!" and "End Segregated Rules in Public Schools" were among the sea of placards bobbing up and down as the crowd

marched from the Monument to the Lincoln Memorial. They stabbed the air in time with the voices of Peter Paul and Mary, Bob Dylan, Leon Bibb, Odetta, and Joan Baez.

By 2 pm, the procession was over and thousands of people stood shoulder to shoulder, cheering loudly when a roll call of celebrities bounced from the speakers. Jackie Robinson, James Baldwin, Marlon Brando, Paul Newman, Harry Belafonte, Sammy Davis Jr., Ossie Davis and Ruby Dee, Diahann Carroll, Burt Lancaster, and even Charlton Heston were among the most popular members of the Hollywood contingent spotted in the crowd.

Between Randolph's opening comments and the benediction by Dr. Benjamin Mays at the close of the ceremony, there were some eighteen remarks, prayers, and vocal selections. As was his due,

King delivers the "I Have a Dream" speech

Some may have been disappointed that there were no boycotts or rowdy disturbances, but most were glad that nothing had occurred to mar the nonviolent assembly. Governmental officials were certainly pleased there were no racial encounters and that peace had indeed reigned. To express his gratitude that things had gone so well, President Kennedy invited a contingent of the march leaders to the White House. Earlier, shortly after the march was over, he had released a statement to the press, expressing his goodwill and warm regards to all involved.

"We have witnessed today in Washington tens of thousands of Americans—both Negro and white—exercising their right to assemble peaceably and direct the widest possible attention to a great national issue," the president stated. "Efforts to secure equal treatment and equal opportunity for all without regard to race, color, creed, or nationality are neither novel nor difficult to understand. What is different today is the intensified and widespread public awareness of the need to move forward in achieving these objectives—objectives which are older than this Nation.

"Although this summer has seen remarkable progress in translating civil rights from principles into practices," he continued, "we have a very long way yet to travel. One cannot help but be impressed with the deep fervor and the quiet dignity that characterizes the thousands who have gathered in the Nation's Capital from across the country to demonstrate their faith and confidence in our democratic

A marcher rests, sitting on his placard, at the March's end

form of government. History has seen many demonstrations—of widely varying character and for a whole host of reasons. As our thoughts travel to other demonstrations that have occurred in different parts of the world, this Nation can properly be proud of the demonstration that has occurred here today. The leaders of the organizations sponsoring the March and all who have participated in it deserve our appreciation for the detailed preparations that made it possible and for the orderly manner in which it has been conducted."

Yet two events of which very few people were aware had threatened the march's peaceful conclusion. On the night before the march, the cables for the public address system had been severely damaged, almost cut in half. When this sabotage was brought to the attention of Walter Fauntroy, one of King's aides in charge of logistics in Washington, D.C., he related the problem to Attorney General Kennedy. Because white segregationists were claiming the government was acting like a co-sponsor of the march, the Kennedys were reluctant to move expediently. But Fauntroy prevailed and the Army Signal Corps was sent in to repair the damage and guarantee that the speakers would be ready to go by noon the next day.

The other problem was a human one. George Lincoln Rockwell, an infamous leader of the American Nazi Party, stood with his constituents in the heart of the black community with banners adorned with swastikas proclaiming "Martin Luther Coon Go Home!" "Their purpose was to provoke something," Fauntroy remembered. "It was all we could do but to circulate in the neighborhood and tell people what they were trying to do. Just laugh at them…don't throw anything. Just laugh at them. But it gave me a fear that there might be provocateurs in the crowd who might precipitate an incident to destroy the effectiveness of what we had planned to do."

Days afterwards the march was still reverberating in the media, and the editorials from the major dailies glowed in their assessments. If Albany, Birmingham, and the struggle in Mississippi had failed to capture the nation's attention, the March on Washington did. Dr. King reached the pinnacle of his activist career, the movement had gained the legitimacy it needed, there was no harm done to the possible passage of the Civil Rights Bill—though many doubted it registered any influence one way or the other—and the Kennedys seemed to be happy about the event.

But what about the Klan and the White Citizens' Council? How did they feel about what had happened? One tragic response from them would occur only weeks later, and it would be one of the most devastating blows to the civil rights movement and an affront to human decency.

16

Four Little Black Girls in White

I t was a little over two weeks since the March on Washington and the peacefulness following that historic event was gradually giving away to a new round of violence. Nowhere was this change more apparent than in Birmingham. Early in the spring of 1963, there had been a rash of bombings, most notably at the Gaston Motel, which was owned by black millionaire A. G. Gaston, who had made his fortune from real estate and the insurance business. On the eve of Mother's Day, segregationists ignited a bomb that destroyed the room where Dr. Martin Luther King and his colleagues had their headquarters during the demonstrations in the city. There were minor reports of fires and Molotov cocktails through the summer, but nothing as disturbing as the early September 1963 bombing of the home of Arthur Shores, a friend of A. G. Gaston. Once more black residents were in the street battling with the police. One black person was killed and twenty-one were severely injured.

That the friends and property of A. G. Gaston, one of the richest black men in the country, were targets of segregationists was no coincidence. Gaston had been an uncompromising opponent of injustice, providing financial support to activists and their campaigns to end segregated schools and public facilities. One evening in early September, after having dinner at the White House with President Kennedy and returning to Birmingham, Gaston and his wife, Minnie, had just retired for the night when a firebomb sailed through a first-floor window of their house. "The bomb exploded and began to burn through the living room, filling the house with smoke," Carol Jenkins and Elizabeth Gardner Hines recounted in their Gaston biography, *Black Titan*. "A. G. Gaston awoke to Minnie's cries: 'I started running for her…she was in the living room, standing beside a burned lamp shade, and tears rolled down her terrified face.'"

When law enforcement officials arrived and conducted investigations, they discovered that two bombs had been thrown. One crashed through the window and the other splattered on the outside of the house. The Gastons concluded that only the flame-retardant material in the drapes and the rugs limited the spread of the fire. Someone was responsible for the crude fire bombs made of milk bottles filled with gasoline and wrapped in rags—and A. G. Gaston had enemies among whites and some blacks who believed he was blocking more militant action against segregation. It prompted the wealthy businessman to employ twenty-four-hour security at his home. The Gastons were fortunate to escape with just a modicum of damage to their property; others, including four little black girls at the Sixteenth Street Baptist Church, were not.

As usual, Denise McNair got up Sunday morning ready for church. Her white dress was neatly pressed and her thick, shoulder-length hair was combed and brushed and matched her sparkling eyes. A collection of dolls stared at her from various parts of the room. On the dresser were two containers full of money she had raised for muscular dystrophy. She was proud of her work and couldn't wait to tell her friends and playmates how well she had done. In a couple of months, on November 17, she would celebrate her twelfth birthday. She was the first child of Chris and Maxine McNair. Her playmates and classmates at Center Street Elementary School called her "Niecie."

"Everybody liked her even if they didn't like each other," said childhood friend Rhonda Nunn Thomas. "She could play with anybody."

Many of the adults in the neighborhood and her teachers at school felt she was a natural-born leader, destined for greatness. Denise and her close friend, Carole Robertson, were always busy trying to improve themselves and to help others. Maybe one day she would be a teacher like her parents.

When Carole Robertson, age fourteen, wasn't reading a book or doing her homework she was usually practicing scales on the clarinet or working on her dance routines. On this Sunday morning before going to church, she was spinning around the room, a fancy heel and toe, mixed with a cha-cha shuffle. She was a good dancer and very nimble on her feet.

Denise McNair, Carole Robertson, Addie Mae Collins and Cynthia Wesley: The Four Little Girls

The altar of the Sixteenth Street Baptist Church is covered in rubble from the bombing

She also liked to model and try different hairstyles. Like Denise, she was excited about their role in Sunday's youth affair, and she really looked forward to showing off her pretty white dress. Other than her girl scout uniform, it was one of favorite outfits.

Each Sunday Addie Mae Collins, age fourteen, got out of bed eager to attend church. This Sunday was special, and she and her sisters had stayed up late on Saturday starching and pressing their dresses. It was a routine she enjoyed, just as she loved knocking on neighbors' doors selling her mother's aprons and potholders. One of eight children, she was often the peacemaker among her siblings. "She just always wanted us to love one another and treat each other right," her sister, Sarah, recalled. "She was a happy person also, and she loved life."

Addie Mae also loved to play hopscotch, and whenever sides were chosen for a softball game, she was picked early, since she was among the best underhand pitchers in the neighborhood. But playing ball was not on her mind this Sunday as her sister, Flora, pressed and curled her short hair.

Cynthia Wesley, age fourteen, was a petite girl with a small, narrow face that always seemed to be smiling. Her birthday was April 30, just six days after Carole's and twelve days after Addie Mae's. An excellent student, she was also a member of the school's band. Cynthia was very popular and made friends easily. One of her closest friends was Rickey Powell. Because September 15 was Youth Day, she had invited Rickey to come to church with her. At first Rickey had agreed to go, but declined when his mother wanted him to accompany her to a funeral. "We were like peas in a pod," Powell said. "That was my best bud."

Sunday school at Sixteenth Street Baptist Church, Birmingham's largest black church, had just let out, recalled Sarah Collins, Addie Mae's sister. Their teacher, Ella C. Demand, had completed their lesson for the day, entitled "The Love That Forgives." Sarah was in the basement with her sister and Denise McNair, getting ready to attend a youth service. "I remember Denise asking Addie to tie her belt," Sarah said. "Addie was tying her sash. Then it happened."

Nineteen sticks of dynamite placed underneath a stairwell exploded and destroyed the northeast corner of the church. "I couldn't see anymore because my eyes were full of glass—twenty-three pieces of glass," Sarah said, after she was dug out from under slabs of concrete and stone. "I didn't know what happened. I just remember calling, 'Addie, Addie.' But there was no answer. I don't remember any pain. I just remember wanting Addie."

Amid the turmoil, the church's pastor, Reverend John H. Cross, with a megaphone in his hands, tried to calm the crowd. "The police are doing everything they can," he pleaded, at the same time trying to control his own tears. "Please go home. The Lord is our shepherd...We shall not want."

While he was making the rounds to survey the church's damage, he encountered a young woman

Workers inspect the ruins of the church

with a brick in her hand. She was preparing to throw it at the policemen who had arrived at the scene. She believed the police were either involved in the bombing or knew who had done it. "I got there in time to grab her arm," Rev. Cross said later. "I told her you can't settle it this way. She started crying, 'I know they did it, I know they did it.' I told her we just have to let justice take its course."

Rev. Cross's daughter, Barbara, who was thirteen at the time of the explosion, was also in the basement, and narrowly escaped injury. "I was in the Sunday school classroom when the bomb went off," she recalled years later, noting that three of the girls who were killed had left the classroom to go to the restroom. "I thought the United States had been bombed, not just our church. It was a horrific sound…and the building shook." Barbara remembered running and screaming before some of the church members ushered them out the front door.

As the panic subsided, the awful task of determining who was buried beneath the basement's rubble began. Denise McNair was the first of the dead girls pulled from the ruins. Then, in tearful succession, the bodies of the other victims were removed. "Addie Mae Collins, Cynthia Wesley, and Carole Robertson were dead, their Sunday dresses shredded into bloody rags, their bodies horribly mangled. 'They were all found almost within the same location,' Reverend Cross said, "as if they had been thrown on top of each other.'"

Later that afternoon, while Sarah's parents comforted her at the hospital, her older sister Junie, age sixteen, who had also miraculously survived the bombing, was taken to the University Hospital morgue to help identify a body. "I looked at the face, and I couldn't tell who it was," she says of the crumpled form. "Then I saw this little brown shoe—you know, like a loafer—and I recognized it right away." As for Sarah, she spent three months in the hospital, ultimately losing her right eye.

"I remember so well arriving in Birmingham about two and a half hours after the bombing and I couldn't believe when I arrived at the church and saw the devastation," SNCC activist John Lewis said. "I remained there for the funeral of the four little girls. And it still pains me when I go and visit Birmingham even today and go back to the site of the bombing."

Ever since the bombing at Gaston Motel, the church had been used occasionally as a meeting place for civil rights organizers. It had been chosen because no one expected it would be targeted by the Ku Klux Klan or radical segregationists. Perhaps that is why there was no security there the night when someone presumably broke in and planted the bombs.

When Rev. Cross was asked if he thought the church was a target, he answered in the affirmative. Diane McWhorter, author of a memoir on growing up in Birmingham, *Carry Me Home*, agreed with the minister.

"It had come to be known as the headquarters of the movement," McWhorter wrote, "because it was big and centrally located. It was right across the street from Kelly Ingram Park, which is where those dogs and fire hose photos were taken. It was a staging ground for the marches. Interestingly though, the Sixteenth Street Baptist was a very snooty church. It was one of the oldest black churches in town. The membership was extremely proud and prosperous. The church was rather withholding when it came to bettering the race, and none of the girls who were killed, ironically, had marched because their parents wouldn't let them. There were a lot of ironies that this church was targeted, but the Klan had stopped making distinctions. At first they were bombing just Shuttlesworth's church, but into the Sixties they were bombing indiscriminately."

Reverend C. T. Vivian, a charter member of the SCLC and who would be a pivotal leader in the Selma, Alabama, demonstrations, expounded on the role of the church as a sanctuary and a meeting place for the movement. "The church was a very important place for us during the civil rights movement," he said. "The Sixteenth Street Baptist Church was a

The removal of a body from the Sixteenth Street Baptist Church

place we operated out of at various times. It was close to the only motel where blacks could stay in Birmingham, if not in the whole region."

The bombing left more than twenty injured, including Sarah Collins. In its immediate wake there was an outbreak of violence in the city, and one black and five whites were hurt in the disorder that morning. Rev. Cross was able to dissuade one distraught woman from hurling a brick, but he couldn't stop others as they pelted the police with rocks. The throwers dispersed when the police fired shotgun blasts over their heads. Alerted to the incident, Rev. Martin Luther King Jr. and other civil rights activists hurried to the city.

By late Sunday afternoon, two African American youths had been killed. "Johnny Robinson, a sixteen-year-old Negro, was shot in the back and killed by a policeman with a shotgun this afternoon," Claude Sitton of the *New York Times* reported. "Officers said the victim was among a group that had hurled stones at white youths driving through the area in cars flying the Confederate battle flags." Robinson had been shot in the back.

Virgil Ware, age thirteen, was shot while riding on the handlebars of his brother's bicycle just outside Birmingham. The police were unable to explain the circumstances of Ware's death, but believed it was related to the rash of disturbances. Two other young people, one black and one white, were also shot, but their wounds were superficial.

As night approached, Alabama Governor George Wallace dispatched more than five hundred National Guardsmen in battle gear and three hundred state troopers. They were there to augment the Birmingham police and the Jefferson County sheriff's deputies. Meanwhile, Birmingham Mayor Albert Boutwell and other city officials appeared on television to urge residents to cooperate in the call for calm, and to "end the senseless reign of terror."

"The bombing came five days after the desegregation of three previously all-white schools in Birmingham," Sitton wrote. "The way had been cleared for the desegregation when President Kennedy federalized the Alabama National Guard and the federal courts issued a sweeping order against Governor Wallace, thus ending his defiance toward the integration step."

There were no immediate arrests. Chief Police Inspector W. J. Haley told reporters that they had spoken to two witnesses who said they saw a car drive by the church, slow down, and then speed away before the blast occurred. Very few black residents were optimistic that anyone would be arrested and charged for the crime. In the fifty reported bombings of African American property in the city since World War II, not one of them had been solved.

"We have a deep-seated kind of suspicion of the criminal justice system when it comes to black folks," said the Reverend Abraham Lincoln Woods, who would be among the most persistent black clergy in Birmingham pressuring the FBI to reopen the church bombing case. "If those four little girls had been another color and the suspects were black, they would have been caught."

More than fifteen hundred spectators stood outside St. John's AME Church and three thousand people crowded the sanctuary on September 17, 1963. Those inside had their eyes fixed on the baby blue casket at the front of the church that held the body of Carole Robertson. She was the first of the four girls to be buried. Several pastors mounted the pulpit to eulogize her. "We live here in a society in which we have not made safe the streets, the homes or the

Reverend Martin Luther King Jr. speaks at the funeral service

churches," intoned Reverend Fred Shuttlesworth. The normally fiery preacher's words were soft and directed straight at Carole's family when he said, "You by your loss, have made a payment on this great thing called freedom."

Carole's minister, John Cross, had the last words, saying, "When the atrocious act was committed on Sunday morning, it was not committed against us but against all freedom-loving people. I believe with my heart that out of this dastardly act, this inhuman deed, somehow we have been brought together as we have never been brought together."

On Wednesday, the day after Carole's funeral, services were held at Sixth Avenue Baptist Church for the other three girls. When it was announced that Dr. King would be delivering the eulogy, more than seven thousand people turned out for the funeral. The majority of them had to listen to Dr. King's words from outside through a loudspeaker. **CD**

DISC 2
TRACK 2

"They are the martyred heroines of a holy crusade for freedom and human dignity," he related to the packed church.

King imagined that the death of the young girls—indeed perhaps the girls themselves—had something to say to America. In a stirring speech that belied his frustration, he called out blacks not involved in the fight, politicians who fed hatred, and a federal government prone to ineffective compromise.

The girls, he said, "say to us that we must be concerned not merely about who murdered them, but about the system, the way of life, the philosophy which produced the murderers. Their death says to us that we must work passionately and unrelentingly for the realization of the American dream."

Condolences came from far and wide to the families of the slain children, but Birmingham's mayor and his administration did not attend the funeral, though a weeping Mayor Boutwell did appear on television, seemingly contrite. President Kennedy was certainly moved and invited Dr. King and several other civic leaders from the city to join him at

the White House. King left the White House feeling positive. The nation's leaders, he believed, had the potential to right the wrongs that had come to be commonplace.

But Dr. King was mistaken. Though a number of FBI agents were assigned to the case, making it one of the largest manhunts by the agency since the days of John Dillinger, there were no immediate results. Two years later in 1965, Birmingham FBI agents recommended that at least four suspects be charged with the bombing. But FBI Director J. Edgar Hoover blocked the prosecution of the suspects, saying the chance of winning a conviction was "remote."

In 1970, Bill Baxley was elected attorney general of Alabama and he promised to reopen investigation of the case. Within five years, despite the hesitancy on part of the FBI to release its files, charges were brought against Robert Chambliss. On November 19, 1977, Chambliss, age seventy-three, a former member of the Ku Klux Klan, was convicted by a jury on a charge of first degree murder in the death of Denise McNair. Having successfully prosecuted Chambliss, Baxley said there were up to four others he was seeking for their role in the bombing. One of the suspects, Herman Frank Cash, died before charges could be brought against him.

Baxley may have had good intentions but it would be almost twenty years before the FBI reopened the case. By that time, Chambliss had died in prison, maintaining his innocence. "It's a crime that has gone unsolved except one local conviction and it remains a sore part of American history that we would like to heal," said Joseph Lewis, FBI special agent in charge in Birmingham. "We feel we have an opportunity to do so this time, and we want to take one last shot at it."

A new probe by the FBI occurred a month after film director Spike Lee released a new documentary about the bombing. Entitled 4 *Little Girls*, the film retold the story of the case through the eyes of survivors, witnesses, defenders, and prosecutors. The FBI said its renewed investigation had nothing to do with the documentary's release.

On May 17, 2000, nearly thirty-seven years after the bombing, Thomas Blanton Jr., age sixty-two, and Bobby Frank Cherry, age sixty-nine, turned themselves in to authorities after they were indicted by a state grand jury. "The prosecutor, United States Attorney Doug Jones, declined to spell out what new evidence prompted the indictments, which follow the reopening of the case against Blanton and Cherry by the FBI in 1996. He did say that the prosecutions were a crucial step in bringing closure, both to the victims, and to the city of Birmingham, which has yet to emerge fully from the shadow of its racist past. Even the FBI seems in search of redemption; the agency is said to have abandoned the case in 1964 at the behest of J. Edgar Hoover, who insisted over the objections of his staff, that no jury could be impaneled which would convict the men," Joy-Ann Lomena Reid reported. Blanton and Cherry were charged with four counts of first-degree murder. Both ex-Klansmen insisted they were innocent.

Over the years, since he was a suspect in the crime, Blanton had offered several alibis on his whereabouts the night the bombs were placed in the church. "He was with his girlfriend at a movie or a restaurant," said Frank Sikora, a reporter for the *Birmingham News* and author of *Until Justice Rolls Down.* "His alibi kept changing. He was a Klansmen, there was no doubt about that."

Blanton, according to Sikora, had poured acid on the front seat covers of a car belonging to a black owner. He used to drive around town with a big Confederate battle flag flying from his car, which was a kind of trademark for him. "That car was seen at the church that morning before the bomb went off," Sikora said in an interview. "They were convinced that he went by the church that morning. The assumption was that he went by to see if the bomb had gone off."

Mourners exit the funeral

In May 2001, Blanton was convicted of murder by a jury and sentenced to life in prison. Almost a year later, the other accused man, Cherry, was convicted of murder and given a life sentence. He had avoided being tried earlier on grounds that he was mentally incompetent, but heated protests from activists pressured the prosecutor to move forward with his trial. Like Blanton, Cherry repeatedly denied his involvement in the perfidious crime. He claimed he was home with his wife, who was suffering from cancer, that evening, watching wrestling. A search of television logs revealed there was no wrestling on television that night. During his days in the Klan, Cherry was noted for his bitter hatred of blacks. He once attacked Reverend Shuttlesworth with a pair of brass knuckles.

Nine white and three black jurors convicted the last of the men believed to have blown up the church.

When Cherry was handcuffed and led off by officers of the court, he told the press that people had lied about him. "I have no idea why I'm going to jail," he snapped. While his relatives stood in shock, some of them in tears, there were tears of joy from members of the family of the victims. "My mother used always tell me that you have to learn to love, live and forget," said Eunice Davis, Cynthia Wesley's sister. "The hard part is going to be to forget. But I can forgive him. Because when people don't know better, they don't do better. And I feel he just doesn't know better."

It took more than a generation to bring some semblance of justice for the murder of four little black girls. If the testimony of black residents in Birmingham is any indication, it will take even longer to forget what happened that fateful morning in September. For many of the members of the Sixteenth Street Baptist Church, there is no intention to forget the tragedy. In fact, to some extent they have embraced it, turning the church into a shrine of the civil rights movement with more than 80,000 visitors annually. Josephine Marshall, a witness at Cherry's trial, is a longtime resident who will keep that memory alive.

"As soon as I walk in this building," she said of the church, "I remember what I saw outside. And as the years pass, it gets a little bit better, but still, you don't forget. I won't forget what I saw that morning."

17

Mississippi Goddam

Upset by the racist violence that took the lives of Medgar Evers and the four little girls in Birmingham, singer/songwriter Nina Simone composed the song "Mississippi Goddam" to commemorate them. The song also captured the continuing hatred that roiled race relations in Mississippi in 1964, marking the state with unrelieved brutality and inhumane treatment of its black residents.

Black Mississippians were still reeling from the assassination of Medgar Evers in 1963 when Student Nonviolent Coordinating Committee (SNCC) workers, including Bob Moses, James Forman, and Lawrence Guyot, began formulating ways to draw national attention to the state. It had done so during previous months when a number of white volunteers had ventured South to aid the voter registration drives of SNCC and the Congress of Racial Equality (CORE).

Moses wrote in his autobiography, "I felt that with increasing automation of the cotton fields, and the White Citizens' Council campaign to export blacks out of the state, with the staff we had blacks were not going to get the vote fast enough to have significant impact if their numbers shrank and the population balance changed in favor of whites." Moses, Forman, and Allard Lowenstein, a white Democratic Party operative who had come to Mississippi shortly after Evers' assassination, drew up plans that would involve recruiting thousands of students, mainly white, to come to Mississippi in the summer of 1964.

The concept was in the discussion stages before it was almost completely derailed following the assassination of President Kennedy in November 1963. Like much of the nation, the civil rights movement was traumatized by the tragedy and just as it was recovering from that setback, the activists, particularly those in Mississippi, were confronted with other challenging obstacles.

Nothing proved more distressing than the murder of Louis Allen. Allen, a logger and farmer, had been an eyewitness two years earlier when the white state legislator, E. H. Hurst, killed Herbert Lee for trying to register black voters. Allen was ready to refute in court Hurst's claim of shooting Lee in self-defense. He told investigators that Lee was killed in cold blood. When he began receiving threats and experienced harassment from local police and other whites, he changed his mind about appearing as a witness against Hurst. This turnabout, however, didn't end the threats on his life. One January night, weeks after the FBI had declined to provide protection, Allen's son, Henry, came home and found him dead in the front yard.

"Oh, he was just mutilated," Henry Allen said. "You shoot a person in the head with a shotgun at close range, I mean—just chaos, man. I never wanted my mama or my little sister to ever see him. My mama wanted to go down to that road, but she'd have stroked, she'd have probably died right there. It's just too much to look at, somebody that close to you. 'Cause we was close people."

Allen's death put an end to the long debate about whether to pursue "Freedom Summer." "It was my decision to move it," Moses said. "And what moved me was Louis's murder. That was it."

FROM "MISSISSIPPI GODDAM" BY NINA SIMONE

Oh but this whole country is full of lies
You're all gonna die and die like flies
I don't trust you any more
You keep on saying "Go slow!"
"Go slow!"

But that's just the trouble
"do it slow"
Desegregation
"do it slow"
Mass participation
"do it slow"
Reunification
"do it slow"
Do things gradually
"do it slow"

But bring more tragedy
"do it slow"
Why don't you see it
Why don't you feel it
I don't know
I don't know

You don't have to live next to me
Just give me my equality
Everybody knows about Mississippi
Everybody knows about Alabama
Everybody knows about Mississippi Goddam

Despite Moses's central role in the project, Lawrence Guyot, a SNCC field secretary who spent a month in the Hattiesburg jail for organizing against segregation, said there was no one person responsible for proposing Freedom Summer. "The Summer Project was a combination of a lot of different ideas," he explained. "Timothy Jenkins came up with the idea of using a Mississippi law that said that people who were not registered to vote should be counted—should be allowed to cast a challenge ballot. Then there was a discussion of Freedom Days in South Africa, and you combine that with a need to bring the country into Mississippi in order to really put the spotlight into Mississippi. So you combine those—which Moses did—and then you have the Freedom Summer objectives. Well, what was this objective? This objective was to bring in [more registered voters]. We had learned from the Freedom Vote, Freedom Election. We had learned both in Hattiesburg and throughout everywhere else that these people would bring with them more FBI agents and more cameras than anything else. That we were being picked off systematically."

Although Moses, Forman, Lowenstein, and Guyot were excited about the initiative, several of their comrades were not, believing that the local leadership would be overwhelmed by the invasion of white volunteers. The idea of having an army of white volunteers was questioned, Guyot said, "because [of] the fact that this is a concession and we have to do this." However, he continued, "Hattiesburg had demonstrated to us that white volunteers bring with them the country, as it relates to press, as it relates to federal government, ad infinitum."

The presence and support of such influential voices as Fannie Lou Hamer from Sunflower County were enough to carry the day and the opposition caved in to the plan, though there were to be a number of critical drawbacks which hadn't been carefully considered. For example, were the white volunteers coming for just the summer or were they going to be there indefinitely? As Forman noted in his study of the movement, "we would pay dearly for this miscalculation." Forman was probably referring to the role of whites in the organization, particularly how their leadership would impact the black members. Later, by 1966, the emerging black nationalism in SNCC brought about an impasse. When the one hundred members who attended the upstate New York meeting submitted their votes on whether whites should stay or be expelled, they were voted out by one vote, nineteen to eighteen. Twenty-four members abstained.

One of the first massive assemblies of volunteers occurred in June 1964 when some eight hundred students, three hundred of them women, from colleges in the North met on the campus of Western College for Women in Oxford, Ohio, for weeklong training sessions sponsored by the National Council of Churches. Most of them were from well-to-do families who could afford to send off a son or daughter with $500 in bail money and sufficient funds to cover their living expenses and transportation home if the going got too rough. "We had to tell these young people exactly what they were getting ready to get involved in," Mississippi native and then-SNCC staff member Hollis Watkins said. "They had to be prepared to go to jail, they had to be prepared to be beaten, and they had to be prepared to be killed. And if they were not prepared for either one or all three of those, then they probably should reconsider coming to Mississippi."

Coming from backgrounds that were markedly distinct from what they were about to encounter in Mississippi, the volunteers had to be drilled on the culture and the oppressive conditions blacks in the state endured. The new recruits also had to be given the proper orientation and tactics that were consistent with the philosophy of nonviolence. Along with these lessons, they were thoroughly instructed on how to survive in the dangerously racist environment. "No interracial groups traveling, day or night, unless absolutely necessary," recalled Bob Zellner, the white SNCC staff member from Alabama. "And if that happened…whoever was in the minority would be hidden, covered with blankets, laying on the floor boards, whatever."

But even before the young volunteers had to face down a redneck sheriff on a deserted back road, they had to overcome their own privileged upbringing and racism. Some of the differences between them and the people they were going to help erupted during the Ohio training sessions. SNCC staff showed a film of a fat, drawling Mississippi county registrar turning away would-be black voters, recalled white volunteer Robbie Osman, then a nineteen-year-old from New York City.

"Someone had tried to register and he was sending them back and being vaguely threatening," Osman says, "and it seemed to us, the young white college students, that this guy was as ridiculous, as pathetic, as caricature a racist as we ever expected to see. And we laughed. And to our complete surprise—I speak for myself, I really didn't expect it—this horrified the SNCC veterans. Folks stood up and said, 'How can we go to Mississippi with you? How can we put our lives on the line with you guys? You really don't have

a clue as to what's going on, do you? You really don't know what this guy represents in the context in which he really lives.' And I think it was a moment in which we all had to stop and realize the gap between us. If we were to reach across it, it was gonna take a lot of reaching."

Moses recalled that nearly all one thousand students who came to Mississippi that summer were white, many of them burdened with unresolved contradictions. Some of them hadn't even fully unpacked their bags when they were told that three civil rights workers were missing, including Andrew Goodman, a twenty-year-old Queens College student from New York City. He had come to Mississippi accompanied by Michael and Rita Schwerner, a white couple from Brooklyn, who had organized CORE's office in Meridian. Michael Schwerner and James Chaney, a twenty-one-year-old native Mississippian, were missing along with Goodman.

According to documents obtained from the Freedom of Information Act, the three men drove to Lawndale on Sunday, June 21, 1964, to investigate

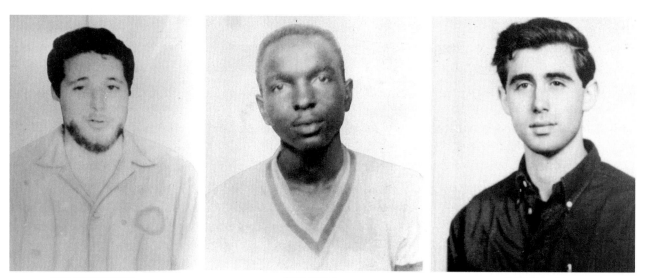

SCHWERNER   CHANEY   GOODMAN

The missing civil rights workers

The workers' burned station wagon, discovered in a remote swampy area

the burning of a church. Apparently some local people objected to their appearance there and noticed they were driving a blue Ford station wagon. Around three pm they were arrested for speeding by Sheriff Cecil Price near the town of Philadelphia, Mississippi, and later released. When the three men failed to call headquarters at the appointed time, their colleagues knew something was wrong.

Reports of the missing workers and volunteer occupied news accounts daily. Since the case now commanded national media attention, Rita Schwerner and other civil rights workers decided to take the matter straight to the White House, demanding an audience with President Lyndon Johnson. Bob Zellner and James Forman went with Rita Schwerner to see Johnson. "Mr. Johnson came in from one side of the room and came over and shook hands with everybody and said, 'I'm glad to meet you, Mrs. Schwerner,'" Zellner related. "And she said, 'I'm sorry, Mr. President, this is not a social call. We've come to talk about three missing people in Mississippi. We've come to talk about a search that we don't think is being done seriously. We've come to talk about what we think are the shortcomings in the federal government in terms of protecting civil rights workers in Mississippi.'"

Alarmed by the abrasive manner of Mrs. Schwerner's remarks, Johnson turned on his heels and left the room. The activists were berated by the president's press secretary, Pierre Salinger, who told them

Deputy sheriff Cecil Price helps unload the body of one of the murdered three

that he didn't think they should have addressed the president in such a manner. "We do," Schwerner said as they prepared to depart.

Shortly after their departure, Johnson amended his seemingly callous attitude and dispatched military personnel to aid the search. "President Johnson has ordered two hundred marines and eight helicopters to join the search for the missing civil rights workers," Mississippi Governor Paul Johnson said at a press conference. "Their presence here is indeed a surprise to me."

President Johnson would later add several hundred more soldiers to the hunt, despite Governor Johnson and Senator James O. Eastland's charges

that the entire incident was a "fraud" and a scheme deliberately concocted to give the movement notoriety with the report of more martyrs. **CD**

Moreover, on July 2, the president signed the Civil Rights Bill that had been initiated by Kennedy. It would mean very little to the men and women knee-deep in the search for the three missing men. Swamps were dragged, rivers dredged, and vast stretches of fields were combed for any evidence of the three. The FBI was soon involved in the intensive search, helping to scour the countryside in and around Philadelphia, Mississippi.

Meanwhile, Senator Eastland, chairman of the Judiciary Committee, vehemently questioned the likelihood the three missing men had been abducted. "Many people in our state assert that there is just as much evidence, as of today, that they are voluntarily missing as there is that they have been abducted," Eastland remonstrated to the press.

Six weeks later Eastland's impressions were proven as wrong as his social policies. On August 4, the bodies of Goodman, Schwerner, and Chaney were found buried together in an earthen dam. Coverage of the murders received national attention. "I personally suspect that if Mr. Chaney, who is a native Mississippian Negro, had been alone at the time of the disappearance, that this case like so many others that have come before, would have gone completely unnoticed," said Rita Schwerner, Michael Schwerner's wife. More than a dozen black Mississippians' bodies were found during the search for the three summer volunteers.

An FBI official reported, "from the time we got into the case following the finding of the burned car, and the fact that the victims were missing until the time that bodies were found on August 4, 1964, we, of course, conducted extensive interviews and during that time picked up additional situations involving alleged violations of Civil Rights Statue concerning victims other than the three murder victims." The FBI, at this stage of the investigation, determined that there was a conspiracy between Sheriff Price and his deputies to deprive "the colored population of their civil rights."

No one faced state murder charges for the murders, though the federal government later prosecuted fourteen men, including several Ku Klux Klan members, for violating the victims' civil rights. Seven defendants were convicted in 1967, with none serving more than six years in prison.

Chaney's brother, Ben Chaney, just a young boy when his brother was murdered, said he believes prosecutors have no intention of ever presenting the case to grand jurors. In earlier cases where civil rights

THE MISSISSIPPI FREEDOM DEMOCRATIC PARTY: THE BEGINNINGS

Several hundred delegates from precinct meetings and county conventions attended the first state convention of the Mississippi Freedom Democratic Party in April 1964. The total attendance was about a thousand, including alternates and observers.

A slate of sixty-eight delegates and alternates was elected to represent Mississippi at the national Democratic Convention. Hattiesburg housewife Victoria Gray was elected National Committeewoman, and Rev. Ed King, white chaplain of Mississippi's private, interracial Tougaloo College, was elected National Committeeman. Dr. Aaron Henry, Clarksdale pharmacist and president of the state NAACP, was named permanent chairman of Convention, and chairman of National Convention delegation. Fannie Lou Hamer, a candidate for Congress in Mississippi's Second District, was named vice-chairman of the delegation. Ella Baker delivered the keynote address at the convention. "Among resolutions adopted were statement of loyalty to National Democratic Party platform and candidates," reported Matthew Zwerling, a friend of the murdered Andrew Goodman.

prosecutions had been successful, prosecutors were pressured by strong, middle-class black communities, which don't exist in rural Neshoba County. "It's sort of like there's a noose hanging around the neck of Mississippi with a big ball and chain," said Chaney, a paralegal who now heads the James Earl Chaney Foundation, a New York civil rights group. "Until this case is vigorously prosecuted, I think the ball and chain will continue to pull the neck of the state down, hold Mississippi back."

The deaths of Chaney, Goodman, and Schwerner were not the only violence lurking in the Mississippi night and countryside. Numerous black churches were torched. Volunteers were shot at by Klansmen. Yet these determined young people were undaunted and continued to venture into peril to get black residents to register to vote as part of their mission to forge a new Mississippi Freedom Democratic Party (MFDP).

The tireless volunteers also dedicated themselves to creating Freedom Schools, unwilling to allow the threats of "night riders" to deter them from their goals. A white New Yorker, Sandra Adickes, who had been recruited by SNCC organizer Ivanhoe Donaldson to teach in one of the Freedom Schools, recalled her experience in the schools during the time of the missing workers. "We knew immediately that they were dead. And someone, I remember one of the presenters, one of the leaders of that training session had worked with Mickey Schwerner and was just devastated by the news…And I think, you know, we were all concerned, but I don't think anybody…nobody left as a result of that. Nobody said, 'Oh, I'm going home. I want to get out of here.' Nobody left."

Not only did the volunteers refuse to leave, they rededicated themselves to the struggle against the menace of the Klansmen, firm in their beliefs that they could defeat the segregationists and change the racist climate of the state. They were courageous idealists who joined forces with the NAACP Legal Defense Fund, the National Lawyers Guild, and the

Price is escorted to his arraignment for violating the civil rights of Freedom Summer workers

President Lyndon B. Johnson at the signing of the Civil Rights Act of 1964

American Jewish Committee to defend the civil and human rights of black citizens from one backwater town in Mississippi to another.

They were so successful in their labors to register voters that by end of August more than 80,000 African Americans were members of the MFDP. Even a few whites applied for membership. "Segregationists in Mississippi watched the mostly upper-middle-class white volunteers with disdain," author and journalist Juan Williams wrote, noting that the White Citizens' Council viewed them with both curiosity and intense resentment.

Not everybody was happy with the presence of this army of white volunteers, as James Forman noted in his memoir. The Summer Project and its interracial element, as he saw it, had "weakened the organization (SNCC)," and just at a time when SNCC was grappling with whether it was going to struggle for reform or revolution, for violence or nonviolence. The internal conflict had become increasingly difficult to suppress, and the factionalism "split the circle of trust asunder."

"We had acquired enormous power there [in Mississippi]," Forman wrote, "a power that called for expansion, a power that could have been greatly increased." He was fearful that powerful forces were circling the organization waiting for an opportunity to intrude and manipulate the movement to its own designs. "If we did not expand our power base there, all kinds of vultures would be waiting to descend on the vacuum thus created—from the NAACP through the unions up to the Democratic Party and the anti-poverty program vultures. And there were many signs that SNCC was going to let that base evaporate."

Even so, there was much to commend Freedom Summer, particularly the impact it had on mobilizing thousands of black Mississippians. Their brave, indefatigable efforts in support of voting rights received national attention, and the accomplishment of the Freedom Schools bolstered the flagging educational initiatives following *Brown v. Board of Education*, now a full decade before. Yet despite all these achievements, one of the main initiatives of Freedom Summer—the Mississippi Freedom Democratic Party—failed to realize its dream.

18

Fannie Lou Hamer and the MFDP

"This little light of mine, I'm gonna let it shine, let it shine, let it shine, let it shine."

In the summer of 1962, as the voter registration campaign gained momentum, the Student Nonviolent Coordinating Committee (SNCC) opened a beachhead in Mississippi's Sunflower County, the home of arch-segregationist U.S. Senator James O. Eastland. On a sultry hot day in Indianola, the county seat, SNCC leader James Forman led a group of canvassers in their quest to get residents to sign a petition stating that if they had been able to vote in the primary that June they would have voted for a black candidate. Not many were willing to sign the petition, and Forman and his frustrated crew prepared to leave town. The scheduled meeting was canceled and they were headed to another sector of the county when they were confronted by the sheriff. They were informed in brusque language that he didn't want "no outside agitators coming into Indianola messing with my negras."

"Before we left the Delta," Forman recalled, "we attended the first meeting in Ruleville, a small town in Sunflower County, where we met Mrs. Fannie Lou Hamer for the first time." Hamer, age forty-five, a short, stout timekeeper and sharecropper who had been picking cotton since she was six years old, was curious about the young people and their audacity. So, when she heard they were going to hold a meeting that evening, she made up her mind to go, the first she had ever attended.

"When they asked for those to raise their hands who'd go down to the courthouse the next day, I raised mine," she later recounted. "Had it up high as I could get it. I guess if I'd had any sense I'd a-been a little scared, but what was the point of being scared. The only thing they could do to me was kill me and it seemed like they'd been trying to do that a little bit at a time ever since I could remember."

The deeply religious but poorly educated Hamer, who could cite chapter and verse from the Bible, didn't have to think long about her actions and whether she was doing the right thing, though she did recall that for many years "the right thing" was the "white thing." "At first I wanted to be white because in my family there was twenty of us—six girls and fourteen boys. We would gather fifty to sixty bales of cotton…gather all that cotton and we wouldn't have food in the wintertime," she said. "I figured then that the white people must be right, but as I got older I said no, there's something wrong,

and if I ever get a chance I'm going to do something about it. But things got worse and worse. The Student Nonviolent Coordinating Committee helped to build confidence in people just as they were about to lose all hope—and that's the truth."

Buoyed by this newfound confidence, Hamer boldly headed for the registrar's office in Indianola the next day, August 31, 1962. "When we got there—there was eighteen of us went that day…there were people there with guns and just a lot of strange-looking people to us," she said. "We went on in the circuit clerk's office, and he asked us what did we want; and we told him what we wanted. We wanted to try to register. He told us that all of us would have to get out of there except two. So I was one of the two persons that remained inside, to try to

Fannie Lou Hamer speaks to MFDP sympathizers

register, [with] another young man named Mr. Ernest Davis. We stayed in to take the literacy test. So the registrar gave me the sixteenth section of the Constitution of Mississippi. He pointed it out in the book and told me to look at it and then copy it down just like I saw it in the book: put a period where a period was supposed to be, a comma and all of that. After I copied it down he told me right below that to give a real reasonable interpretation then, interpret what I had read. That was impossible. I had tried to give it, but I didn't even know what it meant, much less to interpret it."

Hamer wasn't alone in failing the test. Some of the best-educated blacks in the county were told they had failed. Even so, the whites in the county, literate or illiterate, almost without exception passed the test and were registered voters. **CD**

When the group started back to Ruleville, they were stopped by a state highway patrolman and the city police and ordered to get off of the bus. They obeyed. They were then told to get back on the bus and go back to Indianola. Once more they dutifully obeyed. Back in Indianola, one of the SNCC workers with them, Lawrence Guyot, was arrested. SNCC veteran Charlie Cobb, who was also among those who were on the bus, explained, "I kind of remember this driver being arrested for, you know, like something really totally off—like driving a school bus without a license. And Mrs. Hamer, somewhere around this point was on the bus and as the bus was really getting tense, starts to sing. And all of a sudden you kind of look and she has this remarkable voice—it's like coming at you out of nowhere. And it's Mrs. Hamer singing something like 'This Little Light of Mine.'"

By taking the test Hamer had defied the owner of the plantation where she worked. When he heard what she had done, he visited her home that evening and asked her if she had tried to register to vote. "I told him that I did it for myself not for him," Hamer said. "He told me to get off the plantation and don't

be seen near it again. That night I left the plantation and went to stay with Mr. and Mrs. Tucker in Ruleville."

Hamer's husband wasn't with her because he had to stay on at the plantation and work long enough to earn the money necessary to get their possessions from the owner. Amidst potential danger, he came for her soon. Shortly after she left, the Tucker's house was riddled with bullets by night riders. Hamer and her husband then moved on to Tallahatchie County for a brief stay before returning to Ruleville. On December 4, Hamer ventured down to the registrar's office to take the literacy test again. This time she was given a different section of the Constitution to copy and interpret. But because she had been prepared for the test by SNCC workers, she passed it, as she learned that January. Still, she had to hurdle another obstacle. Since she didn't have receipts from two consecutive poll taxes, she was not eligible to vote. It would be nearly two years before she would able to exercise the franchise, and that vote would be cast for herself.

Before that momentous day when she would be able to vote, there were months of work registering others. It was no easy task and fraught with danger. "Well," Hamer said, "it was rough because we would go to places, go in to do voter registration in places, and we talked to people. We would walk the streets in different little areas, and we would tell them we were coming back the next day. And by the next day somebody would be done got to them, and they wouldn't want to talk with us, and this kind of stuff. Some days it would be disgusting, some very disappointing. Some very disappointing. Then we'd go to churches…they was burning up churches. These are the kinds of things we faced."

Despite the violence and turmoil that raged throughout 1963 in Mississippi, and particularly in the Delta, Hamer and her young compatriots were fearless in their campaign to register new voters and create a new political party. In June of that year,

DISC 2
TRACK 4

after attending workshops on how to pass the voter registration and literacy tests, she and her colleagues were traveling home on a Continental Trailways bus to Greenwood from South Carolina. They got off the bus to get something to eat at a bus terminal in Winona, Mississippi. They were soon greeted by police who treated them roughly, then charged them with disorderly conduct and shepherded them off to jail.

The two officers who escorted Hamer to jail cursed her before throwing her into a cell with Euvester Simpson. From her cell Hamer said she could hear horrible screams coming from other parts of the jail. Another member of the group, hustled along by white officers, passed Hamer's cell with a bloody eye, her hair standing up on her head and her clothes practically torn off.

Three of the officers soon approached Hamer's cell. After verifying that she was from Ruleville, as she had told them, they told her that they were going to make her wish she was dead. "They led me out of this cell to another cell," Hamer remembered, "and they gave a Negro prisoner a blackjack and they ordered me lay down on the bunk bed. The Negro prisoner asked them 'Do you want me to beat them with this, sir?' and one of them said 'You damn right, 'cause if you don't, you know what I'll do for you.' So, I laid down on the bunk like he ordered me to do. The Negro beat me until he was exhausted…then the second Negro was given the blackjack…and while the first Negro sat on my feet, the other one beat me. Then the white man started to beat me in the head. I have a blood clot now—in my left eye—and a permanent kidney injury on the right side from that beating. These are the things we go through in the state of Mississippi."

Euvester Simpson, then a teenager, shared a cell with Hamer, and witnessed the brutal attack. "I sat up all night with her applying cold towels and things to her face and hands trying to get her fever

down and to help some of the pain go away. And the only thing that got us through that was that we sang. We sang all night. I mean songs got us through so many things, and without that music I think many of us would have just lost our minds or lost our way completely."

When the Justice Department heard about what had happened to Hamer and her companions, they brought a lawsuit against the five officers involved in the assault. A trial was conducted in Oxford, Mississippi. The prosecution had an airtight case, replete with photos of the victims. Moreover, there were a number of witnesses—a waitress, a bus driver, and others—who testified for the plaintiffs. Even the two men who had beaten Hamer came forward and told the truth. "They told how the white men had them drink corn whiskey before they beat us because they figured that if they didn't have something in them they might do it," Hamer recalled. "They told all that and nothing has been done." The whites who were charged were found not guilty.

If the police believed the beatings would stop Hamer and others, they were wrong. Hamer became all the more determined in her struggle for civil and human rights. By the spring of 1964, she was among the original members of the Mississippi Freedom Democratic Party, forged as an alternative to the main, white-led party that was widely known as "Dixiecrats."

"The way I got involved in the Freedom Democratic Party," Hamer said, "is that we tried to get in the regular Democratic Party. We tried from the precinct level up to the county to the state. I remember when we tried to attend the precinct meeting at the little polling place in Ruleville. Eight of us…went up there and we couldn't get in. We stood on the outside and held our own meeting.…We elected our chairman and secretary, our delegation and alternates, and we passed the law into resolution."

On April 24, in Jackson at the Masonic Temple, the Mississippi Freedom Democratic Party held its inaugural rally. The party was formally launched. In August, sixty-eight delegates were elected to travel to Atlantic City where the Democratic Party was holding its National Convention. Hamer led the assembly in singing "Go Tell It on the Mountain." "Ella Baker gave the keynote address," Bob Moses remembered. "Part of what we wanted to do was challenge the national Democratic Party to recognize us as its legitimate arm in the state and Miss Baker spoke directly to the way the Democrats and the entire nation contributed to the sustenance of white supremacy in Mississippi."

Lawrence Guyot, chairman of the MFDP, which by now had thousands of members, including several whites, recounted how the party had been built along the guidelines established by the national Democratic Party. "We paralleled the state organization of Mississippi where we could, where it was possible to do so and remain alive," Guyot said. "We had our registration form, we conducted precinct meetings, we conducted convention meetings, we conducted county meetings, and congressional district meetings, we elected a delegation. We then put that delegation on the way to Atlantic City."

Moses, Baker, Guyot, Hamer, and the MFDP delegates had been assured by Joseph Rauh, counsel for the United Automobile Workers, that if the regular Mississippi delegation was challenged, they would be unseated. None of the black Mississippians believed this promise would be fulfilled.

Aaron Henry

Empty seats at the Democratic National Convention after whites and African Americans failed to compromise

DISC 2
TRACK 5

But running on hope and faith was nothing unusual for the SNCC workers, who by now had been joined by a complement of activists from Howard University under the banner of NAG (Nonviolent Action Group), with Stokely Carmichael as its leader. Most of the delegates and supporters en route to Atlantic City were already "wore out," as Hamer put it, from working on the voter registration campaign and building the party.

"All of us were physically exhausted from the sheer burden of the organizing work," Carmichael related. "Many more of us than we knew then were totally burned out. Emotionally scarred, spiritually drained from the constant tension, the moments of anger, grief, or fear in a pervading atmosphere of hostility and impending violence."

When the weary band of travelers—with their sixty-four black and four white delegates—arrived in a caravan of buses at the national convention in Atlantic City, New Jersey, they were still in shock from the news of the discovery of the bodies of civil rights workers Andrew Goodman, Michael Schwerner and James Chaney in August 1964. But there was no time to mourn. They had work to do as the Democratic Party prepared to nominate President Lyndon Johnson. Many of the delegates from around the nation had been alerted that there might be conflict with two separate groups vying to represent Mississippi.

The leaders at the convention quickly gathered to see what could be done to keep the peace and unity, and to avoid any divisive rancor. Hamer and the other delegates wasted no time stating their intention of being seated in place of the all-white delegates from the regular state party. Testifying before the credentials committee, the Freedom Democrats argued theirs was the only legitimate delegation from Mississippi. And among these elected delegates on that warm day in August, Hamer's voice rang with passion and conviction. 🆑

"Mr. Chairman, and the Credentials Committee, my name is Mrs. Fannie Lou Hamer, and I live at 626 East Lafayette Street, Ruleville, Mississippi, Sunflower County, the home of Senator James O. Eastland, and Senator [John C.] Stennis," she began. For the next several minutes, the credentials committee was riveted as Hamer told how she became involved in the civil rights movement, the violence she had seen and endured, including the beating she received in Winona. At the end of her speech, she invoked the nation's creed and its professed freedom and liberty. "If the Freedom Democratic Party is not seated now, I question America. Is this America, the land of the free and the home of the brave, where we have to sleep with our telephones off the hook because our lives be threatened daily, because we want to live as decent human beings in America?"

"The clincher was her retelling of her beating in the Winona jail," said Leslie Maclemore, then a young Freedom Democrat delegate from northern Mississippi. "She told it in such a way [that] if you could have stopped the reel right then and there and said, 'Let's take a vote up or down on these Freedom Democrats,' without the intervention by the hardened political pros, Fannie Lou Hamer would have won the day."

Her testimony, televised nationally, proved so compelling that President Johnson immediately requested time from the network to interrupt it with a hastily called press conference "about nothing in particular," Bob Moses recalled. Like her voice in song, her words came from the depths of her soul and the pain she evoked was palpable.

Even the most callous among the white delegates who witnessed Hamer's speech confessed to its power. "But the word had been given," SNCC veteran Charles Sherrod wrote later. "The Freedom Party was to be seated without voting rights as honored guests of the Convention. The Party caucused and rejected the proposed 'compromise.' The slow and now frantic machinery of the administration was grinding against itself. President Johnson had given Senator [Hubert] Humphrey the specific task of dealing with us. They were desperately seeking ways to seat the regular Mississippi delegation without any show of disunity. The administration needed time!" Of paramount importance to Johnson was southern support, which he vitally needed if he was going to defeat Republican Barry Goldwater.

While the administration ruminated, the Freedom Democrats conferred and discussed the issue among themselves, trying to find a way to deal with the compromise. Dr. Martin Luther King, Bayard Rustin, James Farmer, James Forman, Ella Baker, and Bob Moses were among those who voiced their concern about the issue. Some of these leaders, along with Hamer and two other Mississippi Freedom delegates, Aaron Henry and Ed King, met with Humphrey in his suite at the Pageant Hotel to see what could be done. With Humphrey leading the discussion, the Democrats offered the Freedom delegates two symbolic seats. "We rejected it right there in front of Humphrey and [Walter] Reuther," Moses said. There was no way they could accept such offer without the approval of the MFDP. Even so, after debating the issue at a simultaneous, separate meeting of the credentials committee, Walter Mondale, Humphrey's chief aide, went on television and announced that the compromise had been accepted. "I stomped out of the room," Moses said, "slamming the door in Hubert Humphrey's face...I was furious."

Hamer was equally upset about the developments. Her good friend Unita Blackwell recalled her outrage. "Well, we ain't gonna take no two seats," Hamer had declared. "All of us sixty-eight can't sit in no two seats." 🔘

Disc 2
Track 5

It was devastating blow to the sharecroppers, farmers, mechanics, merchants, housewives, and other common folks who comprised the Freedom delegates. Still, they were not finished. On the following night, Hamer, who said she was "sick and tired of being sick and tired," led a contingent of MFDP delegates to the convention floor where with borrowed badges and passes they took the seats set aside for the regular Mississippi delegates. A squad of security men soon arrived and forcibly removed them.

When the Convention ended, there were mixed feelings among the Freedom delegates. Some viewed the experience as just another exercise in futility in the combat against American discrimination and racism, while a few others saw it as a symbolic victory of sorts and a significant step in the march toward freedom. Dr. King felt that the compromise would have been a step in the right direction, and he would have advised them to take it had he been in the delegation. "But life in Mississippi had involved too many compromises already," he said "and too many promises had come from Washington for them to take these seriously."

Dr. King praised the dedication of Fannie Lou Hamer and Aaron Henry, who in Hamer's opinion had tried to convince the other delegates to accept the offer.

"In the end they just didn't have the guts to do it," said former SNCC staff member and MFDP organizer Frank Smith. Democratic Party leaders "agreed with us, they all knew it was wrong, they all knew it violated the Constitution, they all knew it

had to be done sooner or later. They all knew all of the right things. They just couldn't do it at the time. It disillusioned us a great deal. I think it disillusioned, actually, the civil rights movement quite considerably."

Bob Moses lamented the setback, but he relished the bold move by the poor and downtrodden people of Mississippi to assert themselves on a national stage. "When the MFDP challenged the seating of the 'regular' Mississippi Democrats at the 1964…our efforts reached a national audience," he declared. "However, the national Democratic Party and the institutions surrounding it in government, church, and politics rejected any extension of power into the hands of the black and poor. They were not prepared to risk status quo arrangements. But though the MFDP did not

Civil rights demonstrators picket the convention

succeed, the issue of empowerment of the poor for meaningful citizenship has not vanished."

The event also focused the spotlight on a courageous sharecropper from Mississippi, who with her magnificent voice and unflagging devotion to civil rights and justice provided an everlasting model for those gallant freedom fighters who came after her. When they marched in Selma, Alabama, a year later, Fannie Lou Hamer's voice inspired them, and her song lifted them when they stumbled and fell under the vicious assault from law enforcement officers who had no respect for them or their human rights. Hamer was best known for singing "This Little Light of Mine," but she had sizable repertoire of spirituals that were just as inspirational. One of her most moving spirituals contains the words, "I want Jesus to walk with me." In Selma, civil rights marchers would need all the company they could get.

19

Selma, Alabama

I n the summer of 1964, a few weeks before the Freedom Democrats from Mississippi began their journey to Atlantic City for the Democratic National Convention, President Lyndon B. Johnson signed the Civil Rights Bill. "Our generation of Americans has been called on to continue the unending search for justice within our own borders," Johnson told the nation, "We believe that all men are created equal, yet many are denied equal treatment....We believe that all men have certain unalienable rights, yet many Americans do not enjoy those rights. We believe that all men are entitled to the blessings of liberty, yet millions are being deprived of those blessings. Not because of their own failures, but because of the color of their skin....We know how it happened, but it cannot continue." **CD**

The newly elected delegates, formed to challenge the regular delegates from Mississippi, viewed the signing as a good omen. Perhaps the president would supply the pressure they needed to gain recognition at the convention. While their dreams were eventually shattered, there was still hope that the bill would have impact elsewhere, particularly in places like Selma, Alabama, where very few of the city's fifteen thousand blacks of voting age were registered.

Thus Selma, according to the Student Nonviolent Coordinating Committee (SNCC), was a perfect place to see if blacks would be allowed to register and vote without intimidation. It was not exactly a new venue for the young civil rights activists. A small cadre of them had been there for several months trying to convince the reluctant residents to register. The resistance they encountered was based on fear and intimidation from white segregationists who had stifled the majority of blacks there and elsewhere in the South. Registering and voting, the blacks told the

Annie Lee Cooper and police

SNCC workers, were things only white folks did. "We ain't got no business meddling in white folks' business," was a common response from black citizens of Selma.

The blacks who were not fazed by the threats of the White Citizens' Council, the John Birch Society, and the Ku Klux Klan had to take a literacy test that was sure to stop them in their tracks. Governor George Wallace had poured thousands of dollars into the Alabama Sovereignty Commission and its agents, who were assigned the task of applying pressure on registrars around the state, making sure they were properly informed on ways to impede blacks from registering to vote. Their tactics were mainly responsible for thwarting the SNCC workers in their campaign. By the time Dr. Martin Luther King had returned from Oslo, Norway, where he received the

Nobel Peace Prize, the SNCC volunteers were on the verge of halting their initiative in Selma. Their spirits would have been renewed had they heard King's Nobel acceptance speech that touched on the virtues and beliefs he held dear:

"I have the audacity to believe that people everywhere can have three meals a day for their bodies, education and culture for their minds, and dignity, equality, and freedom for their spirit….I still believe we shall overcome."

When Dr. King returned to Atlanta he was visited by a contingent of black citizens from Selma who requested that he come to their city and help them in their struggle for equal rights. It was the opening King and the Southern Christian Leadership Conference (SCLC) had been looking for; he made plans to arrive in the city later that winter. As promised, he came on January 2, 1965, and spoke at Brown's Chapel African Methodist Episcopal Church. More than seven hundred people enthusiastically cheered King's speech. Vowing that blacks would elect those who fought for justice rather than those who impeded it, King demanded, "Give us the ballot!"

King's arrival in Selma was a source of consternation for both SNCC and Mayor Joseph Smitherman and his law enforcement officers, particularly Wilson Baker, the newly appointed public safety director, and big, burly Sheriff Jim Clark.

Smitherman had to make sure his sheriff and his minions didn't go too far in their efforts to contain the minister. Selma was in the national spotlight now, of which the mayor was very much aware, so he felt compelled to keep violence to a minimum, if at all. Meanwhile, in Washington, measures were underway to outlaw the use of literacy tests in voter registration. The Civil Rights Division of the Justice Department had also begun to prepare a lawsuit against the state of Alabama, charging that their test was an obstruction to the civil rights of blacks who sought to register to vote. The city would soon find itself squeezed in a vice of marching protesters and a legal attack from the nation's capital.

There were several demonstrations in January after Dr. King's visit and some arrests were made. More importantly, Baker and Sheriff Clark were unable to keep their composure and maintain their nonviolent approach to the protesters. On at least a couple of occasions they resorted to manhandling women, and both incidents were captured by the media covering the events. One encounter was between Sheriff Clark and a large, fifty-three-year-old woman named Annie Lee Cooper.

"We were as usual, lined up on the courthouse steps—the local men and women waiting to register and people like me and Hosea [Williams] and other SNCC and SCLC people who were there to support and make sure these marchers had all that they needed," John Lewis wrote in his autobiography. "As Clark's men moved in and began pushing people aside, Mrs. Cooper—all 235 pounds of her—confronted him. 'Ain't nobody scared around here,' she said. Clark wasn't one to stand for backtalk, especially from a woman. He shoved Mrs. Cooper, hard. But not hard enough. She came right back and punched the sheriff in the head, sending him reeling.

"Three deputies then grabbed Mrs. Cooper and wrestled her to the ground, where she kept flailing and kicking even as they held her down," Lewis continued. "Clark looked out of his mind with anger. He had his billy club out and looked as if he was about to hit her with it. Then he hesitated. You could see his mind clicking in, the realization that everyone was watching. Us. The reporters. The photographers. Everyone. What happened next was described in the following day's New York Times by reporter John Herbers: 'I wish you would hit me, you scum,' she snapped at the sheriff. He then brought his billy club down on her head with a whack that was heard throughout the crowd gathered in the street.' It took two pairs of handcuffs to hold Mrs. Cooper as she was taken away to jail, blood dripping from a wound over her right eye. Photos of that, too, appeared across the country the next day."

The vicious assault on Cooper gave the movement in Selma the notoriety it sought. On Monday, February 1, 1965, King was back in town and ready to deliver the second punch that could bring the situation to the living rooms of America. Accompanied by 250 protesters, King marched from the church to the courthouse. Commissioner Baker warned them that they were violating a parade ordinance before arresting King and several other demonstrators.

"When the king of Norway participated in awarding the Nobel Prize to me he surely did not think that in less than sixty days I would be in jail," King wrote in his autobiography. "They were little aware of the unfinished business in the South. By jailing hundreds of Negroes, the city of Selma...had revealed the persisting ugliness of segregation to the nation and the world."

When five hundred children were arrested during a march protesting King's arrest, they, too, were jailed. Then on successive days, hundreds more were arrested. The jails were packed. Unlike his letter from the Birmingham jail, King had written a memo for Selma before his arrest, and it spelled out in detail specific assignments for individuals. Bernard Lafayette, Joe Lowery, Walter Fauntroy, and other colleagues of were told exactly what to do and whom to contact. Moreover, King wrote that President Johnson was to be called, demanding that a Congressional committee come to Selma and study the turmoil.

King said nothing about inviting Malcolm X to the fray, which was done by members of SNCC. This was not the first time SNCC had been associated with Malcolm. Earlier, on December 20, 1964, he had participated in a rally in Harlem organized by the MFDP and shared the dais with Fannie Lou Hamer. Though Malcolm chided those advocates who sat around singing "We Shall Overcome," he invited Hamer to join him that evening at the Audubon and deliver the same speech she had given at the rally. Eleven days later, thirty-seven members of a youth delegation from McComb, Mississippi, sponsored by SNCC, came to New York City for their Christmas vacation. Toward the end of their stay they visited the Theresa Hotel and heard Malcolm tell them, "I myself would go for nonviolence if it was consistent...and if everybody was going to be nonviolent. I don't go along with any kind of nonviolence unless everybody is going to be nonviolent. If they make the Ku Klux Klan nonviolent, I'll be nonviolent....I want you to know that we're not in anyway trying to advocate any of kind of indiscriminate, unintelligent action. Any kind of action that you are ever involved in that's designed to protect the lives and property of our mistreated people in this country, we're with you one thousand percent."

As everyone knew, Malcolm was not a proponent of nonviolence, so his appearance in Selma at this critical phase caused a certain amount of apprehension from various sectors of the community. On February 4, seventeen days before he was assassinated in New York City at the Audubon Ballroom, Malcolm spoke at Brown's Chapel. "I'm 100 percent for the effort being put forth by the black folks here," the Muslim minister told the largely Christian gathering. "I believe they have an absolute right to use whatever means are necessary to gain the vote. But I don't believe in nonviolence—no. I don't think anyone expects a sheep to go into the den of the wolf and love the wolf, because the sheep would end up in the stomach of the wolf." Malcolm spoke for more than an hour, telling the crowd that the white people should "thank Dr. King for holding people in check" and suggesting they were lucky since they didn't have to deal with a more radical alternative.

Coretta Scott King was then ushered to the pulpit, partly to muffle the uproar Malcolm had stirred and to reassert the philosophy of nonviolence. "I was impressed by his obvious intelligence," Mrs. King said of Malcolm, "and he seemed quite gentle as he said to me, 'Mrs. King, will you tell Dr. King that I had planned to visit with him in jail? I won't get a chance now because I've got to leave to get to New York in time to catch a plane for London, where I'm to address the African Students' conference. I want Dr. King to know that I didn't come to Selma to make his job difficult. I really did come thinking that I could make it easier. If the white people realize what the alternative is, perhaps they will be more willing to hear Dr. King.'"

No one can say for certain what impact Malcolm's appearance had on the struggle in Selma, but many pondered President Johnson's timing when he called a press conference the day of Malcolm's speech to announce his indignation toward anyone

C. T. Vivian leads a prayer on the Selma courthouse steps

who denied another's right to vote. "I intend to see that that right is secured for all our citizens." On February 5, Dr. King was released from jail. Four days later he was meeting with Vice President Humphrey, where he made it clear that all citizens should have the freedom to exercise their right and responsibility to vote.

While King deliberated with officials in Washington, Sheriff Clark and his deputies grew even more violent in their reaction to demonstrators. There were two savage attacks by deputies on two children, both of whom were severely clubbed by deputies. John Lewis witnessed the incidents and recorded it among his notes: "Sheriff Jim Clark proved today beyond a shadow of a doubt that he is basically no different from a Gestapo officer during the fascist slaughter of Jews. This is but one more example of the inhuman, animal-like treatment of the Negro people in Selma....This nation has always come to the aid of people in foreign

lands who are gripped by a reign of tyranny. Can this nation do less for the people of Selma?"

On February 16, Sheriff Clark demonstrated that his menace was not limited to women and children. Reverend C. T. Vivian, one of the more outspoken leaders of the SCLC, bravely faced off against Clark in front of the courthouse. He referred to the sheriff as Hitler and dared Clark to hit him. Clark took the bait and slammed a big fist into Vivian's jaw, knocking him down the steps. According to Lewis, he hit Vivian so hard that he broke one of his fingers. Vivian was arrested and it precipitated an outcry in the community. Two days later, on the same day Vivian was released from jail, marchers assembled to protest the arrest of James Orange, an SCLC member. Vivian spoke at the rally, and the demonstrators soon marched off to the jail where Orange was being held. The march was at night, which was a rarity for civil rights activists.

The marchers left a tiny church and proceeded toward the jail. "Suddenly the street lights went out," Lewis recalled. "As if on cue, the police and troopers began beating the marchers while a crowd of white onlookers leaped on the press, spraying the TV camera lenses with paint and assaulting the reporters…It was mayhem."

Caught in the middle of the chaos was Army veteran Jimmie Lee Jackson. Stories vary as to why Jackson came into altercation with police. Some reports say he was trying to get his grandfather to the hospital, others say he was fighting back to protect his mother, but the end result was the same—a shot rang out and Jackson crumbled to the pavement. He lay in the streets for more than an half hour before the police finally picked him up and took him to the hospital. Jackson was still clinging to life on February 21 when the nation was shocked by the assassination of Malcolm X. Five days later Jackson died.

During Jackson's funeral procession, Reverend James Bevel suggested that the body be taken to

"MALCOLM," BY SONIA SANCHEZ

Do not speak to me of martyrdom
of men who die to be remembered
on some parish day.
I don't believe in dying
though I too shall die
and violets like castanets
will echo me.

Yet this man
this dreamer,
thick-lipped with words
will never speak again
and in each winter
when the cold air cracks
with frost, I'll breathe
his breath and mourn
my gun-filled nights.

He was the sun that tagged
the western sky and
melted tiger-scholars
while they searched for stripes.
He said, "Fuck you white
man. we have been
curled too long. nothing
is sacred now. not your
white face nor any
land that separates
until some voices
squat with spasms."

Do not speak to me of living.
life is obscene with crowds
of white on black.
death is my pulse.
what might have been
is not for him/or me
but what could have been
floods the womb until I drown.

State troopers use tear gas to break up a demonstration

Montgomery, and that hundreds of people should walk the entire fifty-four miles from Selma and deliver the body on the state capitol steps. Jackson was buried that day, but Bevel's idea, like so many he had during the civil rights movement, did not fade away. Soon, members of SCLC, including Dr. King, began discussing the idea of a march from Selma almost directly east to Montgomery. If the march was to occur it would happen without the involvement of SNCC. Although Chairman Lewis favored the march, he was overruled by the others, who believed the march did not "justify the dangers." In a letter to King, SNCC promised only to provide "radios and cars, doctors and nurses" to the march.

Lewis made it abundantly clear that the letter was from SNCC and not from him. Later, after a heated meeting with other SNCC members in Atlanta, he made his mind up to participate because, as he said, "I'm a native Alabamian…I grew up in Alabama. I feel a deep kinship with the people there on a lot of levels…I'm going to march." The decision, he said, that would alter the course of his life.

Sunday, March 7 was selected as the day of the march. There was a beehive of activity at Brown's Chapel that morning. But on the chosen day, Dr. King was not at the chapel where more than five hundred people had gathered to march. He had decided to post-pone his participation in the march because of previous commitments at his church in Atlanta. Later, it was disclosed that he had received several death threats to be carried out if he proceeded. He would miss the day that would come to be known as "Bloody Sunday."

Andrew Young, Hosea Williams, and James Bevel were among the leaders assembled at the church. After talking to King, they informed those gathered that the march was going to take place and that Williams, by a flip of a coin, would be up front as one of the leaders. When the marchers left the church, walking two abreast, Williams and Lewis were at the front. "I can't count the number of marches I have participated in in my lifetime," Lewis said, "but there was something peculiar about this one. It was more than disciplined. It was somber and subdued, almost like a funeral procession."

The marchers tromped down unpaved Sylvan Street, where small knots of well-wishers had gathered in this black section of town. They snaked along Water Street; there was no singing, just the sound of scuffling feet. Then they walked along the river until they reached the base of the Pettus Bridge that spanned the Alabama River. A long line of white men in hard hats were staring at them with clubs in their hands. As they turned onto the bridge, they were mindful to stay on the narrow walkway. The road had been closed to traffic. When they reached the crest of the bridge, Williams and Lewis came to a halt. Before them, at the bottom of the other side, stood a phalanx of blue-helmeted, blue-uniformed Alabama state troopers, waves of them. Sheriff Clark and his posse backed them up. Beyond them, a crowd of white people waved Confederate flags. Williams and Lewis looked at the landscape of people and then at each other. They were about one hundred feet above the water.

"Can you swim?" Williams asked.

"No," Lewis replied.

"Neither can I," Williams said, "but we might have to."

In a moment or two, the march resumed. They watched as several troopers began slipping on gas masks. As they reached the bottom of the bridge, Major John Cloud, the officer in charge, approached them and bellowed, "this is an unlawful assembly…you are ordered to disperse and go back to your church or to your homes." They were given two minutes to turn around and disband. Williams and Lewis decided that there were too many of them to turn around, but to go forward would be to march into a juggernaut of defiant officers. Only one option existed: kneel and pray. A few had reached their knees when the troopers advanced on them. Then, as Lewis remembered, "all hell broke loose."

"Get 'em! Get the niggers!" screamed the troopers as they swarmed into the mass of marchers, who were trampling each other to avoid the bludgeoning. Lewis was clubbed on the left side of his head and blood began streaming onto his clothes and white trench coat.

He curled into a fetal, or "prayer," position to ward off the blows, but he could not protect his head. The violent mayhem raged around him and then came the tear gas. "I began choking, coughing," he said. "I couldn't get air into my lungs. I felt as if I was taking my last breath. If there ever was a time in my life for me to panic, it should have been then. But I didn't. I remember how strangely calm I felt as I thought, This is it. People are going to die here. I'm going to die here."

Beaten to the ground and soaked in his own blood, Lewis was barely conscious as marchers scampered helter skelter to flee the vicious attack. Even those who had escaped the immediate zone of

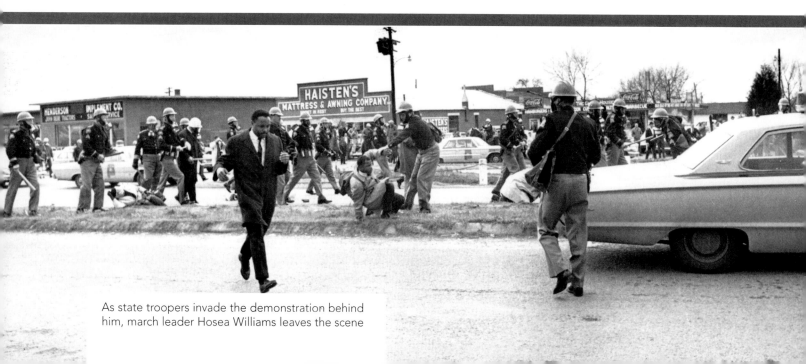

As state troopers invade the demonstration behind him, march leader Hosea Williams leaves the scene

terror were not free from the troopers and Sheriff Clark's deputies. Some were pursued as far as a mile from the epicenter of the melee, still running from the brutal officers. When the tear gas cleared and the troopers tired, seventeen battered and bruised men and women were carted off to Good Samaritan Hospital while others were treated for less serious injuries.

Lewis suffered contusions and a fractured skull, though at the time he was unaware of the severity of his injuries. He was present that evening at a mass meeting where Williams delivered the main speech. With his head still throbbing and his hair matted with blood, Lewis railed against the Johnson administration, intoning, "I don't know how President Johnson can send troops to Vietnam…don't see how he can send troops to the Congo…don't see how he can send troops to Africa, and he can't send troops to Selma, Alabama."

President Johnson didn't deploy any troops, but a veritable army of ministers arrived from all over the country, including Dr. King, who was a bit unnerved about rumors of his cowardice for missing the march and the subsequent melee. On Tuesday, March 9, King and the local leadership of Selma were issued an order by Federal Judge Frank M. Johnson not to march. King was once more faced with a difficult decision. After consulting with his lawyers and advisors he felt it was imperative that he seek a confrontation with Sheriff Clark and his deputies at the foot of the Edmund Pettus Bridge. 🄲🄳

The march, King believed, had to proceed. More than two thousand people assembled for the second march that Tuesday, and there was some trepidation as they neared and then crossed the Pettus Bridge. "Five hundred yards away a double line of state troopers stood across the road," a reporter from the *New Republic* magazine wrote. "The marchers approached them and stopped. Major John Cloud told them that they could not proceed. King asked if they might pray and sing; Cloud agreed."

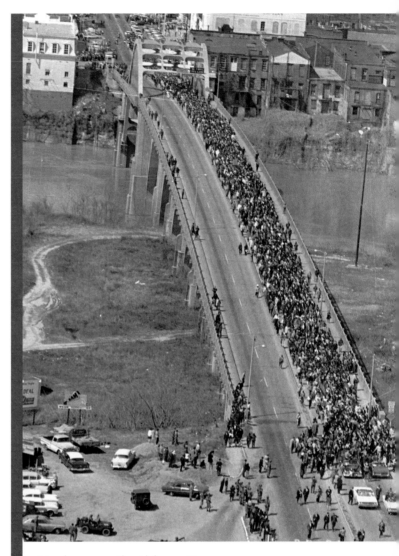

Marchers cross the Alabama River

Sunday's march had shown the face of raw brutality and on Tuesday the marchers demonstrated that the potential for violence was still very much a part of Selma. King promised that the march to Montgomery would eventually go ahead as planned. Some of his enthusiasm was muffled on March 11 when he learned that white minister Reverend James Reeb, who had been severely beaten two days prior, had died. But soon things were back in motion and the date of March 21, 1965, had been approved by the court for the march to Montgomery.

DISC 2
TRACK 6

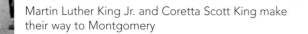

Martin Luther King Jr. and Coretta Scott King make their way to Montgomery

DISC 2
TRACK 6

Once more Brown's Chapel was the assembly point and Dr. King offered these words of instruction before setting out for Montgomery: "It has been estimated that almost ten thousand people who will be marching out of Selma today…Now, our first stopping point will be about seven or eight miles out of the city…where we will camp tonight."

J. D. Reese, one of the march's organizers, recalled that momentous day, saying, "a group of people had charted a plane and came on bus to Selma and came through that door. They said 'we're here after hearing the call from Dr. King and seeing him on television and what transpired across the bridge. We're here to lend our bodies and to lend our assistance to the people of Selma.' That was one of the most exhilarating moments of the movement that day."

"Ain't Gonna Let Nobody Turn Me Around" and "We Shall Overcome" rippled louder and louder as the arriving throng grew in size. "There was a moment of excitement when Dr. King and other speakers assembled on the steps, but a succession of long, rhetorical, and, to a certain extent (when press helicopters buzzed too low or when the microphone went dead), inaudible speeches put a damper on that," wrote *New Yorker* reporter Renata Adler. 🔘

As the thousands walked along the highway, there were federal marshals and troops stationed at various points, and helicopters whirled above them. King was asked by a reporter if had expected such an escort. "We thought we'd be able to make this march and probably get at least a modicum of protection from the state," he said. "We had no idea that it would turn out like it did."

A little more than seven miles from Selma the marchers, their ranks thinned considerably, reached the campsite for the night. Most of the marchers had returned to Selma by a special train; only about three hundred were chosen to make the entire trip. The limit had been stipulated by a court order to not violate a stretch of the two-lane highway where only three hundred marchers were permitted at one time. By sunset, four large tents were pitched and nearly three tons of spaghetti were prepared for supper. As the marchers got ready for bed, there were rumors about what lay ahead, particularly the hundreds of snakes they might encounter as they passed through Lowndes County.

On the second night the campsite was set at Rosa Steele's farm, and it was a restless night, given the rumors of snakes and bombs that may have been planted by Klansmen. Tuesday brought a downpour of rain and it continued for the rest of the day. That night they rested at a farm owned by A. G. Gaston, the millionaire businessman from Birmingham. Wednesday, the fourth day of the march, turned sunny, and so to did the disposition of most of the marchers. By noon, many of them were sunburned.

Two black men, their faces daubed with sunburn lotion, inscribed "vote" on their foreheads. That evening became a night of jubilation with a gallery of entertainers now in the camp, including Shelley Winters, Sammy Davis Jr., Tony Perkins, Tony Bennett, Nipsy Russell, Mike Nichols, Elaine May, Dick Gregory, and Nina Simone.

By the time the marchers reached Montgomery on Thursday, their numbers had swelled to more than twenty-five thousand. Reporter Jimmy Breslin recalled the scene as the marchers arrived at their destination, noting, "the sidewalks were nearly empty, with only small groups of Negroes watching, but the white faces were everywhere. They were at the lobby doors of the Jefferson Davis Hotel. And they were looking out from the street level windows of the Dixie Office Supply Company and McGehee's

Malcolm X speaks to young African Americans

Drug Store and Weiss Opticians. And they looked down from opened windows at the Whitley Hotel and the Exchange Hotel, and the big First National Bank building was twelve stories of white faces pressed against windows and looking at the street below."

As they marched up Montgomery Street, the difference between the black section of town and the white section of town was discernible as they moved from the mud road to asphalt. They passed the huge fountain where Montgomery turns into Dexter Avenue with the white capitol building at top of the hill. The mixed band of marchers had accomplished their mission in five days. Ministers, school teachers, carpenters, rabbis, civil servants,

writers, doctors, lawyers, blacks, whites, young and old had bonded on the fifty mile trek and stood as one before the state capitol building on this sunny but cool day.

With the media out in full force, a pantheon of civil rights leaders followed King to the top of the capitol steps, including A. Philip Randolph, Roy Wilkins, Whitney Young, John Lewis, and Rosa Parks. "So I stand before you this afternoon with the conviction that segregation is on its deathbed in Alabama and the only thing uncertain about it is how costly the segregationists and Wallace will make the funeral," King told the crowd stretched out down Dexter Avenue and beyond. In the near distance he could see the church where he got his start in the

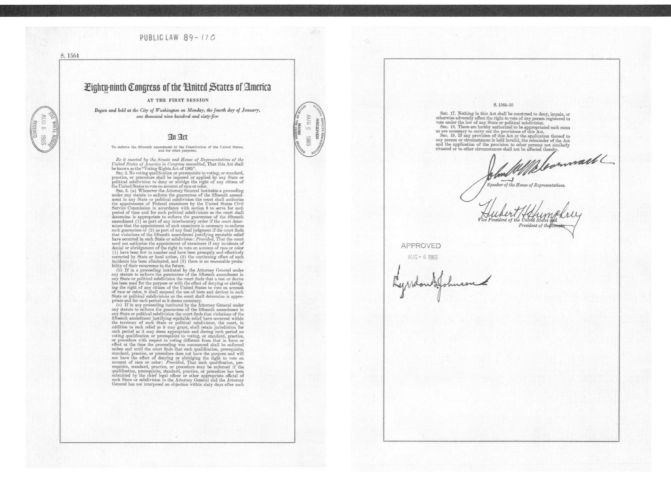

Voting Rights Act (1965): "No voting qualification or prerequisite to voting, or standard, practice, or procedure shall be imposed or applied by any State or political subdivision to deny or abridge the right of any citizen of the United States to vote on account of race or color."

ministry, and where much of the organizing for the Montgomery Boycott occurred.

While his words resounded over the multitude, as it was later reported Governor Wallace peeked out of his window at the throng, maybe even hearing King's eulogy to Jim Crow. King's speech then turned to his repetition of "How Longs." "How long? Not long, because mine eyes have seen the glory of the coming of the Lord, trampling out the vintage where the grapes of wrath are stored. He has loosed the fateful lightning of his terrible swift sword. His truth is marching on. He has sounded forth the trumpets that never call retreat. He is lifting up the hearts of men before His judgment seat. Oh, be swift, my soul, to answer Him. Be jubilant, my feet. Our God is marching on."

Later that evening, this glorious moment of triumph would be washed away by the news that one of the volunteers driving marchers back to Selma had been slain. Viola Liuzzo, a white homemaker from Detroit and a student at Wayne State University, had dropped off several marchers at Brown's Chapel and was returning to Montgomery to pick up others with Leroy Moton, a black activist.

Gary Thomas Rowe, a Federal Bureau of Investigation informant and a member of the Ku Klux Klan, was at the scene of the crime and disclosed the events that led to Liuzzo's death. According to his court testimony, after the passengers were delivered, he and three other members of a KKK "missionary squad"—Collie Leroy Wilkins Jr., William Orville Eaton, and Eugene Thomas—spotted Liuzzo and Moton stopped at a traffic light in Selma. They followed her car for twenty miles. About halfway between Selma and Montgomery, the four men pulled their car up next to hers and shot at her. Liuzzo was killed instantly. Moton escaped injury—the blood the assailants thought was his belonged to Liuzzo.

After the Klansmen departed, Moton hailed a passerby and reported the incident to law enforcement officials. Because Rowe was with the three other men, the FBI was able to track them down and arrest them almost immediately. President Johnson announced their capture on national television.

On August 6, 1965, the president signed the Voting Rights Bill. One of the most significant provisions of the bill was the guaranteed presence of federal examiners at elections. The marchers in Selma must have felt a measure of satisfaction that their commitment might have influenced this act. And they must have been thrilled to learn that since the bill was passed more than nine thousand blacks had registered to vote in Dallas County, Alabama.

Jimmie Lee Jackson, Reverend James Reeb, and Viola Liuzzo were the martyrs of Selma and they will always be remembered for their selfless devotion to justice. "Selma brought us a voting bill," Dr. King said in his summary of events in Selma, "And it also brought us the grand alliance of the children of light in this nation and made possible changes in our political and economic life heretofore undreamed of." The Voting Rights Act of 1965 was a landmark federal law. Though it held many gains, where it did not go far enough, King knew he could rely on nonviolent protest on the road to victory.

20

Black Power!

There were a number of hopeful signs for the civil rights movement in 1966. Congress had passed and President Johnson had signed the Voting Rights Bill the previous summer, thousands of newly registered African Americans voted for the first time in Dallas County, Alabama, and the black civil rights organizations had agreed to meet in Memphis to see what could be done to continue an initiative James Meredith had begun. His "March Against Fear" on the back roads of Mississippi was a walk that would evoke the state's true nature when he was shot and seriously wounded by a sniper. Meredith crumpled to the highway on June 6, near Hernando, Mississippi, after covering just thirty miles of his proposed walk from Memphis to Jackson, Mississippi.

Meredith had moved on his own without consultation with any of the significant black leaders, but the summit meeting planned in Memphis to carry on his mission included Whitney Young of the National Urban League; Roy Wilkins, executive secretary of the NAACP; attorney Floyd McKissick of CORE; Stokely Carmichael of SNCC; and Dr. Martin Luther King, representing the SCLC. Despite Carmichael's attempts to ingratiate himself and disarm Wilkins' reputed haughtiness, a difference between them arose at the appearance of the Deacons for Defense and Justice, an armed militant group from Louisiana, who had volunteered to provide security for the march. Eventually, Wilkins and Young would withhold their support and denounce the project as one that had been "taken over by militants."

Carmichael recalled in his autobiography, *Ready for Revolution*, that Wilkins "clearly had no respect for the experience and contributions of mass activism or the intelligence of any of us, not just SNCC. In his mind, whatever the movement had accomplished—the legislation—was entirely because of the insider contacts and skillful influence of the NAACP. It never occurred to him that they had never been able to get any legislation—not as much as anti-lynching law—until masses of black people had taken to the streets in nonviolent direct action."

Dr. King didn't offer anywhere near as much detail on the meeting as Carmichael, merely recalling that there was a brief conference among McKissick, Carmichael, and him, in which they agreed that the march would be jointly sponsored by CORE, SNCC, and SCLC. Staff assignments were made, then four cars were dispatched to the location where James Meredith had been shot the day before. The march was on.

At the end of the first day of the march, everybody returned to Memphis and spent the night in a black-owned motel because the tents had not been purchased. That night before they retired, many of the march participants assembled and continued the discussion that had begun on the road, mainly the issue of nonviolence and the presence of whites. Both issues were disturbing to Dr. King, who did what he could to mollify the mounting dissent, particularly among the younger, more militant marchers. He reminded them that they had neither the means nor the skills to win a violent confrontation. King repeatedly stressed the importance of unity during the march, and that they should not be divided over the questions of tactics and color. McKissick and Carmichael gradually conceded to King's wishes and the next morning they held a press conference affirming that the march would be nonviolent and that whites were welcomed.

King failed to note in his autobiography an incident that happened on the first day where he was

Above: A 1967 Black Power pamphlet

Left: A marcher places a U.S. flag on a bust of Jefferson Davis

James Meredith, in white hat, and supporters on the March Against Fear

knocked down by a policeman who had commanded them to stay off the highway and walk along the roadbed. Perturbed by the cop's overzealousness, Carmichael quickly responded and was prepared to retaliate when several marchers nearby restrained him. Rather than compliment Carmichael for his reaction, King chastised him for disobeying the tenets of nonviolence. The incident triggered much of the heated debate about strategy and tactics that night at the motel. For Carmichael, the debate was never one about nonviolence. "It was about self-defense," he insisted.

In each town the marchers were greeted by residents, many of them cheering them on and offering them food and water. In Grenada, Mississippi, about ten days from the march's starting point, white citizens watched with "disciplined fury" when a black marcher stuck a U.S. flag behind the bust of the president of the Confederacy, Jefferson Davis, in the town square. "As a direct result of the march,"

reporter Paul Good noted, "more than thirteen hundred Grenada Negroes registered as the county graciously provided extra registrars, even colored ones. Of course, barely had the march moved out of town and Negroes were arrested for trying to integrate a theater and rights workers left behind to set up a permanent movement were being attacked."

The organizing tactic had been devised by SNCC, and workers in each town had their share of stories to tell of how they were followed by Klansmen and chased down the highway. Carmichael and the SNCC workers marched into Greenwood to a boisterous, welcoming crowd, many of whom knew them from their organizing in the region. But the warm welcome from the black residents was soon obscured by Carmichael and Cleveland Sellers's arrests. They had become agitated when the police tried to stop a group from erecting a tent on school yard. "By the time I got out of jail," Carmichael recalled, "I was in no mood to compromise with racist arrogance.

The rally had started. It was huge. The spirit of self-assertion and defiance was palpable. I looked over the crowd, that valiant, embattled community of old friends and strugglers. I told them what they knew, that they could depend only on themselves, their own organized collective strength."

Up to that point there was nothing remarkably new about a Carmichael speech. The usual sing-song effect was present, his way of ending a sentence with a rising cadence or a lowering sarcasm filled the Mississippi evening. There was typical response that always gravitated to a call-and-response routine, as if a preacher was exhorting his flock. Then came the rhetorical bomb that he and Willie Ricks, a SNCC colleague, had been discussing.

"Drop it now," Ricks told Carmichael. "The people are ready. Drop it now."

"It's time we stand up and take over, take over," Carmichael said, after citing the years of black Americans begging the government for its rights. "We have to do what every group in this country did. We've got to take over the communities where we outnumber people so we can have decent jobs, so we can have decent houses, so we can have decent roads, so we can have decent schools, so we can have decent justice. Every courthouse in Mississippi ought to be burned down tomorrow, to get rid of the dirt in there, and the filth. From now on when they ask you what you want, you know what to tell them....We been saying freedom for six years and we ain't got nothin'. What we gonna start saying now is 'black power.'"

Having primed the crowd and without missing a beat, Carmichael asked the crowd:

"What do you want?"

The response was "Black Power!"

"What do you want?"

"Black Power!"

With each question the response grew louder until the exchange seemed to take on a life all its own. 🆑

Judy Richardson, a veteran SNCC organizer who was at the rally, remembers the excitement of that moment and its impact on the audience. "We had been talking about it [Black Power] within the organization...and as we moved through each town during the march....Just before the tear gassing of all these people who had been marching he began talking about what we need is some black power. It was wonderful since we were already going that way in the organization."

Later, in October in Berkeley, California, Carmichael, as he would do on many occasions, explained to an audience what he meant by black power. "We maintain the use of the words Black Power—let them address themselves to that," he said, chiding those white detractors who took exception to the term. "We are not going to wait for white people to sanction Black Power. We're tired of waiting; every time black people try to move in this country, they're forced to defend their position beforehand. It's time that white people do that. They ought to start defending themselves as to why they have oppressed and exploited us....White people associate Black Power with violence because of their own inability to deal with blackness. If we had said 'Negro power' nobody would get scared. Everybody would support it. If we said power for colored people, everybody'd be for that, but it is the word 'black' that bothers people in this country, and that's their problem, not mine. That's the lie that says anything black is bad."

"I had reservations about its use," Dr. King said when asked his reaction to the term. "I saw it bringing about division within the ranks of the marchers. For a day or two there was fierce competition between those who were wedded to the Black Power slogan and those wedded to Freedom Now." He went on to explain, "I don't believe in black separatism, I don't believe in black power that would have racist overtones, but certainly if black power means the amassing of political and economic power in order to gain our just and legitimate goals, then we all believe in that."

DISC 2
TRACK 8

To some extent, Carmichael, in a speech two years later, agreed with King about amassing political and economic power, adding the cultural component. "We have to constantly move on those three levels at the same time," he said in a speech in Oakland, California. "We can't move on one level and disregard the other two." But over the course of the preceding two years, Carmichael had extended his notion of black power, adopting an ideology of guerrilla warfare as a member of the Black Panther Party.

James Forman, who had recently relinquished his post as executive secretary of SNCC to Ruby Doris Robinson, was not in Greenwood when Carmichael shouted "Black Power." However, he was there on the last day of the march in Jackson. "[Willie] Ricks and others had been chanting 'Black Power' and the words were becoming more and more popular, although some activists seemed frightened by them. John Lewis, for example, urged me to stop Ricks—he didn't like the phrase, it didn't make sense, he said."

Lewis said the phrase was not new, that Ricks had been using it in his speeches to rile up audiences. It was a shortened version of a SNCC campaign slogan "Black power for black people," he recalled. In his estimation, Carmichael merely expropriated it from Ricks and made it his own. "The way I had always understood the phrase," he said, "it had more to do with self-reliance than with black supremacy, though that distinction was hard to see, especially through the fire and spit with which Stokely and some of the others tended to deliver their message. The way he was using it, I thought tended to create a schism, both within the movement itself and between the races. It drove people apart rather than brought them together. He was out to stir things up. He delighted in scaring white people, and this did the trick."

The day after Carmichael's speech, on the steps of the Greenwood Courthouse, there was a minor clash between the forces of SNCC and SCLC. "Get that vote and pin that badge on a black chest," Hosea Williams, one of King's point men, said to a throng

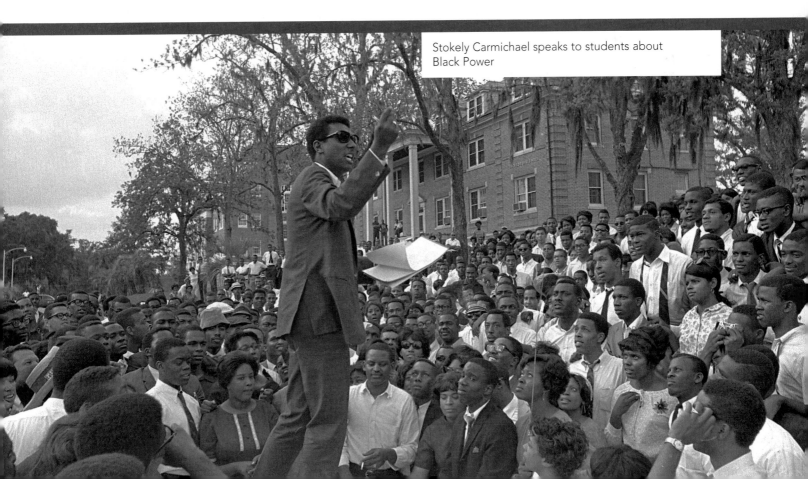

Stokely Carmichael speaks to students about Black Power

Carmichael, at Berkeley, denounces the draft

gathered below them. "Get that vote…Whip the policeman across the head." To these words, King quickly sought to muffle any notion of violence in Williams' words. "He means with the vote," he said. Standing nearby, Carmichael chimed, "they know what he means."

The following morning, Dr. King, sensing a growing split between the civil rights organizations, called a powwow in Yazoo City, not far from Jackson. King pleaded with the others to drop the Black Power slogan. When Carmichael noted that all the other ethnic groups in America had achieved power but black Americans, King retorted, "that is just the point." He said the Jews, Italians, and the Irish had never chanted a slogan of Irish Power or Jewish Power. They merely worked hard and achieved it. "That's what we must do," he concluded.

Still, Carmichael and McKissick stuck to their positions, insisting they needed a powerful slogan to galvanize their forces for social and political change.

The only concession King could wring from his obstinate confederates was the promise that they would not urge the chanting of the slogan for the remainder of the march.

The distance from Yazoo City to Philadelphia, Mississippi, stretches some one hundred miles due east. It was June 21, 1966, the second anniversary of the murders of James Chaney, Andrew Goodman and Michael Schwerner in Neshoba County. The march was entering its second week. "We had to pay our respects to the memory of the three martyrs," Carmichael said, "but it was too far for the entire march to go. So we decided that the march leaders would drive over with a group of marchers, hook up with the local folks, and have a public memorial service. Dr. King would conduct the service in front of the courthouse after we marched from the black section."

When they arrived in Philadelphia on June 22, they were greeted not with cheers but with derisive jeers and a hail of rocks and firecrackers from a unruly white mob that had gathered along the streets. Observing the possible violent response from some of the marchers, King reminded them to keep calm, even as he was struck by a bottle. After the marchers departed, the Klan drove into the black community and attempted to intimidate them with rounds of gunfire. Instead of cowering behind closed doors as many of them had done during previous raids, black residents responded with their own bullets. The Klan didn't come back.

Two days later, the group merged into a single unit again when the marchers crossed the Pearl River and arrived in Canton. It was the city where Andrew Jackson met with the Choctaw chief Pushmataha in 1820 and signed the treaty of Doak's Stand. In order to preserve peace, the Choctaws, under duress, ceded acres of homeland to the U.S. government. If there were any such similar détente between the marchers and the law enforcement officers assigned to protect them, it was seriously violated when King and his cohorts were told they couldn't pitch their tents on a particular school yard. Soon there was a standoff between the two adversaries, one determined to raise the tents, the other content to raise some hell.

"We were working by flashlight, trying to erect the tent," Carmichael recounted. "Tired, hungry people are milling around. Suddenly the scene is lit by searchlights out of the surrounding darkness. A bright, white, blinding light. A voice amplified by a bullhorn commands us to disperse. It was dark. We had no place for 150 marchers to go, and they knew that."

For several minutes Carmichael and Dr. King tried to talk to the disembodied voice from the darkness. Blinded by the searchlights, King pled for peace. He said he was sick and tired of violence. The words were hardly out his mouth when the assault began. The marchers had but a moment's notice—seeing the uniformed troopers donning their gas masks—before the canisters began raining and exploding all around them.

"I took a direct hit in the chest from a canister and was knocked to the ground," Carmichael remembered. "Semiconscious and unable to breathe; my eyes were tearing. My ribs felt as though crushed. Gas in my lungs was always my weakness….I could hear screams, shouts, and Dr. King calling on people to remain calm amid the sickening thud of blows."

While the marchers gasped for air, the white officers pummeled them unmercifully, hitting women, children, whomever they could make out through the suffocating fog of gas. Reporter Paul Good witnessed the entire attack. For him, it was Selma redux. While there were fewer casualties than at Selma, the ferocity of the assault was just as intense. Good recalled, "A heavyset Negro woman in her late 30s, Mrs. Odessa Warrick, was stunned from the gas and as she tried to hold herself up a patrolman kicked her in the back, yelling, 'Nigger, you want your freedom, here it is!' She was hospitalized with a possible spinal fracture. A white man, Morris Mitchell, who was seventy-one that day, had brought to the march some students from an interracial Quaker school on Long Island. He saw a patrolman beating a man on the ground with a rifle butt [Apparently Charles Meyer, a white pre-med student who suffered two fractured ribs and a 20 percent collapse of one lung] and said to the patrolman: 'You should be ashamed of yourself.' The patrolman replied to the white-haired Mitchell: 'You get back or I'll put it into you.'"

With the last vapors of gas drifting from the school grounds where the marchers lay bruised and in disarray, Carmichael was on his feet, trying vainly to rally his beaten comrades. While he was screaming for them to prepare for another attack, King and the other advocates of nonviolence pleaded with him to calm down, lest he provoke the very thing he feared. There were no more attacks on the already wounded bodies of the marchers. It was only a few more miles to their destination, but many wondered whether they could make it.

King could not understand why he had not heard from anyone in the Johnson administration.

"It's terribly frustrating and disappointing," he told a reporter. "The federal government makes my job more difficult every day…to keep the movement nonviolent." And how did he feel about black power now, after the battering and disillusionment at Canton? "I don't think that has touched many of us," he answered. "It has been used on this particular march and I think people generally just use a slogan that anybody projects. I prefer not to use it, not because I don't understand its denotative reasons but because it has connotative implications. I don't use the term 'Black Power' but I do know the Negro must have power if we're gonna gain freedom and human dignity."

Though the marchers had their heads bloodied, they remained unbowed, and when on the next day hundreds more arrived to beg for a repeat performance from the menacing police, a compromise had been reached. A permit was granted for a rally on the school grounds, but no tents would be erected. That wasn't possible anyway, since they had already been shipped on to Tougaloo, just outside Jackson.

On June 26, 1966, the march concluded at the Mississippi state capitol before an integrated crowd of about fifteen thousand. The crowd, which included many young marchers, heard from King and a host of other luminaries—even the injured James Meredith had rejoined the march to participate in the final twenty miles. One luminary not allowed to speak was Charles Evers, Medgar's brother, and top brass for the NAACP. The combined votes of SNCC, CORE, and the MFDP prevented Evers from addressing the crowd. Apparently his ongoing feud with the more militant activists had not dissipated. Rather than "Bloody Sunday" in Selma, it was "Glorious Sunday" in Jackson.

The marchers had a lot to cheer about as a band played countless choruses of "When the Saints Go Marchin' In." Among the achievements they could boast were the four thousand new voters added to the rolls; attempts at a cooperative merger among the various civil rights organizations; and the emergence of black power as a concept that would have a larger, more effective impact on the young black men and women in the northern ghettoes.

"After the success of the Meredith march I felt we'd made a real breakthrough," Stokely Carmichael reflected. "At least to the extent of commanding the attention of the media, and therefore the nation….I had reason to feel that things were on schedule so far as advancing SNCC's program within the national movement and to the larger political community. So everything seemed according to plan. The next big task: begin to organize the African American community nationally."

21

King in Chicago and Against the War

As early as 1965, Dr. Martin Luther King considered opening a northern front for his civil rights crusade. He had dispatched Hosea Williams to survey the situation and see how they could accomplish their boast of registering one hundred thousand new voters. King and the Southern Christian Leadership Conference (SCLC) had not ventured north on their own whim and caprice. They had come at the invitation of black leaders who requested their assistance in the mission for quality integrated education. All the while King was marching in Selma and through Mississippi, Chicago was a festering challenge, one he knew would soon be on his agenda.

By the end of June, after a relatively successful "March Against Fear" in Mississippi, King was off to Chicago, ready for his first major offensive in the North, though his appearance in the Watts area of Los Angeles right after the uprising in August 1965 must be seen as his initial foray into conflict beyond the South. He had been told that his visit might be fruitless, that the people of Watts were in no mood for preachers espousing nonviolence. But King had been to Watts before and wanted to hear directly from the people what they thought the reasons for the riots were.

What the riot was all about, wrote journalist/activist Nelson Peery, was a people's reaction to living in a virtual police state. "The police in Watts were an army of occupation," he concluded. "There were daily arrests and beatings over trivial misdemeanors. Black motorists were constantly stopped, harassed, and humiliated. Rape of black women by the cops was well known. Just before the uprising, two cops stopped a young black couple and forced the woman into the squad car. Her escort, facing their drawn guns, was given the choice of leaving the area or getting arrested. After the rape, the woman got the license of the squad car. Nothing was done.

"This incident," Peery continued, "happened only a few weeks after two cops raped a black woman who worked for the police department. She had the training to get the numbers and identify the rapists. One cop was fired and the other given a reprimand. There were no criminal prosecutions. The rapid development of the fighting was due to a rumor that the cops had raped another woman. Watts was a tinderbox waiting for the spark."

That spark was fully ignited when a highway patrolman halted a young black driver for speeding. According to the police, the young man appeared intoxicated, and he was arrested. The incident attracted several pedestrians. Soon there was crowd

DISC 2
TRACK 9

and more law enforcement officers were called in. One officer administered a clubbing and a black woman was dragged into the middle of the street after she spat on an officer. After the police left, some of the people who witnessed what had happened sought revenge and began throwing rocks at passing cars, overturning some of them and beating the drivers and passengers.

The potential explosion was quelled, but only until evening of the next day. Thirty hours after the early disturbance, wide-scale vandalism, looting, and arson began. For six days Watts raged. It was the largest racial disturbance the nation had seen since the Detroit riots of 1943. When the violent disorder was finally subdued, there were thirty-four fatalities, almost one thousand injured, more than four thousand arrested, and property losses in the millions. **CD**

A shoe store burns to the ground in the midst of the Watts riots

Dr. King was glad he had gone to Watts, despite encountering heckling and boos from residents of northern ghettos not used to his nonviolent tactics. Malcolm X's influence was pervasive among the militants, and many of them vocally expressed their opposition to King's passive resistance. It was the northern baptismal King felt he needed in preparation for his sojourn in Chicago.

Several months before settling into Chicago, King had visited the city, the kind of reconnaissance that was often his practice. During one of his famous sermons, "A Knock at Midnight," he had evoked the city and how it affected him. "I've seen my dream shattered as I've walked the streets of Chicago…and seen Negroes, young men and women, with a sense of utter hopelessness because they can't find any jobs. And they see life as a long and desolate corridor with no exit signs."

When Dr. King began his actual organizing work in Chicago, it was under the aegis of the Coordinating Council of Community Organizations, which was a coalition of local civil rights groups, forged by Al Raby, a former public school teacher in the city. While King's focus was on the deplorable education provided by the city's schools, he was clearly aware that they were symptomatic of a system suffering from economic and spiritual deprivation. To get to the crux of the problems in Chicago, King could call on Hosea Williams, Raby, and James Bevel. An eager young man, then twenty-four, elbowed his way into a prominent position next to King. His name was Jesse Jackson.

Raby wasn't pleased to be paired with Jackson in preparing the way for King. He was preoccupied with trying to keep the various groups together in the coalition. Jackson's energetic zeal and sometimes singular pursuits were additional headaches that he confessed he didn't need.

"Jackson and Raby couldn't have been more different," historian Gary Rivlin wrote. "Where Jackson was brazen and brash, Raby was deliberate, respectful,

Rioters in Watts

and wise beyond his years. Jackson burned with one idea after another; Raby was the sort who, in meetings, offered the sobering perspective that they could only accomplish so much, so let's set some priorities. If Raby had one skill above all others that won him the task of organizing on King's behalf, it was his ability to keep peace among large and unwieldy groups."

Reverend Jackson was given the assignment to round up the clergy and to make it easier for King to reach them and earn their support. This was not an easy task since King, for many of the city's preachers, came as an outsider. Nonetheless, Jackson coordinated the job with speed and aplomb, thoroughly enough that he was given the privilege of introducing

Dr. Martin Luther King Jr. helps to clean up a neglected Chicago neighborhood

Dr. King during a major downtown rally. Rather than a short, perfunctory introduction, Jackson commanded the rostrum for several minutes—longer, in fact, than King's speech.

Even more annoying to his associates was Jackson's propensity for the grand statement that would draw the media to him. His remarks that King would be marching in the all-white suburb of Cicero shocked all who heard it, particularly Dr. King, who knew nothing about such a march. Don Rose, who also worked with King, recalled that announcement came one night when the Jackson was holding forth before a bank of cameras. "It was like Jesse couldn't resist saying something sensational that would get his name in the paper," Rose said. Whatever others may have

thought of Jackson, King reserved his opinion.

When the King family moved to Chicago they deliberately chose to live in the ghetto. King said it was the best way to feel and experience what his brothers and sisters there felt. "Right after the Mississippi march ended, Martin and I took the children to our slum apartment [in Chicago]," Coretta Scott King wrote. "It was pretty difficult living there with four children." Amidst the summer heat, noise and crowded chaos of their urban quarters, the King family carried on.

On Sunday, July 10, 1966, a major rally took place at Soldier Field. By now, the King family had been thoroughly acclimated to their new surroundings, having truly given time and attention to their neighbors and their plight. Fifty thousand people responded to the call and more than half of them followed King on a march downtown. Except for Dr. King leading a march to City Hall and nailing his demands to the Hall's closed door—as Martin Luther had done with his ninety-five theses at Wittenberg in 1517—the rally and march were uneventful. The following day, King and several community leaders met with Mayor Richard Daley to discuss the demands, including a plea for adequate housing and an end to price gouging by local merchants. Daley rejected them without consideration.

Black Chicagoans were livid when they heard what Daley had done. That night was one of the hottest of the summer, with the temperature soaring above ninety degrees. Another mass meeting was slated, but given the heat, some thought it would be best to postpone it. But it was on, and the Kings, accompanied by Mahalia Jackson, were on their way to the meeting when they encountered gangs of young men ranting and raving in the streets. They were reacting to the police who had turned off the fire hydrants where children were trying to cool themselves with sprays of water. "When we got to the meeting," Mrs. King remembered, "everyone was upset and angry. Several black youths had been badly

National Guard troops aim at Chicago rioters

beaten, and others had been arrested. Two groups, the Cobras and the Vice Lords, had gathered across the street from the church, and they sent a delegation to the church saying that if the prisoners were not released immediately, they were going to tear up the city."

That promise did not materialize until the following evening, July 13. Unlike the previous day, the rock throwing, looting and fire-bombing intensified, particularly on the west side of the city. The next several days featured violence, random gunfire, and media reports of "guerrilla warfare" in the streets. Before order was restored, scores of civilians and law enforcement officers had been injured. More than five hundred people were arrested, including 155 juveniles. Three black people were killed by stray bullets, it was reported,

among them a thirteen-year-old boy and fourteen-year-old pregnant girl.

On several occasions Mrs. King and the children had to scurry from trouble as the riot spread to the north side of the city. Soon after the riots were over, Mrs. King took the children back to Atlanta. But Dr. King traveled back and forth to the city three or four times a week. Now the movement had shifted its focus to open housing, which would permit African Americans to live wherever they could afford. King took the demonstrations to the streets, including an open-housing demonstration in Gage Park, where he was struck in the head with a rock. Knocked down but not seriously injured, he rose and continued on.

Not only had King taken a lump on the head, his movement was being assailed and discredited after the riots. Various news accounts and editorials pinned the blame on them. Despite the accusations, King and his colleagues struggled on, pressing their nonviolent crusade even more vigorously.

King may have been hurt more by the Chicago Housing Authority. The agency repeatedly rebuffed King's demand for open-housing. But finally a breakthrough occurred. A ten-point agreement on open-housing was reached. It called for various measures to strengthen the enforcement of existing laws and regulations with respect to housing. The city would enforce its 1963 open housing ordinances and Mayor Daley agreed to work for statewide open housing legislation. "We felt we had achieved a victory after a long struggle," Mrs. King recounted. "Unfortunately, the agreement was never properly implemented. The city officials failed to keep their promises."

One promise that was kept came from the SCLC with the founding of Operation Breadbasket, which advised merchants, "If you respect my dollar, then you must respect my person." Jesse Jackson was put in charge of the program which gave rise to other social and political campaigns in the city, including the subsequent election of Harold Washington as the city's first black mayor.

For King and other leaders, 1966 was both a pioneering year and one of great education for Southerners who had now taken the fight to Northern cities. Working with local leaders through advancements and setbacks, King saw the hard truth. "We found ourselves confronted by the hard realities of a social system in many ways more resistant to change than the rural South," he said.

While King was fighting on several domestic fronts against segregation, disenfranchisement, urban violence, and poverty in places like Los Angeles, Chicago, and Cleveland—where he had gone to mediate a disturbance—he kept a keen eye on America's international policy. Many feel that his statements against the war in Vietnam were a sudden development late in his life, but as early as the summer of 1965, King had voiced his opposition to the bombing of North Vietnam. And on January 10, 1966, he strongly endorsed Georgia State Senator-elect Julian Bond's right to oppose the war. But it was his speech on April 4, 1967, at New York's Riverside Church that brought his position fully before the American public.

Many of King's earlier doubts about the war were either a private matter or disclosed in meetings with such powerful figures as United Nations Ambassador Arthur Goldberg, where he requested that negotiations rather than military might be the answer to the turmoil in southeast Asia. Gradually, he became more public about his feelings, no longer relying on his wife to represent him on foreign affairs.

Both friends and enemies, blacks and whites, harshly questioned why King was expanding his message to include opposition to the war in Vietnam. "I was chided," he wrote, "even by fellow civil rights leaders, members of Congress, and brothers of the cloth for 'not sticking to the business of civil rights.'"

Several indications of his controversial views appeared before his momentous speech at Riverside, particularly long, in-depth conversations with his colleagues and advisors at the SCLC, with his wife and members of his family (his father vehemently disapproved), and finally with himself. None of those who disagreed with his stepping into the peace movement were harder on him than he was on himself as he mulled the consequences and absorbed more and more literature about the war. One evening he read an article entitled, "The Children of Vietnam," that discussed U.S. atrocities against Vietnamese people. It was the final piece of justification he needed to betray what had been his silence up to that moment. "I came to the conclusion that there is an existential moment in your life when you must decide to speak for yourself; nobody else can speak for you," he wrote.

Deciding to come out against the war placed King at odds with many of his associates in the SCLC, but he was in step with the more militant stance announced by the Student Nonviolent Coordinating Committee (SNCC). During the "March Against Fear" in Mississippi, King had often engaged members of SNCC in debates about the rapidly emerging war in Vietnam, especially with Stokely Carmichael.

"Ever since we'd made our statement on the war, SNCC had been out there isolated from the other civil rights organizations," Carmichael wrote. "The press had beat up on us, vilified us…and a lot of the brothers suddenly started to receive draft notices. Dr. King knew this because I'd made a point of telling him. Where were the other organizations on the question? I'd ask."

In January 1967, after long and careful deliberation, King felt he was ready to go public with his conscience at a conference in Los Angeles. His wife remembered the speech he delivered: "The promises of the Great Society have been shot down on the battlefields of Vietnam. The pursuit of this widened war has narrowed domestic welfare programs, making the poor, white and Negro, bear the heaviest burden….It is estimated that we spend $322,000 for each enemy we kill, while we spend in the so-called war on poverty in America only about $53 for each person classified as poor….We must combine the fervor of the civil rights movement with the peace movement."

King marches against the Vietnam conflict

This talk was but the prelude to his speech at Riverside in April in which Vietnam was not just a footnote, but the theme. While many deem King's "I Have A Dream" speech his most remarkable, others contend that he reached his full political maturity on both domestic and foreign policy with his speech at New York's Riverside Church. The event was an anti-war rally sponsored by Clergy and Laymen Concerned about Vietnam.

"It was a cool, clear evening, and more than three thousand people showed up," said John Lewis who had not seen Dr. King since he left SNCC. "The scene was loose, boisterous, colorful, almost like a happening, with dozens of religious leaders of all denominations streaming into the church. There were several speakers on the agenda, but the one everyone had come to hear was Dr. King. This was the night he would finally take a stand on the war."

King explained his intentions, that the speech was not pro-Vietnam or pro-Washington, but meant for the people of America. After years of struggle on behalf of the poor and disenfranchised, he had begun to see some hope. Then came Vietnam. King told the crowd that he now saw a direct link between the build-up of a war abroad and the shortcomings of a movement at home. Though the speech began with slow, measured tones, his cadence quickened as he explained the connection to the crowd.

"I knew that America would never invest the necessary funds or energies in rehabilitation of its poor so long as adventures like Vietnam continued to draw men and skills and money like some demonic, destructive suction tube," he explained. "So I was increasingly compelled to see the war as an enemy of the poor and to attack it as such."

It was not until he began enumerating measures to end war and evoking the Geneva Agreement of 1954 that his speech was interrupted with applause. Then there would be moments of sustained applause as he reprimanded America for being "the greatest purveyor of violence in the world."

"I came away from that evening inspired," Lewis said. "I still believed, in the face of so much that seemed to be falling apart, that slowly, inexorably, in ways I might not be able to recognize or figure out, we were continuing to move in the direction we should, toward something better."

Lewis was not alone among the ministers who supported King's position. Of course, the hundreds of ministers in attendance at Riverside backed him, including the event's organizers Dr. Henry Steele Commager, Rabbi Abraham Herschel, and Reverend John C. Bennett.

"I was always sorry that more black leaders did not share the outrage of Martin Luther King Jr. about the war, for—in spite of inherited deprivations and handicaps—articulate blacks could have had considerable influence on public opinion and on the federal government," Bennett charged.

But others were less complimentary, including black columnist Carl Rowan, who suggested King was "creating the impression that the Negro is disloyal." *Life* magazine said King's speech "sounded like a script for Radio Hanoi" and President Johnson was advised by a confidant that "King—in desperate search of a constituency—has thrown in with the commies." Given the climate and the growing anti-war movement that the speech helped fuel, the president couldn't have been too pleased.

"The Johnson Administration seemed amazingly devoid of statesmanship, and when creative statesmanship wanes, irrational militarism increases," King observed later. "President Kennedy was a man who was big enough to admit when he was wrong—as he did after the Bay of Pigs incident. But Johnson seemed to be unable to make this kind of statesman-like gesture in connection with Vietnam….What I was concerned about was that we end the nightmarish war and free our souls."

Obviously Dr. King was not too concerned about what the Johnson administration felt, because by November he was still voicing his strong dissent about the war. "I say to you, this morning, that if you have never found something so dear and so precious to you that you will die for it, then you aren't fit to live," King said in a sermon from his pulpit at Ebenezer Baptist Church. Even without the mention of Vietnam, the congregation knew what he was talking about.

22

Black Panther Party

For the leadership of the Student Nonviolent Coordinating Committee (SNCC), the emergence of a Black Panther Party in Oakland, California, was nothing new. In fact, they were aware of its growth plans long before a platoon of them, bearing rifles, barged into the state capitol building in Sacramento in the spring of 1967. The origins of the Party, at least from the standpoint of its name, evolved from the civil rights movement. As Stokely Carmichael often related, the Party would have never come about had it not been for the march from Selma to Montgomery in 1965. Because the route of the march cut across the swamp-like region of Lowndes County, the members of SNCC—as they had done in every town through which they passed—actively engaged local residents, cajoling them to register to vote.

Carmichael recalled his experience during a brief layover in the town. "When the march left Lowndes, so did we," he said. But unlike the other marchers, he returned, along with other SNCC workers as they had promised the residents they met that first time. When they returned the townsfolk remembered them. "Hey, as soon as we arrived, we got a house," Carmichael continued. "We just walked into a house." Their new friends even provided them armed protection. Many of the farmers there had prior experience with radical politics stemming from the 1930s when members of the Communist Party recruited in the area. "That's the reason Lowndes County went so fast. Within one year we had that county completely organized," Carmichael boasted.

Achieving such a phenomenal feat would not have been possible without the tireless energy and dedication of such freedom fighters as John Hulett. He helped facilitate the recruitment process that brought local residents into the organizational structure of the Lowndes County

Voters League, later to be called the Lowndes County Freedom Organization or the Black Panther Party.

The panther designation had come about when members chose the black panther as its symbol to be placed on the ballot. "The black panther was a vicious animal, who, if he was attacked, would not back up," Hulett explained. "When we chose that symbol, many of the people in our county started saying we were a violent group who is going to start killing white folks. But it wasn't that, it was a political symbol that we was here to stay and we were going to do whatever needed to be done to survive." The party was criticized and derisively called communists and black nationalists.

On May 22, 1966, Hulett delivered a speech in Los Angeles in which he explained the history and intentions of his party. "Too long Negroes have been begging, especially in the South, for things they should be working for. So the people in Lowndes County decided to organize themselves—to go out and work for the things we wanted in life." This was not only for people in his county, he added, "but for every county in the state of Alabama, in the southern states, and even in California."

Hulett purposefully mentioned California because almost since the inception of the Lowndes County Black Panther Party, rival groups in California and elsewhere had been vying to use the name. The rivalries got so bad that Carmichael had to go to California to keep the groups from becoming violent. At first, he considered the idea of forming a united Black Panther Party that would incorporate all of the disparate groups, but that was a pipe dream. So, it was off to the West Coast.

"Two brothers from Oakland were representing, far as I could see, no established group," Carmichael said. "They were together so I guess they represented themselves. They were militant and political, and one of them, Huey [Newton], seemed very serious. When I first met them, he was the one that impressed me. He didn't say much, whereas his partner, Bobby Seale, rarely stopped."

Carmichael reported to Atlanta that the differences between the groups were so deep and intense there was no way for him to determine which should be the legitimate Black Panthers. He left the Bay Area and went to Los Angeles for ten days. When he returned to Oakland he discovered the problem had been solved. Huey P. Newton and Bobby Seale were the only ones still interested in retaining the name. Later, Newton would write a letter to the Lowndes County Black Panthers formally requesting the use of the name. But there was never any formal granting of the name since the Lowndes County activists felt they didn't own it. The name, they said, belonged to the people.

Newton, however, contradicts Carmichael's version of what happened. "Bobby and I together had chosen the Party's name," he said, "taking it from the symbol of the black panther party used by the Lowndes County Freedom Organization....We never asked Stokely's advice...we were organized before we met him."

In several months the slogan "Power to the People!" would reverberate from one black community to another as the Black Panther Party for Self-Defense grew in size and significance. According to Newton, it all began after he read a pamphlet about voter registration and how the people in Lowndes County had armed themselves against violent attacks. So, they had the symbol they wanted, and from the readings of Frantz Fanon, Che Guevara, Mao Tse-Tung, Malcolm X, and Robert Williams, whose "Negroes With Guns" would prove influential, the two students of Merritt Junior College had a sampling of the theory and practice they needed to begin organizing what they called the "lumpen proletariat."

But before recruiting members, they had to lay out a program of action—"What We Want" and "What We Believe." Newton began reciting the points and

Seale quickly jotted them down. "All in all, our ten-point program took about twenty minutes to write," Newton said. Among the ten points were a demand for freedom, full employment for black people, an end to exploitation and police brutality, reparations, decent housing and education, and that black men be exempt from military service. Seale has a slightly modified take on those first organizational moments, saying, "Huey and I racked our brains as to how to get some community-based organization going, and especially how to properly deal directly with the police. We decided we would need to watch the police, patrol the police; black brothers were getting brutalized and arrested. Huey and I knew we could do it, but we'd have to do it armed." Newton suggested they arm themselves with a law book, a tape recorder, and a shotgun, which they knew was legal to carry so long as it wasn't concealed.

Minister of Defense Newton and Chairman Seale's first recruit was fifteen-year-old Bobby Hutton, whom they called Li'l Bobby. He was among the teenagers who hung around the two founders, absorbing their ideas about politics and culture. From the pool halls and bars, they began to add more members to the Party. With several more Panthers in tow, they began to patrol the police, whom they viewed as nothing more than an army of occupation.

"The police are not in our community to promote our welfare or for our security," Newton explained. "They are here to contain us, to brutalize

BLACK PANTHER PARTY: OCTOBER 1966 PLATFORM AND PROGRAM

What We Want
What We Believe

1. We want freedom. We want power to determine the destiny of our Black Community.
2. We want full employment for our people.
3. We want an end to the robbery by the white man of our Black Community.
4. We want decent housing, fit for shelter of human beings.
5. We want education for our people that exposes the true nature of this decadent American society. We want education that teaches us our true history and our role in the present-day society.
6. We want all black men to be exempt from military service.
7. We want an immediate end to police brutality and murder of black people.
8. We want freedom for all black men held in federal, state, county, and city prisons and jails.
9. We want all black people when brought to trial to be tried in court by a jury of their peer group or people from their black communities, as defined by the Constitution of the United States.
10. We want land, bread, housing, education, clothing, justice, and peace. And as our major political objective, a United Nations–supervised plebiscite to be held throughout the black colony in which only black colonial subjects will be allowed to participate for the purpose of determining the will of black people as to their national destiny.

us, to murder us because they have their orders to do so, just as the soldiers in Vietnam have their orders to destroy the Vietnamese people….They couldn't possibly be in our community to see that we receive due process of law for the simple reason the police themselves deny the due process of law."

An end to police brutality was one of the most important of the ten points, and they stressed this view in the first weeks of the Party's existence. The normal procedure was to merely stand by and observe what a police officer did when accosting a citizen. On several occasions they came close to violent confrontations with officers who longed for an opportunity to charge them with interfering with an arrest. But Newton and Seale taught their young recruits how to stand back and watch, ever ready with a law book lest they were approached, a shotgun if necessary, and a tape recorder to make sure everything that happened was documented.

Their policing of the police was soon all the rage in the community. Their tactics had also become a widely known among the nation's law enforcement agencies. It was only a matter of time before the Panthers' aggressive monitoring would provoke a response from nervous police officers. Not long after the Panthers opened their first office in Oakland on January 1, 1967, police accosted Newton and Seale in a car with other Panthers parked in front of their office. With his cohorts as the audience, Newton displayed a daring, if somewhat reckless performance, and he never blinked.

"What are you doing with that shotgun?" an officer asked Newton, after following him from his car into Panther headquarters.

"What are you doing with your gun?" Newton snapped back. "Because if you try to shoot at me, or if you try to take this gun, I'm going to shoot back at you, swine."

Such bravado caught the officer off guard. He was clearly unnerved by Newton's defiance. For several minutes the two had sharp exchanges, much to the delight of the other Panthers. Soon the word got out about the showdown with the officer. The Panthers quickly garnered a reputation as an organization that would stand up to the police. It was what Newton and Seale needed to bolster their ranks.

But if the Party was going to really attract attention, they also needed a big name, someone with a background that could be respected by young men in the streets. One evening that winter Seale called Newton and asked him to meet him at a radio station; he wanted him to meet Eldridge Cleaver. Cleaver had been released on parole from prison in December 1966 after serving nine years of a sentence for rape. He would later ride a crest of popularity with the publication of his book *Soul on Ice*, which included intimate love letters to his attorney as well as prescriptions for militant political activism. **CD**

The purpose of the meeting was to recruit Cleaver into the Party, but he was noncommittal, merely nodding at their recitation of the ten-point program and the Party's overall intentions. They would meet again a month later when a coalition of groups, including one calling itself the Black Panther Party of Northern California, had planned to honor the anniversary of the assassination of Malcolm X. This was one of the groups that Carmichael had talked about during his attempts to mediate between the factions. Security guards were needed to escort Malcolm X's widow, Betty Shabazz, to the rally, and Newton and the Panthers were given the responsibility.

After picking up Dr. Shabazz from the airport, Newton and his entourage took her to the offices of *Ramparts* magazine, a radical, white-owned publication, where she was to be interviewed. A fracas occurred at the office between Newton and a cameraman. Things got a bit rowdy and Newton commanded the other Panthers to remove Malcolm's widow from the scene. The police were on the scene and their attention went immediately to Newton, who was wielding his shotgun. Some reports say he dared the police to make the first move.

DISC 2
TRACK 10

"If you start drawing, this will be a bloodbath," Newton cried.

The cops froze and Newton walked off, entered a car, and drove away with Cleaver and Seale. Unbeknownst to Newton, Cleaver was very impressed by Newton's stand. As Newton remembered, Cleaver asked then if he could become a member of the Party. Cleaver offered a different story. "I fell in love with the Black Panther Party immediately upon my first encounter with it; it was literally love at first sight," Cleaver enthused, then age thirty-three and working at *Ramparts* as an editor.

"It happened one night at a meeting in a dingy little storefront on Scott Street in the Fillmore District, the heart of San Francisco's black ghetto. It was February, 1967…I spun around in my seat and saw the most beautiful sight I had ever seen; four black men wearing black berets, powder blue shirts, black leather jackets, black trousers, shiny black boots— and each with a gun!"

By April, the Panthers had published their first paper, edited by Cleaver. Through the paper, they increased their membership both locally and nationally. The group also gained wider reconnaissance and recognition from the police, whom they referred to as "Pigs." Even so, they remained primarily a California organization.

But that was to change on May 2, when they marched into the State Capitol Building at Sacramento. When the caravan of cars came to halt outside the Capitol Building, thirty Panthers—twenty-four men and six women—emerged. All of them were dressed in black and some had bandoliers stuffed with shotgun shells criss-crossing their bodies, with rifles

A member of the Black Panther Party speaks to Assemblyman Willie L. Brown in the Capitol

Armed Black Panther Party members stand in the corridor of the Capitol in Sacramento, after arriving to protest a bill restricting public carrying of weapons

and shotguns pointed down to the ground or straight up into the air. Li'l Bobby Hutton, wearing a stingy brimmed hat, a shotgun nestled in his right arm, led the way. Behind him was Seale brandishing a holstered 9mm pistol that was strapped to his waist. The Panthers fanned out and walked toward the building. Suddenly, from out of nowhere came a veritable army of reporters. Lights from the TV cameras and flashbulbs illuminated the band of young Panthers as they went from room to room, looking for the State Assembly meeting hall.

Onlookers were stunned at the procession, gawking and muttering to each other, "who in the hell are these crazy Negroes?" The Panthers were unaware that one of the shocked, baffled spectators was Governor Ronald Reagan. Entering the Assembly floor,

Seale was surprised that Cleaver was there and even more surprised when he joined the Panthers as they filed down the aisle. The Panthers stopped and Seale unrolled the paper he had clutched in his hand and read the Party's "Executive Mandate Number One."

"The Black Panther Party for Self-Defense calls upon the American people in general and the Black people in particular to take careful note of the racist California Legislature which is now considering legislation aimed at keeping the Black people disarmed and powerless at the very same time that racist police agencies throughout the country are intensifying the terror, brutality, murder, and repression of Black people," it read in part.

Media across the country picked up the story. It was not the words that kept eyes riveted to the reports; it was the image of black men bearing arms. It was a dazzling show of force, but the audacious act backfired. Rather than halting the push for gun-control laws then on the minds of many legislators, the invasion precipitated new measures to check the possibility of another Panther embarrassment.

Executive Mandate Number Two, dated June 29, 1967, and issued by the Party, was an attempt to bring even more notable figures into their ranks. It was addressed to Stokely Carmichael. "Because you have distinguished yourself in the struggle for the total liberation of black people from oppression in racist white America," it began and included several paragraphs of praise and admiration, "you are hereby drafted into the Black Panther Party for Self-Defense, invested with the rank of Field Marshal, delegated the following authority, power, and responsibility: To establish revolutionary law, order and justice in the territory lying between the Continental Divide East to the Atlantic Ocean; North of the Mason-Dixon Line to the Canadian Border; South of the Mason-Dixon Line to the Gulf of Mexico....So let it be done."

By the time it was done, Carmichael had apparently been promoted to Prime Minister, or head of the Party, which, as Newton said, would have in effect given the leadership of the Party to SNCC. "We even considered moving our headquarters to Atlanta, where we would be under SNCC, in their buildings, with access to their duplicating equipment and other sorely needed materials."

The merger also included the induction of H. Rap Brown as Minister of Justice and James Forman as Minister of Foreign Affairs. The Panthers were seeking an alliance with SNCC, but, as Newton would later discover, the feeling was not mutual. Despite the overtures, none of the SNCC inductees or other leaders ever deemed the merger a serious one. There was too much distrust for them to ever become partners, some SNCC members related. "There were just too many contradictions,"

Carmichael concluded, "serious contradictions. The similarities between SNCC and the Panthers were as obvious as were the differences."

To be sure, both organizations were youth oriented, idealistic, and fiercely committed to ending oppression, but they emerged from different exigencies and in different places. "SNCC had been fortunate in ways the Panthers were not," Carmichael observed. "To start with, the Panthers did not have the benefit of the highly experienced, politically activist adult mentorship that we had. No Bayard [Rustin], no Ella [Baker], no James Lawson, no Dr. King." Nor did the Panthers have the benefit of a shared experience through organizational work. They were essentially a quasi-military group of ex-gang members, and a "product of an alienated, urban ghetto culture." Whatever perfect notions many outsiders envisioned were offset by the realities, and eventually compounded by the machinations of COINTELPRO (Counter Intelligence Program), devised by J. Edgar Hoover's Federal Bureau of Investigation. The "dirty tricks" campaign of the agency exacerbated any differences, ultimately pitting the potential allies against one another.

Carmichael spent only a year with the Panthers before he left. His exit was hastened, he said, when he heard that Forman had been held at gunpoint and his life threatened. Moreover, a rumor was afloat that Carmichael might have had something to do with it. It was never absolutely clear if the incident ever occurred—Forman denies it—or if it did, who the perpetrators were. Nonetheless, Carmichael ended his affiliation with the Panthers and was soon enmeshed in a fight to deflect rumors that he was an agent for the Central Intelligence Agency.

When the merger attempt fell apart, Newton said he was glad it didn't work out because he never really trusted Carmichael. "You never knew where he was coming from," Newton recalled. "Stokely says one thing one day and another the next." There are some scholars who contend that the riots that raged across

America in the summer of 1967 might have been avoided if the merger between the two groups had occurred. That was certainly Newton's contention. But the uprisings, according to Cleaver, were inevitable and an outgrowth of class war and aggressive police behavior. "All those riots are making our lives miserable," he told interviewers. "They really don't want to focus in on the fact that it's the pigs and their mentors, the people who control the pigs, the power structure, the bald-headed businessmen at the chamber of commerce."

By the fall of 1967, the differences between SNCC and the Panthers would pale in comparison to the antagonism between the Panthers and the Oakland police. One evening Newton was on his way home from a party celebrating the end of his probation when Officer John Frey in his patrol car asked Newton to pull over. From the car's license plate, the officer knew the car was registered to one of the Panthers.

"Well, I'll be. If it isn't the great Huey Newton," Officer Frey is purported to have sang. "Let me see your driver's license and registration." Frey took the documents, glanced over them, passed his license back and headed for his car with the car's registration. It was clear he had called for backup when Officer Herbert Heanes showed on the scene. Having completed his check on the registration, Frey asked Newton and his companion, Gene McKinney, to get out of the car.

While Newton was being led to the patrol car, he began reciting the law. "You can take that law book and shove it up your ass," the officer reportedly snapped. Within a few seconds their sharp exchanges apparently evolved into a scuffle, gunfire erupted, and when the shooting was over, Newton had been

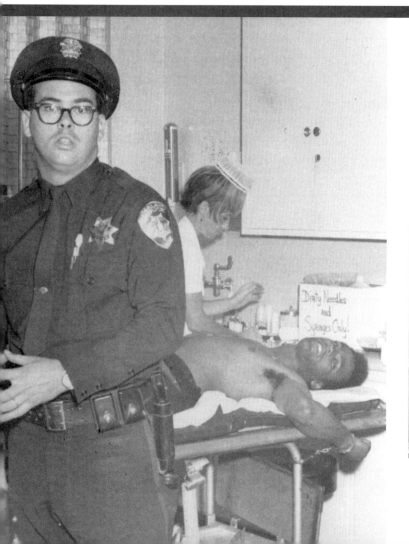

Left: Huey P. Newton is treated for a gunshot wound to the stomach while handcuffed to a hospital table

Above: Newton in jail

shot in the stomach. Officer Heanes had multiple wounds and Officer Frey was dead. McKinney had fled the scene, according to a man named Dell Ross, who claimed he happened to be passing by when Newton and McKinney flagged him down. He said he was forced at gunpoint to drive them to David Hilliard's house. Hilliard was the Party's chief of staff and he drove Newton to the hospital. When the police learned that Newton was at the hospital they proceeded there heavily armed, grabbed him, and slammed him roughly against the gurney to which he was handcuffed. Photos of Newton, stripped to the waist, appeared in newspapers all over the country.

A grand jury brought a three-count indictment against Newton. He was charged with first degree murder, assault with a deadly weapon, and the kidnapping of Dell Ross. The Panthers had their first *cause célèbre*. "Free Huey" was the latest slogan to resound across the land. "In less than a week we're in action, borrowing a psychedelically painted double-deck bus from one of the local white political communes, cruising the streets blaring 'Free Huey, Free Huey! Can a black man get a fair trial in America—even if he was defending his life against a white policeman?'" Hilliard recalled.

Soon the chants of "Free Huey or the sky's the limit!" were heard outside the Alameda Courthouse, where Newton's trial was scheduled. Supporters arrived from all over the world for the rallies and thousands of dollars were raised to get Newton the best lawyers available. Most of the rallies were attended by hundreds of Panthers, and at their boisterous best they presented a choir of voices singing, "No more pigs in our community. Off the pigs! No more pigs in our community. Off the pigs!"

Meanwhile, the police stepped up its harassment and raids on Panther offices and homes. In the first week of April 1968, both the militant and nonviolent advocates were jolted with the news of Dr. King's assassination in Memphis and the police attack on Eldridge Cleaver and other Panthers two days later. Cleaver was leading a convoy of cars filled with Pan-

Eldridge Cleaver outside the bullet-riddled window of the Black Panther headquarters

thers on patrol when they were accosted by the police. Though reports vary on the exact details of the fracas, reports are that everyone was asked to get out of the cars, but before they could, gunfire erupted and raked the night. Cleaver and Li'l Bobby Hutton scrambled into the basement of a nearby house, bullets flying over their heads. For about an hour and a half, a shootout raged. Unable to roust them from the basement, the police hurled tear gas canisters through a window. One of them hit Cleaver in the chest. He had already been shot in the foot. Suddenly, the house was on fire. They had no choice but to surrender. After dropping their weapons, Cleaver and Hutton clambered out of the basement. Cleaver was half-naked with his hands thrust in the air.

They were ordered to drop to the ground and spread eagle. Once they were down, the cops dragged them to the squad cars and began beating them. Then they were told to run to a cop car in the middle of the street. Cleaver, because of his wounded foot, told them he was unable to run. "Then they snatched Little Bobby away from me and shoved him forward, telling him to run for the car," Cleaver said. "It was a sickening sight. Little Bobby, coughing and choking on the night air that was burning his lungs as my own were burning from the tear gas, stumbled forward as best he could, and after he traveled about ten yards the pigs cut loose on him with their guns." A fusillade of bullets ripped through his back and he crumbled in a pool of blood.

The Party's first recruit was now its most prominent martyr. Having survived the shootout, Cleaver, now a parole violator, was taken to state prison. He was charged with three counts of attempted murder of policemen and three counts of assault with a deadly weapon. But his lawyers exploited a loophole in the law and two months later he was released. The Panthers' minister of information was free, but the minister of defense was awaiting trial on July 15, 1968. At the end of eight weeks of often conflicting testimony and a divided jury, Newton was convicted of voluntary manslaughter of Officer Frey. He was sentenced to four years in prison.

It should be noted that Carmichael had not yet fully severed his ties to the Panthers, because in August 1968 he was in Oakland extolling Newton and quoting him as he promoted guerrilla warfare. "Guerrilla warfare is where we have to go," he declared, clearly denouncing the tactics of SNCC and the other civil rights organizations. "And if armed with the correct political ideology and employ it, we recognize where we must move. If we were reading brother Huey P. Newton he explains very clearly. He said: 'In the beginning there are above ground groups, but this above ground groups are always forced underground. It is clear, as it should be clear in all our minds, that the man is moving to break up and destroy all groups that are above ground.'" The speech came a few months before he left the Party and later was expelled from SNCC. Carmichael said nothing about Newton's incarcera-

tion as he began to advance a notion of Pan-Africanism that would absorb his remaining days.

After stops at several prisons, including Vacaville and Soledad, Newton was locked up in the notorious California Men's Colony. He spent twenty-two months at this "hell hole," as it was known by the inmates, before he was notified in May 1970 that his sentence might be reversed. Ninety days later, on August 5, Newton completed the process to walk to freedom. He had served a little over two years in prison, but it seemed like a lifetime for someone as active as he was.

"Cut off from all this [society] for a few years, life around me at first seemed jerky and out of synchronization," Newton admitted. "All the sounds, movements, and colors coming on simultaneously—television, telephone, radio, people talking, coming and going, doorbells, and phones ringing—were dizzying at first. Ordinary life seemed hectic and chaotic, and quite overwhelming. I even had to figure out what to eat and what time I was going to bed. In prison, all this had been decided for me."

Though he had kept abreast with current events, particularly as they impacted the Party, it still took a while for him to adjust to the outside world that had witnessed the death of Li'l Bobby Hutton; the deaths of Panthers Alprentice "Bunchy" Carter and John Huggins in southern California, allegedly by members of Maulana Karenga's US (United Slaves) organization; the ordeal of the Panther 21 in New York City; the police infiltration of the Chicago Panthers that led to the murders of Fred Hampton and Mark Clark in December 1969; a memorandum from FBI Director J. Edgar Hoover asserting that the Panthers "were the greatest threat to internal security in the country"; the New Haven debacle and the trials of Seale, Lonnie McLucas, and Erika Huggins; Jonathan Jackson's failed attempt to free his revolutionary brother, George, from prison; and, perhaps most distressing for Newton, the killing in 1969 of nineteen Panthers with the jailing or arrest of some 745 others. 🆑

In short, the Party was in disarray when he was finally released. He quickly gathered that a massive rebuilding process was necessary. Most urgently, it was less than a month before preliminary sessions of the Revolutionary Constitutional Convention to be held in Philadelphia. Largely inspired by Cleaver, the convention was called to write a new Constitution of the United States. To Newton, it was a pointless exercise since they had no power to implement it. By now Cleaver was living in Algeria, having fled the country. Through telephone calls, Newton tried to impress upon Cleaver the more critical work of defending Seale and others in New Haven as well as the Soledad Brothers. Fresh out of prison, Newton had his hands full, especially the speech he had to deliver in the city of Brotherly Love on Labor Day weekend.

"Two centuries ago when the United States was a new nation, conceived in liberty, and dedicated to life, liberty, and the pursuit of happiness," Newton began, "the conditions prevailed in the nation and the assumptions upon which the foundation was built...to make sure the United States would come to its maturity under circumstances, which means that for a substantial portion of citizens life is nothing more than a living death. Liberty is nothing more than a prison of poverty, and the only happiness we enjoy is laughing to keep from crying."

On the civil rights movement, Newton noted that it could not produce the necessary foundation for a new Constitution because "of the nature of the U.S. society and economy." Toward the end of his ten-minute speech he brought the audience to its feet. "It is our conclusion that a slave who dies a natural death will not balance two dead flies on the scales of eternity. We will have our manhood, even if we have to level the face of the earth....I would like to say that we are one tonight, let us be one in the future, and power to all of the people."

Newton's apprehension about the Constitutional Convention was vindicated by the time of the sec-

A 1968 Black Panther poster. The bottom left corner reads: "Retaliation to Crime: Revolutionary Violence"

ond session in Washington, D.C., which, unlike the one in Philadelphia, failed to draw or to inspire the participants. Since it had been Cleaver's idea, it only exacerbated the rupture between him and Newton that began over their differences about how to deal with the murder of Fred Hampton and Mark Clark in Chicago. Cleaver called for armed retaliation; Newton felt that retaliation was adventuristic and suicidal. The agents of COINTELPRO, recognizing the growing split between the two leaders, applied further provocation with a disinformation campaign evident in FBI memos like one from May 1970, reading, "To create friction between Black Panther Party (BPP) leader Eldridge Cleaver in Algiers and BPP headquarters, spurious or fake letter concerning an internal dispute was sent Cleaver, who accepted it as genuine. As a result, the international staff of the BPP was neutralized when Cleaver fired most of its members."

Neither Newton nor Cleaver was aware of the plot to make them bitter enemies. Factions loyal to one or the other began months of violent intimidation and rivalry that became the source of further internecine fatalities.

But by the spring of 1971 the Panthers had virtually become an underground organization, from which sprang the Black Liberation Army. With the Party spinning into a web of dissolution, the leaders had no recourse but to suspend armed self-defense. To some degree, greater emphasis was given to a free breakfast program for children and free health clinics for the elderly. Later came the purges of members (particularly the highly respected Geronimo Pratt, David Hilliard, and Michael Tabor), Newton's fruitless attempt as an entrepreneur, his penthouse retreat, and his downward spiral into drugs, paranoia, and hallucination.

In 1972 and 1973, what remained of the shattered Party leadership threw itself into electoral politics.

Huey P. Newton speaks at a 1970 convention

From left: Ben Stewart, George Murray, and Bobby Seale speak at a news conference

"The BPP invested in local electoral politics in an unprecedented way," observed historian Dr. Ollie A. Johnson. "However, the decision to close virtually all of the Party's chapters and mount an electoral campaign precipitated a nearly irreversible process of organizational contraction and decline. In Oakland, Panthers worked around the clock registering voters, organizing, and mobilizing the Black community, attending and promoting rallies, and participating in countless campaign meetings."

Neither Bobby Seale's mayoral quest in Oakland nor Elaine Brown's bid for the council was successful. Even more debilitating, Seale left the Party in 1974 and Newton was in exile in Cuba. Elaine Brown was tapped to lead the splintered and practically depleted organization.

"The Black Panther Party had given me a definition," Brown wrote. "I had learned that racism and other oppressions bore down deep into the fabric of lives like mine and crippled them. And I had found peace in this knowing. I had found strength in the party's commitment to fight oppression."

She had also found the authority that would give her an opportunity for revenge on a member of the Party who had beaten her. "Brown demonstrated, upon her elevation, that the abuse of power was not a male prerogative," wrote Mumia Abu-Jamal. "She brooked no questioning of her role and relished the opportunity to 'discipline' a member of the Los Angeles underground who had the misfortune to have beaten her several years earlier."

There were a host of omens in the mid-seventies that would signal not only the downfall of the Black Panther Party but the sad destruction of lives that at one time expressed great potential for social and political change. Only a special few of them lived particularly long lives, and only a few of those retained the fire that made them such potent fighters for freedom. They were among the thousands dressed in black who devoted their lives, though often misguided, to extending the civil rights movement into the struggle for black liberation. And in many respects, given some of the societal advances, they did not fight or die in vain.

23

I've Seen the
Promised Land

While the Black Panthers in Oakland, California, were demanding that their leader, Huey P. Newton, be freed from jail after a October 1967 shootout that left one police officer dead, Dr. Martin Luther King Jr. convened a meeting of his nonviolent followers in Atlanta.

In November 1967, Dr. King and the Southern Christian Leadership Conference began discussions that would broaden the movement and address the true problems America faced. "We made a decision," he wrote. "The SCLC would lead waves of the nation's poor and disinherited to Washington, D.C., in the spring of 1968 to demand redress of their grievances by the United States government and to secure at least jobs or income for all."

The decision was a momentous step for Dr. King. Already he had advanced the civil rights movement to the international arena with his fervent stands against the war in Vietnam. Now he was making plans to broaden his fight against segregation and Jim Crow policies to economic matters that affected more than black Americans, but poor Americans of all colors. Gradually, in slow but significant increments, he was learning what tactics were necessary to bring about change in an obstinate society. Campaigns and marches in Albany, Selma, Birmingham, Chicago, in Mississippi and elsewhere were like primers instructing him on ways to best dramatize an issue, to best get the attention of the American people, particularly the power brokers and the leaders of the nation.

During his deepest moments of concern and reservation, King hoped this new strategy would not lead to further repression and would inspire those who sought a better America. He hoped the campaign for the poor and the dispossessed would receive a sympathetic understanding, and not the often brutal reaction that had accompanied his previous rallies and demonstrations. No matter the response, however, he was determined to forge ahead and "build militant nonviolent actions until that government moved against poverty."

What King envisioned was a massive "march on Washington," one that would stress the need for jobs, an end to the war in Vietnam that was robbing the economy and thereby depriving many Americans of a decent living, and pressure the government to live up to its longstanding ideals of democracy, liberty, and justice. It was a challenging assignment, but King and his associates—and this time he planned for them to be truly representative of America—were ready to embark on the historic mission,

one that would surely bring the nation to a new level of morality and social consciousness.

To get the ball rolling, Dr. King agreed to a rigorous schedule of speaking engagements. During one week alone in March 1968, for example, he delivered some thirty-five speeches, beginning in Grosse Pointe, Michigan, a suburb of Detroit. Wrote Paul Lee, a scholar noted for his research on the life of Malcolm X, "Dr. King appeared in Grosse Pointe Farms on March 14, 1968, to address a meeting at Grosse Pointe High School. He was probably briefed on the community beforehand, but his remarks suggest that, while he intended to be respectful, he felt no compulsion to defer to its more reactionary tendencies."

King's speech was less than monumental, as he received one of the worst hecklings he had ever experienced. The hecklers were led by Donald Lob-

Striking sanitation workers are surrounded by National Guard troops in Memphis

singer, whose racist, anti-Semitic diatribes were well-known in and around Detroit. It was not an auspicious debut for a series of speeches King was to deliver on his new policy.

Dr. King had other speaking engagements in the Detroit area, which went off without rancor. Then it was on to Los Angeles where he had more stops to make, including three sermons at churches, and then he flew to Memphis. Unlike Detroit and Los Angeles, Memphis was caught in the throes of a crippling strike. The issue, as it was explained to him, was the refusal of the city of Memphis to be fair and honest in its dealings with its sanitation workers, most of them black. More than one thousand of them were on strike and they were not about to make any concessions until their demands were met. Some had been foolish enough to think that new Mayor Henry Loeb would side with them, which was not the case.

Even before King arrived there were harbingers of an ill wind. Black sanitation workers were demanding improved safety measures after two black men were crushed in the disposal units of their trucks. On February 1, 1968, twenty-two black sewer workers were sent home without pay because of bad weather, while white workers were kept on the job. This sparked the strike eleven days later. Attempts were made to resolve the situation, but Mayor Loeb refused to negotiate until the strikers returned to work.

Among the workers' demands were better wages and working conditions. The average pay was roughly $1.80 an hour. The wages were so low that forty percent of the workers qualified for welfare and many worked second jobs. They lifted leaky garbage tubs into decrepit trucks and were treated unfairly. There were neither benefits, nor vacation, nor pension. The sanitation department refused to modernize ancient equipment used by the black workers. Black sanitation workers were called "walking buzzards."

Almost two weeks later, while King was in New York giving a speech commemorating the birthday of the late W. E. B. Du Bois, Memphis police, using billy clubs and Mace, attacked a small, peaceful march of sanitation workers. The incident triggered a larger response from the union that quickly united behind the local chapter, and Rev. James Lawson of the SCLC helped give the issue a citywide appeal.

This was the background that compelled King to alter his travel plans and head for Memphis. The decision was not endorsed by the board at the SCLC; they saw such a trip as a diversion from the Poor People's Campaign. Dr. King believed otherwise. He didn't feel that he could in good conscience turn his back on the plight of the black workers. Moreover, he concluded, being there was consistent with the overall objectives of the campaign.

On March 18, Dr. King spoke to a crowd of seventeen thousand at the Masonic Temple. Among his promises, he said he would return to the city on the 22nd to lead them in a march. A heavy snowstorm, about sixteen inches and the second largest in Memphis's history, postponed his appearance and the march. Meanwhile, mediation talks continued, though within a few days they would collapse. Reverend Ralph Abernathy arrived in Memphis on March 27 to see what could be done to resume negotiations, but to no avail. He informed the press that on the next day Dr. King would be arriving in the city.

Wrote Coretta Scott King, "I was just getting ready to board a plane from Washington to Atlanta when I decided to call our Washington office to express my regrets for not having been able to drop by, and to establish some personal contact since Martin had asked me to mobilize support from women's organizations for the Poor People's Campaign. As soon as I called, the director of our Washington office…informed me that while my husband was leading the demonstration in Memphis, violence had erupted."

Because his plane was late, King arrived in Memphis after the march had begun, but was quickly rushed by car to the front of it. He was immediately

A confrontation between a Memphis police officer and a suspected looter

aware that the protest was not very well organized; the more than five thousand participants marching from Clayborn Temple to city hall were spread out helter-skelter across Beale Street.

King had been in the march only a few minutes when chaos erupted. Some attributed the blame for the disturbance to a group called the Invaders, a youth-oriented organization interested in nurturing boys into manhood. According to reports, they held signs deriding Mayor Loeb and screamed chants of "Black Power," which particularly annoyed King and his SCLC members. The situation became so unruly that Mayor Loeb called in the National Guard, which further angered the protesters. Many of the union men, adorned with signs that read "I Am a Man," were pummeled by the police. Sixty-two people were seriously injured and one young man died after being shot in the back.

King was quickly escorted away while six hundred police dispersed the marchers with tear gas and nightsticks, arresting more than 150. The FBI circulated a memo to newspaper editorial offices across the country citing a breakdown of nonviolent principles in Memphis that were likely a precursor to what would occur in the Poor People's Campaign. King and many others believed the march had been undermined and sabotaged. It was the first time in King's life he was forced to leave a civil rights march.

On returning home to Atlanta, King was frustrated to know that as the most public figure involved, he would be held responsible for the fracas.

In his response to the riot, President Johnson stopped short of blaming King. "The tragic events in Memphis yesterday remind us of the grave peril rioting poses," he began in a statement to the press. "This nation must seek change within the rule of law in an environment of social order. Rioting, violence, and repression can only divide our people. Everyone loses when a riot occurs. I call upon all Americans of every race and creed, the rich and the poor, the young and old, our governments, businesses, unions and churches to obey the law and to preserve conditions of social stability which are essential to progress. I urge local law enforcement to deal firmly, but always fairly and without fear, with every infraction of law—to work unceasingly to prevent riots, and to train diligently to control them should they occur. I urge state law enforcement to prepare full support for local law enforcement whenever aid is needed to maintain order. Order must be preserved."

At a news conference a day after the riot, Dr. King said he would lead another "massive" civil rights demonstration in Memphis. He conceded that he had been "caught with a miscalculation" in the March 28 protest. "If I had known there was a possibility of violence yesterday, I would not have had that particular march," he declared. King, however, reaffirmed his determination to conduct his "Poor People's Campaign" in Washington beginning April 22. "We are fully determined to go to Washington. We feel it is an absolute necessity," he said.

Two days later, at a press conference in Washington, he offered the Johnson administration and Congress a way out. King said that either the president or Congress might be able to persuade him to call off the campaign by making "a positive commitment that they would do something this summer" to help the country's slums. But, he said, "I don't see that forthcoming."

Nor did King anticipate President Johnson's surprising address to the nation on March 31. "I shall not seek, and I will not accept, the nomination of my party for another term as your President," Johnson said at the end of his announcement, which was mostly geared toward the war in Vietnam. "But let men everywhere know, however, that a strong, a

From left: Hosea Williams, Jesse Jackson, Martin Luther King Jr. and Ralph Abernathy on the balcony of the Lorraine Motel, April 3, 1968

confident, and a vigilant America stands ready tonight to seek an honorable peace—and stands ready tonight to defend an honored cause—whatever the price, whatever the burden, whatever the sacrifice that duty may require." There was no mention of the pressing issues on the domestic front, especially the recent turmoil in Memphis.

On Wednesday morning, April 3, 1968, Reverend Ralph Abernathy met Dr. King at his home. King kissed Coretta goodbye and promised to call her later that evening. When he arrived in Memphis, he decided to take a room at the black-owned and -operated Lorraine Motel on Mulberry Street. He had been criticized for previously staying at the more fancy Holiday Inn. Plus, the motel was closer to the march's starting point. As promised, he later called his wife and told her things were proceeding as planned, though Mayor Loeb had obtained a federal injunction forbidding any "nonresidents" from participating in the march that was scheduled for that coming Monday, April 8. But King said they were going ahead with the march no matter what the mayor said. "I'll call you tomorrow night," he promised.

A violent rainstorm ripped through Memphis that evening when King was scheduled to speak at Clayborn Temple. Believing the inclement weather would curb attendance, King decided he would stay at the motel and allow Abernathy to substitute for him. When Abernathy arrived at the church, two thousand people were crammed in the pews, determined to hear King. Abernathy knew what he had to do. He called King and told him he'd better get over to the church, that the people were eager to hear him. **CD**

After an unusually long introduction by Abernathy, King began what was to be his last public speech. At its start, he used a rhetorical question to launch a mental flight across time and space as if the "Almighty asked me what age I would like to live in?" After citing several historic stops from Egypt to Greece to Rome and choosing not to stop at any of them, he chose to stop in the "second half of the

twentieth century," where people across the world were rising up seeking freedom.

Again and again he was interrupted with applause and people talking back to him in choruses of agreement. King, the master orator, set up his conclusion by dwelling on his mortality, his close calls with death, and then declaring he was ready, whatever the outcome: "Well, I don't know what will happen now. We've got some difficult days ahead. But it doesn't matter with me now. Because I've been to the mountaintop....I've seen the promised land. I may not get there with you. But I want you to know tonight, that we, as a people, will get to the promised land."

His final words were barely audible above the roar of the crowd. "I had heard him hit high notes before," Abernathy recalled of the speech, "but never any higher. The crowd was on its feet, shouting and applauding—even some of the television crew. It was a rare moment in the history of American oratory, [a moment] to file along with Washington's Farewell Address and the Gettysburg Address. But it was something different than those speeches because it was an eloquence that grew out of the black experience, with its similarities to the biblical story of captivity and the hard-won freedom. Everyone was emotionally drained by what he had said, including Martin himself, whose eyes were filled with tears."

The next day, April 4, King was in a cheerful mood, lounging in his brother's room at the motel, kidding with his associates, even having a pillow fight with Andrew Young, executive director of the SCLC. Young had spent the day in court and King kidded him about not being there to keep him abreast on what was going on in the world. "He threw a pillow at me," Young recalled, "and I threw one back at him. The next thing I knew they [the rest of the entourage] had all jumped on me and put me down between the two beds and piled all the pillows on me. It was just childish play having fun. Somebody came and knocked on the door and said

DISC 2
TRACK 11

they were there to pick him up for dinner. And he went up to his room to dress. We were standing out in the courtyard and it was getting cold, and since he had a cold, I told him he should bring his topcoat. Next thing I know, I thought a firecracker had gone off. I looked up and he wasn't there."

Reverend Jesse Jackson, who was with King when the bullet ripped through his jaw and throat, called Mrs. King to tell her the news. Dr. King's wife recalled, "'Coretta,' he said, 'Doc just got shot. I would advise you to take the next thing smoking.' It hit me hard—not surprise, but shock—that the call I seemed subconsciously to have been waiting for all our lives had come. I asked for details, and Jesse, trying to spare me, said, 'He was shot in the shoulder.' I sensed that it was quite serious, and I wanted to ask how seriously hurt he was, but I was afraid. I said, 'I'll check the next flight.'"

While Abernathy attended to his fallen friend, who only moments before was talking to him from the motel's balcony, Young, Jackson, and others tried to figure out where the bullet had come from, pointing to a distance beyond the motel. Finally an ambulance arrived and King was taken from the second floor of the motel to St. Joseph's Hospital, where he was pronounced dead less than an hour later.

Senator Robert Kennedy of New York was among the first elected officials to be informed of King's death. "I have sad news for all of our fellow citizens and people about peace all over the world," Kennedy announced, impromptu, to an audience in Indianapolis. "That is, that Martin Luther King was shot

Ralph Abernathy, Andrew Young, and Jesse Jackson stand with police over the body of Martin Luther King Jr.

and killed," he continued, but his last words were obscured by screams from the listeners. 🔘

Reporter Earl Caldwell had witnessed most of the incident from his room on the first floor of the motel. "After the shot," he wrote, "Mr. [Solomon] Jones [King's driver] said he saw a man 'with something white on his face' creep away from a thicket across the street....Police were reported to have chased a late-model blue or white car through Memphis and north to Millington." Mayor Loeb announced that he was taking every precaution to prevent any acts of disorder.

Other mayors were taking the same precautions, but often to no avail as riots raged in more than one hundred cities. While many of the folks in the street rampaging were merely expressing a hostility born of poverty and despair, others were heartbroken, believing that if they had killed a man of peace,

there was no hope left for reconciliation and goodwill. The "Kerner Report," which had meticulously chronicled the civil disorders of the sixties, had been published the month before, in March. If it had taken a little longer, it might have had additional pages of turbulence and disaster to prove what it had concluded—that this was a nation divided.

The eruption in Detroit was typical of the urban distress that exploded across America. Four thousand National Guardsmen and four hundred state policemen were sent to the city on April 5 to help 4,200 city police quell violence. Mayor Jerome P. Cavanagh proclaimed a state of emergency and ordered an 8 pm to 5 am curfew. Two blacks were killed by policemen in looting incidents and Governor George Romney said one looter was killed "accidentally." 1,483 persons were arrested from April 5–9; 802 of the arrests were for

Chicago buildings burn in the widespread riots following Dr. King's death

Mules carry the casket of Dr. Martin Luther King Jr.

curfew violations. Twelve persons were injured, and 378 fires were reported.

"White America killed Dr. King and they had absolutely no reason to do so," Stokely Carmichael told reporters. "He was the one man, in our race, who was trying to teach our people to have love, compassion, and humility for what white people had done."

President Johnson, who at one time embraced King and his movement but had grown disenchanted with him since his anti-war remarks, was compelled to speak to the nation the day following the tragedy. "Once again the heart of America is heavy," he began. "The spirit of America weeps for a tragedy that denies the very meaning of our land. The life of a man who symbolized the freedom and faith of America has been taken. But it is the fiber and fabric of the republic that is being tested. If we are to have the America we mean to have, all men of all races, all regions, all religions must stand their ground to deny violence its victory in this sorrowful time, and all times to come. Last evening after receiving the terrible news of Dr. King's death, my heart went out to his family and to his people, especially to the young Americans who I know must sometimes wonder if they are to be denied a fullness of life because of the color of their skin."

To Dr. King's widow the president said, "I want you to know how deeply Mrs. Johnson and I feel for you and your family. I'm getting ready to go on television to make a statement." In the statement he announced that he would call an extraordinary joint session of Congress to hear him outline a program of constructive—not destructive—action in this hour of national need. 🆑

As the president prepared his initiative, the SCLC planned to go forward with its scheduled march in Memphis. Harry Belafonte, who had been consoling the grieving widow, suggested that Mrs. King attend the march. She agreed. On Monday, April 8, 1968, with her children by her side and thousands of people looking on, she talked about her husband's ideas of redemptive suffering.

DISC 2
TRACK 11

The Poor People's Campaign crosses Pennsylvania Avenue, carrying out the work of King after his death

In closing she asked a question and made a hopeful statement: "How many men must die before we can really have a free and true and peaceful society? How long will it take?

"If we can catch the spirit and true meaning of this experience," she said, "I believe that this nation can be transformed into a society of love, of justice, peace, and brotherhood where all men can really be brothers."

Dr. King's funeral took place the next day at Ebenezer Baptist Church in Atlanta and was followed by a memorial service at Morehouse College. At the front of the cortege were Coretta Scott King and her children; A. D. King, Martin's brother; and the Reverend Ralph Abernathy. King's bier was placed on a flatbed wagon pulled by two mules, a symbol of the planned Poor People's Campaign. Hosea Williams was in front of the entourage of fifty thousand people, guiding the mules down the street. Andrew Young walked in back of the wagon. At Morehouse, Dr. Benjamin Mays delivered the eulogy. King was temporarily laid to rest at South View Cemetery. Later his body would be placed in a tomb at the King Center in Atlanta.

The nation mourned as the drum major for peace and justice was no longer alive to lead the charge against segregation, racism, and bigotry. Those hundreds of people who were close witnesses to his legacy stood around his grave site, weeping both for his absence and their loss. But there was still work to do, Dr. King would probably advise them, still a crusade to wage, a campaign to complete.

Afterword

The era between the lynching of Emmett Till in 1955 and the assassination of Dr. Martin Luther King Jr. in 1968 marked a generation of struggle for civil rights. A pantheon of activists and leaders—A. Philip Randolph, Bayard Rustin, Thurgood Marshall, James Farmer, Rosa Parks, Ella Baker, Bob Moses, James Forman, John Lewis, Diane Nash, and Stokely Carmichael (Kwame Ture)—provided the movement with insight and urgency. Even those outside the movement such as Malcolm X and Robert Williams served as important militant counterweights, making the demands of nonviolent advocates easier to accept.

If the civil rights movement and its fight to end segregation could be characterized as a battle between David and Goliath, then Goliath had won. Dr. King was dead and his most immediate legacy, the Poor People's Campaign, did not achieve its purpose. Still, the war was not over. For the next decade or so, the fight would rage, mainly in urban ghettoes where radical activists sought "by any means necessary" to carry on the ideas of Malcolm X and Robert Williams. Malcolm had been killed in 1965, and by 1969, Williams was back in the United States after living in exile for almost eight years. His book *Negroes with Guns* had influenced a number of groups who proposed armed self-defense as a method of ending white supremacy and racial oppression.

Black militancy had aided and abetted the civil rights movement, and it continued to provide a counterbalance through the seventies as more blacks were elected to fill seats in city and state governments. They represented a portion of the dream King had when he met with his colleagues in November 1967 and planned the Poor People's Campaign.

In 1966, Stokely Carmichael called for "Black Power," and by the early 1970s it had begun to take root, at least in the political arena. Members of Congress such as Shirley Chisholm, Charles Diggs, Andrew Young, Barbara Jordan, and Parren Mitchell were among the black elected officials whose overall number increased from 1,185 in 1969 to 3,979 in 1976, according to the Joint Center for Political Studies. Several major cities—Detroit, Cleveland, Atlanta, and Los Angeles—elected their first black mayors.

In 1972, in Gary, Indiana, the National Black Political Assembly, spearheaded by Ron Daniels, brought together proponents of black nationalism and former civil rights activists to discuss the possibility of an independent black political party. The gathering was reminiscent of the Negro Convention Movement of the 1800s, and like those conventions in the past, this one in Gary failed to galvanize the disparate participants.

At the very beginning of the civil rights movement, education was a critical issue, symbolized by the legal fight around *Brown v. Board of Education*. Twenty years after the 1954 decision there had been a considerable increase in the number of blacks enrolled at higher educational institutions. The anticipated economic gains never materialized among black Americans, but they were pleased to know that black studies were becoming a integral part of high school and college curricula.

Affirmative action, a concept first cited by President Kennedy in the spring of 1961 to ensure that hiring and employment practices were free of racial bias, was given additional impetus by the Johnson administration in the mid-sixties. By the time of President Richard Nixon in 1969, federal contractors were required to show affirmative action to meet the goals of increasing minority employment. Any contractor receiving federal funds was required to comply with the mandate or risk losing the contract.

The debate on affirmative action continued without great rancor until a Supreme Court decision in the late seventies. Division began when Allan Bakke, a white applicant, was twice rejected by the medical school at the University of California at Davis in 1973 and 1974. He charged that he had been discriminated against when blacks with lower test scores were admitted in front of him. His complaint went all the way to the Supreme Court.

On June 28, 1978, in a landmark decision, the Court placed limitations on affirmative action, establishing that providing greater opportunities for minorities should not come at the expense of the rights of the majority. Affirmative action, the justices decided, was all right so long as it did not lead to reverse discrimination. The UC Davis Medical School had two separate admissions pools, the primary one being for standard applicants. However, sixteen of its one hundred places for were reserved for a second pool, one made up of minority and economically disadvantaged students. In this instance, the Supreme Court ruled that although race could factor into admissions considerations, rigid quotas could not.

The notion of "quotas" would be raised again and again by opponents of affirmative action. As recently as June 2003 it remained a bone of contention that reached critical mass at the University of Michigan. In the end, the Supreme Court upheld the right of universities to consider race in admissions procedures in order to achieve a diverse student body. In two lawsuits challenging University of Michigan admissions policies, the court ruled 5–4 in favor of the law school and, by a vote of 6–3, reversed, in part, the University's undergraduate policy, while still allowing for the consideration of race in admissions. The ruling, in effect, revisited the words of Justice Powell who cast the deciding vote in 1978 and wrote, "the goal of achieving a diverse student body is sufficiently compelling to justify consideration of race…under some circumstances."

In other words, quotas were impermissible, but the use of race as a "plus factor" in the pursuit of racial diversity could be allowed.

The civil rights movement also played a significant role in the "black consciousness movement" and the flowering of artistic expression, particularly in music, literature, art, dance, and theater. And there were hundreds of artists such as Harry Belafonte, Sidney Poitier, Archie Shepp, Max Roach, Amiri Baraka, Woodie King, Hoyt Fuller, Sonia Sanchez, Haki Madhubuti, Dudley Randall, Margaret Walker, Alice Walker, and Jacob Lawrence who fused their creativity with political activism.

The 1980s and the arrival of the Reagan administration were not good news for black Americans. President Ronald Reagan was barely in office before his Assistant Attorney General for Civil Rights William Bradford Reynolds told a congressional committee that "compulsory busing of students in order to achieve racial balance in the public schools is not an acceptable remedy." Reynolds, supported by Reagan, harped on this theme whenever dispatched to discuss civil rights. Blacks, he insisted, were better off in segregated schools and neighborhoods. Consistent with this thinking, he was opposed to affirmative action and other basic principles of the civil rights movement.

To ward off the momentum of retrenchment, branches of the Black United Front, a political formation meant to challenge the intensely sharp rightward drift of the government's policies, emerged in several cities. But they proved relatively powerless to halt the mean-spirited assault from Washington that eviscerated the housing, health, and welfare programs so critical to the impoverished black community. In 1991, to show how generally bad conditions were had become for black Americans in three walks of life, ABC's *PrimeTime Live* presented dramatic evidence that racial discrimination was a current disease, not merely a "legacy." Producers dispatched two evenly matched, well-dressed, well-spoken college graduates—one white, one black—to seek jobs through the same employment agency, apartments from the same landlords, and a car from the same dealer.

Again and again, hidden cameras recorded how the black man was lied to or turned away.

A decade or more later, black America is no better off economically than it was when Dr. King announced the Poor People's Campaign. The income and wealth disparities between black and white Americans are as wide as ever, according to a recent Current Population Survey, a joint project of the Bureau of Labor Statistics and the U.S. Census Bureau. Median earnings for black men working at full-time jobs came to $560 per week, 76.9 percent of the median for white men ($728) in the fourth quarter of 2003. Among women the difference was less, with black women's median earnings ($502) reaching 87.2 percent of those for whites ($576).

The current job picture for black Americans is equally bleak. Unemployment among blacks is rising more rapidly than for other workers, and more sharply than in any downturn since the recession of the mid-1970s, according to recent labor statistics. In 2000, blacks constituted a little over 10 percent of the twenty million factory workers in the United States. During the recession that started in March 2001 an estimated three hundred thousand, or 15 percent, of factory workers who are black lost their jobs. This compares with 10 percent of factory workers who are white. While the black middle class has quadrupled in size, more than 40 percent of black children live at or below the poverty line.

If the recent incidents of police brutality against Africans and African Americans in New York City are representative of the national picture, then we are experiencing an epidemic. In 2003, there were four high profile homicides in which the misconduct or the overzealous aggressiveness of white officers was the cause. In the first month of the new year, an unarmed black youth, Timothy Stansbury, was killed by a white housing officer in Brooklyn. A recent study revealed that black men were four times more likely to be victims of police homicide than were white men.

Compounding the social malaise is the ever-expanding prison industrial complex. More than eight hundred seventy-five thousand African Americans are incarcerated nationally, and a startling one of every seven black males between the ages of twenty-five and twenty-nine is incarcerated on any given day.

Moreover, these inmates are increasingly exploited by multinational corporations at the expense of unionized workers. Some of the companies that use such labor are IBM, Motorola, Compaq, Texas Instruments, Honeywell, Microsoft, and Boeing, according to activist and professor Angela Davis. "But it is not only the high-tech industries that reap the profits of prison labor," Davis says. "Nordstrom department stores sell jeans that are marketed as 'Prison Blues,' as well as T-shirts and jackets made in Oregon prisons. Maryland prisoners inspect glass bottles and jars used by Revlon and Pierre Cardin, and schools throughout the world buy graduation caps and gowns made by South Carolina prisoners."

Even those African Americans beyond the reach of the prison industrial complex find it difficult to make ends meet. Gainfully employed blacks are profiled daily wherever they venture. There has been a rash of incidents in major department stores in which black shoppers have been wrongfully apprehended and accused of shoplifting by security guards. On certain turnpikes and expressways, black drivers are disproportionately stopped by highway patrolmen or state troopers.

Blacks with steady income and collateral are often denied bank loans, which continues to be an obstacle for those seeking to purchase their first home or jump start a business. Insurance can be a problem also, as exemplified by the allegations of sixteen black residents of Kansas City, Missouri, claiming large insurance companies refused to offer or renew homeowner's insurance, charged higher insurance premiums, or offered only inferior insurance policies in minority neighborhoods. These federal court cases, filed in 2003, are still in motion.

Whether seeking a loan, a job, an apartment to rent, or a car, blacks remain repeatedly discriminated against. In 2000, class-action lawsuits were filed in federal court against major automakers' financing companies alleging a higher price markup for blacks than whites. "Debby Lindsey, a business professor at Howard University, analyzed thousands of loans from GMAC (General Motors Acceptance Corporation) and NMAC (Nissan Motors Acceptance Corporation) and concluded that blacks ended up much more in dealer markup than whites paid. For example, in a sample of 9,400 NMAC borrowers of all races, whites paid an average of $508 in markup, while blacks paid an average of $970. For a sample of 4,900 GMAC customers, the figures were: $643 markup for whites, $959 markup for blacks," wrote Holden Lewis for Bankrate.com.

What is to be done? One response to the persistent inequities is to resume the demonstrations and rallies that pressured the status quo in the sixties. Over the last score of years, Reverends Al Sharpton and Herb Daughtry of House of the Lord Church in Brooklyn have been exceedingly vigilant, calling protests each time a black or Hispanic youth has been killed unjustifiably by a police officer. Their efforts have inspired several other organizations, including the October 22 Coalition, the Black Radical Congress, and the New Jersey-based People's Organization for Progress, led by Larry Hamm. Under the leadership of Kweisi Mfume, the NAACP has mobilized its troops to halt the police's rampant abuse.

Mfume and Marc Morial, president and CEO of the National Urban League, criticized the police handling of an incident involving the death of Nathaniel Jones in November 2003. The beating death of Jones, a black man, by police officers was captured on videotape. Morial said, "Too often police conduct has left black Cincinnatians feeling that too many police officers consider the lives of black males expendable. To renew the confidence of all of Cincinnati's citizens in its local police force and our nation's justice system, an independent federal civil rights investigation by the U. S. Justice Department into the death of Mr. Jones seems a reasonable first step."

In 2002, Judson Jeffries, a professor of political science at Purdue University conducted a study that provided more than anecdotal evidence of police brutality across the nation. His study focused on incidents of white police officers assailing black citizens. "More than 25 percent of white officers interviewed in Illinois and 15 percent in Ohio stated that they had observed an officer harassing a citizen 'most likely' because of his or her race," Jeffries wrote. "In Los Angeles such brutality appears to be the order of the day. Officer John Mitchell, who worked out of South Central's 77th division, said that most of the officers that he worked with were racist and moreover, 'extremely eager to be in a shooting.'"

Los Angeles is not the only city where policing tactics have been called into question, Jeffries added. "Investigations of police departments in Buffalo, Charleston, West Virginia, Cleveland, Detroit, Houston, New Orleans, Orange County, Florida, Philadelphia, and Selma, Alabama, have revealed that racism and brutality are widespread and often tolerated by department commanders. In Selma, police harassment of black males had become so prevalent that black leaders installed a telephone hotline for people to report police use of excessive force. While such findings and personal testimony may appear anecdotal and case specific to some, they still provide some insight into the dynamics of white police use of excessive force against black males throughout the United States."

Sharpton, Daughtry, Hamm, Mfume, and Morial are well aware that merely marching and calling for investigations will not bring an end to the violence and injustice that continue plague our society. Empowerment through the courts, workplace, schools, and neighborhoods is a demand that com-plements the campaign for reparations, which is becoming increasingly popular among activists and in the media.

No one can predict where the next spark will light and renew the movement for social and political change. Many thought the protests against the Bush administration and its war in Iraq would unite various sectors of the society, giving momentum to the fight against AIDS, invigorating the mobilization for affirmative action, and undergirding the general demand for universal civil and human rights.

At its peak, the civil rights movement was a powerful force that swept millions into its wake. Native Americans, women, gays and lesbians, and Chicanos received their inspiration from the nonviolent struggle against Jim Crow and white supremacy. Another march on Washington? If so, it'll have to do more than the previous protests, and draw more people than Million Man March. Another Poor People's Campaign? That may be part of the answer since the first attempt was stillborn.

The real solution may rest in a thorough examination of the strategies and tactics that worked for Dr. King and his followers. If there's to be another civil rights movement, it must be strong and large enough to fight on more than one front. It must be prepared to deal with both domestic and international issues; it must embody the spirit of Dr. King, the boldness of Rosa Parks, the integrity of Malcolm X; it must be a movement that is interracial and intergenerational, and it must be one forged for the long haul because that's what it's going to take. We can't afford to repeat the mistakes of the past if we want a future free of exploitation, sexism, and racism. That future was the real, ultimate promise of the civil rights movement.

Herb Boyd
August 2004

Acknowledgments

Writing this book and researching the civil rights movement was truly inspirational, pushing me to produce a narrative I hope is representative of the phenomenal courage of the participants. While I was reluctant to take this project when it was first offered to me, believing there were enough books on the movement, my editor, Hillel Black, explained that the book would include two CDs—a veritable soundtrack to the movement. This and the early stories I encountered convinced me that something more could be said about those turbulent days, and particularly about the hundreds of yet unnamed, but valiant, freedom fighters.

Once I began to dig into the research, other interesting facets of the movement were revealed. From the outset, I was concerned about giving more discussion to the countless number of unheralded people who had participated in the movement. Discovering them and allowing them to speak, or to speak for them in many cases, was very fulfilling. It was equally rewarding to encounter so many new biographies and autobiographies of some of the movement's major voices, particularly Dr. King's autobiography, completed posthumously by Clayborne Carson, the autobiography of Stokely Carmichael (Kwame Ture), which was finished by his co-author Michael Thelwell, and John Lewis and Barbara Ransby's always engrossing study of Ella Baker's life.

Those of you who truly delve into the book will find how significant these works and others were to me toward framing a perspective, shaping my analysis, and generally coming to grips with a generation of struggle that helped to topple the walls of segregation and white supremacy. *We Shall Overcome* allowed me to revisit and to update the Emmett Till case, *Brown v. Board of Education*, and the murders of Chaney, Goodman, and Schwerner.

We gathered the audio clips and sound bites that comprise the soundtrack from a multitude of sources. We listened to hundreds of hours of material, recognizing quickly that distilling everything down to two hours could hardly represent the scope of the movement, nor include all the incredible things we heard. We hope this book and these CDs tell some captivating stories and can become a starting point for you in your reading, listening, and research, and we've provided a bibliography and a resources section to give further ideas.

While on the topic of audio, let me thank the dedicated work of Marie Macaisa and Todd Stocke in this endeavor, as well as their creativity in composing the narration delivered so knowingly by Ossie Davis and Ruby Dee. Todd, Sarah Tucker, and Hillel were a resourceful trio in keeping the project in focus while winnowing the wheat from the chaff. Samantha Raue drove the photos and documents you see here and was responsible for guiding each and every page to the end, and many on the Sourcebooks editorial and design teams put their able hands on this work, including Megan Dempster, Taylor Poole, Matt Diamond, Derek Wegmann, Jenna Jakubowski, Erin Rogers, Dan Bulla, and Dawn Crowther.

Many graciously gave us their time and talents on the audio, photo, and research front. We couldn't have done it without them: Brian Fulford at CNN; Cathy Carapella and the team at Smithsonian Folkways; Nancy Cole, Elena Brodie, and Sarah Donna at NBC; Margaret Burke at BBC Library and Pearl Lieberman at CBS News Archives; Leslie Chavous and the wonderful team at Intellectual Properties Management and the King Estate; the John F. Kennedy Library; the Harry S. Truman Library; the Dwight D. Eisenhower Library; researchers and archivists at the Library of Congress and the National Archives; Thad Allton and Tricia Johnston at the *Topeka Capital-Journal*; Lynn Ewbank at the Arkansas History Commission; Walter Naegle; Vinnie Maressa at Sony Music; Lynne Okin Sheridan and Jeff Rosen at Special Rider Music; Margaret A. Compton, Mike Richmond, and Ruta Abolins at the University of Georgia; Diane Lamb from the *Greensboro News & Record* news library; Juliette Perez at WB Music; the fabulous and gracious Sonia Sanchez; Lylian Morcos and Joe Basile at Thirteen/WNET; Linda VanZandt at the University of Southern Mississippi Center for Oral History; Mark H. Danley, PhD, at the McCain Library and Archives at the University of Southern Mississippi; Claudia Anderson at the LBJ Library and Museum; Brian DeShazor and Arline Chang at Pacifica; Anne Prichard at the University of Arkansas Library; Congressman John Lewis and Mario Collins in his DC office; Kay Mills, author of *This Little Light of Mine: The Life of Fannie Lou Hamer*; Loretta Fellin at the Richmond Organization; Brenda Billips Square at the Amistad Research Center at Tulane University; Gary Handman in the Media Resources Center at UC Berkeley; Don Fleming from the Alan Lomax Archives; Anne Skilton at the University of North Carolina at Chapel Hill; John Shaw at the Vincent Voice Library; the many voices you hear speaking or singing on these CDs; and many, many others we've probably missed.

There is a slew of resourceful folks I only encountered momentarily during a visit to the Sourcebooks headquarters in Naperville, Illinois, but it was an opportunity to meet them and their visionary leader, Dominique Raccah, whose enthusiasm for this project remains undiminished. Joel Roberts, who conducted an author's workshop in preparation for book tours, is an extremely helpful consultant I now count among my friends.

It was my close and dearest friends who, as always, were most important when neither the flesh nor the spirit was willing. My wife, Elza—my alter ego, confidant, and eternal lover—made sure I was properly nourished in the kitchen and concise with my writing. Indeed, she supplied food and thought. Marie Brown, my agent, is that other woman in life, whose editorial skills and management are invaluable. Another Brown, Vicky, my publicist, wasted no time getting the promotion gears in motion. And

there's Katherine Brown, my mother, who is just as alert and feisty today as she was when I was a teenager more than a half-century ago. Much gratitude is due to my brother Charles, who taught me the art of self-defense, and to my sister, Corliss McAfee, who taught me not to be offensive.

Consultation for this project, as in most of my writing assignments, benefited from conversations with a gallery of knowledgeable writers, editors, teachers, and activists. Daily talks with my attorney Robert Van Lierop and my partners Don Rojas and Ron Daniels were absolutely necessary, keeping me abreast of both the big picture of world events and those little, vital pieces of information that suddenly threw light on a murky portion of the project. Mike Thelwell, Playthell Benjamin, Percy Sutton, Dan Aldridge, Malik Chaka, Elinor Tatum, and the gang at the *Amsterdam News*, Todd Burroughs, Aziz Adetimerin, Bob Belden, Clarence Atkins, Gordon Parks, Yusef Lateef, Ron Williams, Cleophus Roseboro, Charles Moore, Jules Allen, Margot Jordan, Frederick Hudson, Linn Washington, Kermit Eady, Dr. Rae Alexander Minter, Ron Lockett, and others are my lifelong friends who make it such a joy to share in public and private discourse.

But the greatest acknowledgment goes to the fearless civil rights participants, hundreds and even thousands of whom faced death in order to bring about change in a racist society. It is your remarkable story I have tried to tell once again, hoping there are no grievous errors and that the book matches the fervor and devotion you gave in the heat of battle.

Bibliography

Books

Abernathy, Ralph David. *And The Walls Came Tumbling Down.* New York: Harper & Row, 1989.

Abu-Jamal, Mumia. *We Want Freedom.* Cambridge: South End Press, 2004.

Allen, Robert L. *The Port Chicago Mutiny.* New York: Amistad, 1989.

Anderson, Jervis. *Bayard Rustin: Troubles I've Seen: A Biography.* New York: HarperCollins, 1997.

Baldwin, James. *Price of the Ticket.* New York: St. Martin's Press, 1985.

Balkin, Jack M., ed. *What Brown v. Board of Education Should Have Said.* New York: New York University Press, 2001.

Bolden, Tonya. *The Book of African-American Women.* Avon: Adams Media Corporation, 1997.

Branch, Taylor. *Parting the Waters.* New York: Touchstone Books, 1989.

Breitman, George, ed. *Malcolm X Speaks.* New York: Grove Weidenfeld, 1965.

Brown, Elaine. *A Taste of Power.* New York: Pantheon Books, 1993.

Carmichael, Stokely. *Ready for Revolution.* New York: Scribner, 2003.

Cottrol, Robert J., Raymond T. Diamond, and Leland B. Ware. *Brown v. Board of Education: Caste, Culture, and the Constitution.* Kansas: University Press of Kansas, 2003.

Doyle, William. *Inside the Oval Office: The White House Tapes from FDR to Clinton.* Tokyo: Kodansha International, 1999.

DuBois, W. E. B. *Black Reconstruction in America.* New York: Macmillan, 1935.

Due, Patricia and Tananarive Due. *Freedom in the Family: A Mother-Daughter Memoir of the Fight for Civil Rights.* New York: Ballantine Books, 2003.

Forman, James. *The Making of Black Revolutionaries.* Seattle: University of Washington Press, 1997.

Foster, William Z. *The Negro People in American History.* New York: International Publishers, 1954.

Franklin, John Hope. *From Slavery to Freedom.* New York: Alfred Knopf, 1980.

Garrow, David J., Bill Kovach, and Carold Posgrove, eds. *Reporting Civil Rights: American Journalism 1941-1963.* New York: Library of America, 2003.

Garrow, David J., Bill Kovach, and Carold Posgrove, eds. *Reporting Civil Rights: American Journalism 1963-1973.* New York: Library of America, 2003.

Goldman, Peter. *The Death and Life of Malcolm X.* Chicago: University of Illinois Press, 1979.

Grant, Joanne, ed. *Black Protest: 350 Years of History, Documents, and Analyses.* New York: Ballantine Books, 1996.

Greenberg, Cheryl Lynn, ed. *A Circle of Trust: Remembering SNCC.* New Brunswick: Rutgers University Press, 1998.

Hampton, Henry, and Steve Fayer. *Voices of Freedom: An Oral History of the Civil Rights Movement.* New York: Bantam, 1991.

Hilliard, David, and Lewis Cole. *This Side of Glory.* New York: Little, Brown, 1993.

Hornsby, Jr., Alton. *Milestones in 20th Century African-American History.* Detroit: Visible Ink Press, 1993.

Huie, William Bradford. *Three Lives for Mississippi.* Jackson: University Press of Mississippi, 2000.

Jenkins, Carol and Elizabeth Gardner Hines. *Black Titan: A.G. Gaston and the Making of A Black American Millionaire.* New York: Ballantine, 2004.

Johnson, Charles, and Robert Adelman. *King: The Photobiography of Martin Luther King, Jr.* New York: Penguin, 2000.

Jones. Charles E., ed. *The Black Panther Party Reconsidered.* Baltimore: Black Classic Press, 1998.

Katz, William Loren. *Eyewitness: A Living Documentary of African-American Contribution to American History.* Englewood: Jerome S. Ozer Publications, 1999.

Keppel, Ben. *The Work of Democracy: Ralph Bunche, Kenneth B. Clark, Lorraine Hansberry, and the*

Cultural Politics of Race. Cambridge: Harvard University Press, 1995.

Kerner, Otto. *The Kerner Report*. New York: Pantheon Books, 1988.

King, Coretta Scott. *My Life with Martin Luther King, Jr.* New York: Henry Holt and Company, Inc., 1993.

King, Jr., Martin Luther. *The Autobiography of Martin Luther King, Jr.* New York: Warner Books, 2001.

King, Jr., Martin Luther. *Why We Can't Wait.* New York: New American Library, 2000.

Kluger, Richard. *Simple Justice*. New York: Vintage, 1977.

Kranz, Rachel. *The Biographical Dictionary of Black Americans*. New York: Facts on File, 1991.

Lynn, Conrad. *There is A Foundation: The Autobiography of a Civil Rights Lawyer.* Westport:

Lawrence Hill and Company, 1979.

McFeely, William S. *Frederick Douglass*. New York: W.W. Norton, 1991.

McWhorter, Diane. *Carry Me Home: Birmingham, Alabama: The Climactic Battle of the Civil Rights Revolution.* New York: Simon & Schuster, 2002.

Meredith, James Howard. *Three Years in Mississippi*. Bloomington: Indiana University Press, 1966.

Metress, Christopher, ed. *The Lynching of Emmett Till: A Documentary Narrative.* Virginia: University of Virginia Press, 2002.

Moody, Anne. *Coming of Age in Mississippi*. New York: Laurel Leaf, 1992.

Moses, Robert P. *Radical Equations*. Boston: Beacon Press, 2002.

Nalty, Bernard C. *Strength for the Fight: A History of Black Americans in the Military.* New York: The Free Press, 1986.

Newton, Huey P. *Revolutionary Suicide*. New York: Writers and Readers Publishing, 1995.

Newton, Huey P. *To Die for the People: The Writings of Huey P. Newton.* Ed. Toni Morrison. New York: Writers and Readers Publishing, 1995.

Parks, Gordon. *Voices in the Mirror: An Autobiography.* New York: Doubleday, 1990.

Parks, Rosa. *My Story*. New York: Puffin, 1999.

Pattillo-Beals, Melba. *Warriors Don't Cry*. New York: Washington Square Press, 1995.

Peery, Nelson. *Black Fire: The Making of an American Revolutionary.* New York: The New Press, 1994.

Ransby, Barbara. *Ella Baker and the Black Freedom Movement.* Chapel Hill: University Press of North Carolina, 2003.

Rivlin, Gary. *Fire on the Prairie: Chicago's Harold Washington and the Politics of Race.* New York: Henry Holt and Company, 1992.

Salter, Jr., John R. *Jackson Mississippi: An American Chronicle of Struggle and Schism.* New York: Exposition Press, 1979.

Seale, Bobby. *Lonely Rage: The Autobiography of Bobby Seale.* New York: Times Books, 1978.

Sharpiro, Herbert. *White Violence and Black Response.* Amherst: University of Massachusetts Press, 1988.

Till-Mobley, Mamie, with Christopher Benson. *Death of Innocence: The Story of the Hate Crime that Changed America.* New York: Random House, 2003.

Whitman, Mark, ed. *Removing A Badge of Slavery.* New York: Markus Wiener Publishing, Inc., 1993.

Williams, Juan. *Eyes on the Prize*. New York: Penguin, 1988.

Wilmore, Gayraud S., and James H. Cone, eds. *Black Theology: A Documentary History, 1966-1979.* New York: Orbis Books, 1979.

Articles

Adler, Renata, "Letter From Selma," *New Yorker*, 10 April 1965.

Caldwell, Earl, *New York Times*, 26 March 1965.

Good, Paul, *New South*, Summer 1966.

Halberstam, David, *The Reporter*, 31 March 1960

Hicks, Jimmy, *Amsterdam News*, 28 September, 1957.

Kopkind, Andrew, *The New Republic*, 20 March 1965.

Lee, Paul, "Martin Luther King, Jr. in Grosse Pointe," *The Black World Today*, 19 January 2004.

Leonard, George B., T. George Harris, and Christopher Wren, "How A Secret Deal Prevented A Massacre at Ole Miss," *Look*, 31 December 1962.

McMillan, George, "Peace for Justice in Aiken," *The Nation*, 23 November 1946.

Peery, Nelson, "Historical Significance of Watts Uprising," *People's Tribune*, August 2000.

Rowan, Carl T., "Martin Luther King's Tragic Decision," *Reader's Digest*, September 1967.

Rozier, Jr., Albert, *The Register, North Carolina A & T*, 5 February 1960.

Sitton, Claude, *New York Times*, 13 June 1963.

Sitton, Claude, *New York Times*, 16 September 1963.

Tuttle, Rick, *Miami Herald*, 2 October 1962.

Williams, James, *The Afro-American (Baltimore)*, 28 September 1963.

Websites

CNN. "Burden of Proof." *CNN.com Transcripts*. http://www.cnn.com/TRANSCRIPTS/0005/18/bp.00.html

CNN. "FBI reopens probe into 1963 church bombing." *U.S. News Story Page*. http://www.cnn.com/US/9707/10/church.bomb/index.html

Court TV. "Death in the Ruins." *Crime Library*. http://www.crimelibrary.com/terrorists_spies/terrorists/birmingham_church/5.html?sect=22.

FBI. "MIBURN (Mississippi Burning) part 1." *Freedom of Information Act*. http://foia.fbi.gov/miburn/miburn1.pdf

Jackson Sun. "White Citizens' Councils Aimed to Maintain 'Southern way of life.'" *Jackson Sun*. http://jacksonsun.com/civilrights/sec2_citizencouncil.shtml

Library of Congress. "With All Deliberate Speed." American Treasures of the Library of Congress. http://www.loc.gov/exhibits/treasure/images/vc_103bp2.jpg

McGuffey Foundation School. "Freedom Summer." *History in Oxford and Butler County, Ohio*. http://w3.iac.net/~mcguffey/OxfordHistory/Freedom_summer/

Minnesota Public Radio. "Oh Freedom Over Me." *American Radioworks*. http://www.americanradioworks.org/features/oh_freedom/story4.html

Unitarian Universalist Association. "Viola Liuzzo." *Dicitonary of Unitarian & Universalist Biography*. http://www.uua.org/uuhs/duub/articles/violaliuzzo.html

University of Illinois, Urbana-Champaign. "About the 1963 Birmingham Bombing." *Modern American Poetry*. http://www.english.uiuc.edu/maps/poets/m_r/Randall/birmingham.htm

University of Southern Mississippi. "An Oral History with Fannie Lou Hamer." *Civil Rights in Mississippi Digital Archive*. http://www.lib.usm.edu/~spcol/crda/oh/hamer/htm

University of Southern Mississippi. "An Oral History with Lawrence Guyot." *Civil Rights in Mississippi Digital Archive*. http://www.lib.usm.edu/~spcol/crda/oh/guyot.htm

University of Southern Mississippi. "Interview with Honorable Charles Evers: Mayor of Fayette, Mississippi." *Civil Rights in Mississippi Digital Archive*. http://anna.lib.usm.edu/%7Espcol/crda/oh/oheverscp.html

Wayne State University. "I AM A MAN: Terrible Thursday." *Walter P. Reuther Library*. http://www.reuther.wayne.edu/man/7Dignity.htm

Wayne State University. "I AM A MAN: Walking Buzzards." *Walter P. Reuther Library*. http://www.reuther.wayne.edu/MAN/2Memphis.htm

Additional Civil Rights Resources

Museums and Historic Sites

Birmingham Civil Rights Institute
   520 Sixteenth Street North
   Birmingham, AL 35203
   (866) 328-9696, ext. 203
   www.bcri.org/index.html
Civil Rights Memorial
   Montgomery, AL
   (334) 956-8200
   www.tolerance.org/memorial
International Civil Rights Center and Museum
   301 N. Elm Street, Suite 303
   Greensboro, NC 27401
   (800) 748-7116
   www.sitinmovement.org/default.asp
Martin Luther King Jr. National Historic Site
   450 Auburn Avenue, NE
   Atlanta, GA 30312
   (404) 331-5190
   www.nps.gov/malu/
Mary McLeod Bethune Council House National
   Historic Site
   1318 Vermont Avenue NW
   Washington, DC 20005
   (202) 673-2402
   www.nps.gov/mamc/
Mount Zion Albany Civil Rights
Movement Museum
   326 Whitney Avenue
   Albany, GA 31706
   (912) 432-1698
   www.cr.nps.gov/nr/travel/civilrights/g3.htm
National Civil Rights Museum
   450 Mulberry Street
   Memphis, TN 38103
   (901) 521-9699
   www.civilrightsmuseum.org

National Voting Rights Museum
   1012 Water Avenue
   Selma, AL 36702
   (334) 418-0800
   www.voterights.org/
Ralph Mark Gilbert Civil Rights Museum
   460 Martin Luther King Jr. Boulevard
   Savannah, GA 31401
   (912) 231-8900
   www.sip.armstrong.edu/CivilRightsMuseum/
   Civilindex.html
Rosa Parks Library and Museum
   251 Montgomery Street
   Montgomery, AL 36104
   (334) 241-8661
   www.tsum.edu/museum/

Films

Citizen King, directed by Orlando Bagwell and
   Noland Walker, PBS American Experience,
   2004.
The Murder of Emmett Till, directed by Stanley Nel-
   son, PBS American Experience, 2003.
The Untold Story of Emmett Louis Till, directed by
   Keith Beauchamp, Till Freedom Comes Produc-
   tions, 2004.
4 Little Girls, directed by Spike Lee, 40 Acres & A
   Mule Filmworks, Inc., 1997.
Scottsboro: An American Tragedy, directed by Daniel
   Anker and Barak Goodman, PBS American
   Experience, 2001.
Brother Outsider: The Life of Bayard Rustin, directed
   by Nancy Kates and Bennett Singer, PBS Amer-
   ican Experience, 2003.
Eyes on the Prize: America's Civil Rights Years, pro-
   duced by Blackside Productions, PBS 1987.

Audio

Freedom is a Constant Struggle: Songs of the Mississippi Civil Rights Movement, released by Folk Era Records, 1994.

Sing for Freedom: The Story of the Civil Rights Movement Through its Songs, released by Smithsonian Folkways, 1990.

Voices of the Civil Rights Movement: Black American Freedom Songs 1960-1966, released by Smithsonian Folkways, 1990.

Books

Children of the Movement: The Sons and Daughters of Martin Luther King, Jr., Malcolm X, Elijah Muhammad, George Wallace, Andrew Young, Julian Bond, Stokely Carmichael, Bob Moses, James Chaney, Elaine Brown, and Others Reveal How the Civil Rights Movement Tested and Transformed by John Blake, Lawrence Hill Books, 2004.

The Civil Rights Movement: A Photographic History, 1954-68 by Steven Kasher, Abbeville Press, 1996

The Eyes on the Prize Civil Rights Reader: Documents, Speeches, and Firsthand Accounts from the Black Freedom Struggle by Clayborn Carson, David J. Garrow, Gerald Hill, Vincent Harding, and Darlene Clark Hine, Penguin Books, 1991.

Freedom: A Photographic History of the African American Struggle by Manning Marable and Leith Mullings, Phaidon Press Limited, 2002.

Freedom's Daughters: The Unsung Heroines of the Civil Rights Movement from 1830 to 1970 by Lynne Olson, Scribner, 2002.

My Soul Looks Back in Wonder: Voices of the Civil Rights Experience by Juan Williams, Sterling Publications, 2004.

A Traveler's Guide to the Civil Rights Movement by Jim Carrier, Harvest Books, 2004.

Voices in Our Blood: America's Best on the Civil Rights Movement edited by John Meacham, Random House, 2003.

Websites

The African-American Odyssey http://memory.loc.gov/ammem/aaohtml/

The American Civil Rights Institute www.acri.org

The Citizens' Commission on Civil Rights www.cccr.org

The Congress of Racial Equality www.core-online.org

Greensboro Sit-Ins: Launch of a Civil Rights Movement www.sitins.org

The National Association for the Advancement of Colored People www.naacp.org

Voices of Civil Rights www.voicesofcivilrights.org

We Shall Overcome: Historic Places of the Civil Rights Movement www.cr.nps.gov/nr/travel/civilrights/

Audio Credits

In all cases, we have attempted to provide archival audio in its original form. Some audio segments have been edited for time and content. While we have attempted to achieve the best possible quality on the archival audio, some audio quality is the result of source limitations. Archival audio research by Marie Macaisa and Herb Boyd. Narration script and audio editing by Todd Stocke and Marie Macaisa. Narration recording by Tarik Solangi at Prime Time Studios in Yonkers, NY. Audio engineering and mastering by Christian Pawola at Music & Sound Company, DeKalb, Illinois.

Archival audio provided by and copyright of: CBS News Archives; NBC News Archives; CNN; National Archives and Records Administration; the Library of Congress; Lyndon Baines Johnson Library and Museum; John F. Kennedy Library and Museum; Harry S. Truman Library; Dwight D. Eisenhower Library; the *Greensboro News & Record* and sitins.com; the University of Georgia; Smithsonian Folkways; WGBH Boston; Congressman John Lewis; the University of Southern Mississippi Center for Oral History; Thirteen/WNET New York; the University of Arkansas Library; Pacifica Radio Archives, North Hollywood, CA.
"We Shall Overcome" (Horton, Carawan, Hamilton, Seeger) courtesy of Ludlow Music, Inc.
Bob Dylan's "Only a Pawn in Their Game" courtesy of Sony Music/Columbia and Special Rider Music.
Martin Luther King Jr. audio courtesy of Intellectual Properties Management and the Estate of Martin Luther King Jr.

Print Permissions

"Malcolm" by Sonia Sanchez used by permission of the author.
"Mississippi Goddam" by Nina Simone, copyright (c) 1964 (renewed) WB Music Corp. (ASCAP), all rights reserved, used by permission
"The Death of Emmett Till" by Bob Dylan, copyright (c) 1963 by Warner Bros. Inc. Copyright renewed 1991 by Special Rider Music. All rights reserved. International copyright secured. Reprinted by permission.
"Oxford Town" by Bob Dylan, copyright (c) 1963 by Warner Bros. Inc. Copyright renewed 1991 by Special Rider Music. All rights reserved. International copyright secured. Reprinted by permission.

Photo Credits

Every effort has been made to correctly attribute all the materials reproduced in this book. If any errors have been made, we will be happy to correct them in future editions.

Index

About the Author

Photo by Christopher Griffin

Herb Boyd is an award-winning author and journalist who has published eleven books and countless articles for national magazines and newspapers. *Brotherman: The Odyssey of Black Men in America – An Anthology*, co-edited with Robert Allen, won the American Book Award for nonfiction. Boyd is also the author of *Race and Resistance: African Americans in the 21st Century*, *The Harlem Reader* and the forthcoming *Sugar in Harlem*, a biography of Sugar Ray Robinson.

In 1999, Boyd won three first place awards from the New York Association of Black Journalists for his articles published in the *Amsterdam News*. Boyd is also the National Editor of *The Black World Today*, one of the leading publications on the Internet, and he teaches African and African American History at the College of New Rochelle in Manhattan.

About the Narrators

Photo by Anthony Barboza

Ossie Davis and Ruby Dee have long been at the forefront of civil rights, in addition to their long list of credits on the stage and screen. Throughout their careers, they supported Martin Luther King Jr., participated in the March on Washington, eulogized Malcolm X, and have been active in social causes including sickle-cell disease research and black voting rights.

Ossie Davis is an actor, writer, producer and director. He made his Broadway debut in 1946 and was inducted into the Theater Hall of Fame in 1994. He has appeared in such films as *Do the Right Thing*, *Jungle Fever*, *Grumpy Old Men*, and *Get on the Bus*, and has directed five feature films. He received Emmy Award nominations for his work in *Miss Evers' Boys*, *King* and *Teacher, Teacher*.

Davis has received many honors and citations, including the New York Urban League Frederick Douglass Award, the NAACP Image Award, and the National Medal of Arts. He is the author of three children's books, *Escape to Freedom*, *Langston*, and *Just Like Martin*.

Ruby Dee grew up in Harlem and began her career as an actor, writer, and producer as a member of the American Negro Theatre. On Broadway, she has appeared in such plays as *Jeb*, *A Raisin in the Sun*, and *Checkmates*. Her film credits include *No Way Out*, *The Jackie Robinson Story*, and *St. Louis Blues*.

She received Emmy Award nominations for her work in *The Nurses*, *Roots: The Next Generation*, Gore Vidal's *Lincoln*, *China Beach*, and *Evening Shade*. In 1991, she was awarded the Emmy for her performance in *Decoration Day*. She is the author of two children's books, *Tower to Heaven* and *Two Ways to Count to Ten*, and a book of poetry and short stories. Dee and Davis have written a joint biography, *With Ossie & Ruby: In This Life Together*.

In December 1998, Davis and Dee celebrated their 50th wedding anniversary. They received the Screen Actors Guild Life Achievement Award in 2001.

Photo by Bruce Davidson

Ossie Davis, Ruby Dee, and their children protest at a CORE (Congress of Racial Equality) peace demonstration, New York City, 1966.